The Long Game

The Long Game

U.S. MEN'S SOCCER AND ITS SAVAGE, FOUR-DECADE JOURNEY TO THE TOP, OR THEREABOUTS

Leander Schaerlaeckens

VIKING

VIKING
An imprint of Penguin Random House LLC
1745 Broadway, New York, NY 10019
penguinrandomhouse.com

Illustrations by Dan Leydon (danleydon.com).

DESIGNED BY CLAIRE VACCARO

Library of Congress control number: 2026008337
ISBN 9780593653876 (hardcover)
ISBN 9780593653883 (ebook)

Printed in the United States of America
1st Printing

The authorized representative in the EU for product safety and compliance is Penguin Random House Ireland, Morrison Chambers, 32 Nassau Street, Dublin D02 YH68, Ireland, https://eu-contact.penguin.ie.

For Steph and Lukie
En voor Ingrid

Contents

Author's Note

I set out to write this book ahead of the 2026 FIFA World Cup because the remarkable story of one of its hosts, the United States men's national team, had never been fully told. The World Cup, which will pit forty-eight nations against each other and sprawl across North America for almost six weeks, will be the biggest sporting event ever staged in terms of footprint, revenue, cultural relevance, attendance, and probably in discourse and controversy as well.

Yet the underdog tale of the home team is barely known—going from total anonymity to a regular place in the top 20 of the 211 nations ranked by FIFA in the world's most popular and competitive sport. Over the course of a decade and a half of covering the USMNT for various major American media outlets, I fell in love with this story: How, exactly, did the U.S. men's team manage to toil from being bereft of talent, money, and attention in the early 1980s, playing just one game a year if that, to a perch from where it can conceivably go on a significant run in the summer of 2026?

This book does not attempt to predict the USMNT's future—sorry, gamblers—but rather to tell you how the team got here, how a cast of larger-than-life coaches shaped the team's story over the past four decades, and how some of the team's contemporary players offer a new story. The ascent of the American men is something akin to a sporting miracle.

The Long Game weaves two stories—that of the *team*, and that of the *players*. The arc of the United States men's national team's past, careening from dysfunction to brief moments of real promise, back to incompetence or irrelevance and toward something constructed on a solid foundation at last, is interspersed with the accounts of a half-dozen players: Tyler Adams, Matt Turner, Ricardo Pepi, Christian Pulisic, Antonee Robinson, and Weston McKennie. Theirs are not only the stories of how six national team careers were made, but also reflections of the problems and progress of the American men's game writ large, of its changes and challenges. All six may not be on the field for the 2026 World Cup, but they were all, in their own ways, central to the remaking of the USMNT.

And that's what this book is ultimately about: how a diverse nation built a national team program capable of competing at the World Cup.

The Long Game

Prologue

Two games into the U.S. men's national team's first World Cup in the better part of a decade, legitimate questions lingered. Was this team overhyped? Was it really ready for the biggest stage in the sport? And would it do any better than the previous incarnations of the USMNT, which had sparked less buzz but had actual track records?

Was globalization at work in sending so many young American players to Europe's biggest soccer clubs, or had the world's game bent toward the United States at last? Did the stateside burst of soccer interest and media attention play a role, feeding all those new fans the narrative of global belonging that they craved?

Was this really a golden generation? Or just a shimmering mirage?

If anything had really changed, if things were truly different, the time to prove it was now, here, at the Al Thumama Stadium in Doha, in this new edifice with its forty-four thousand seats, cloaked in a white facade made to look like a gahfiya, the woven cap worn throughout the Gulf region. Excitement alone would no longer do. Even a very young team could coast on its potential for only so long. If these players really were special, as everyone seemed to think, now would be a fortuitous time to deliver some evidence of that specialness. Because at some point, they would have to actually win a game at the 2022 World Cup in Qatar.

The U.S. had looked confident and competent in its tournament opener against Wales eight days earlier, with one teenager and just two players older than twenty-five on the field. Every American man on the field was making his debut at the pinnacle of the sport, the quadrennial mega-event that soccer keeps time by. U.S. captain and midfielder Tyler Adams was only twenty-three; star forward Christian Pulisic was just twenty-four, same as midfielder Weston McKennie. They zinged daring passes to one another all the same. They treated the substantial U.S. crowd in the stands to backheels and stepovers and other assorted trickery. It all reeked of an unearned confidence, of a swagger that comes only from knowing that you are young and good and exactly in the place you belong.

During the long World Cup qualifying ordeal, the USA's average age of 23.8 made it the youngest team to reach Qatar by more than two years. Only Ghana brought a younger roster to the World Cup proper—and by a matter of days. The Americans had less experience than everybody else. Just one player on the roster, the reserve right back at that, had been there when the U.S. last played a World Cup in 2014, in Brazil. And that player, DeAndre Yedlin, wasn't even on the field to start the Wales game.

This team was predicated on assertiveness and fearlessness, on competing, as head coach Gregg Berhalter put it, "like fucking dogs." In the thirty-sixth minute, Christian Pulisic sprang Tim Weah through the Welsh defense and Weah scored calmly. The goal-scorer tore toward the luxury box of VVIPs—a term invented by FIFA for heads of state and, of course, the biggest of its own bigwigs—toward his father, George Weah, the president of Liberia, who had never made it to the World Cup himself despite having been one of Africa's greatest players.

An experienced team might have put the game away before halftime, but the Americans failed to score again. And the Welsh still had their languid thirty-three-year-old star, the man-bunned, alabaster Gareth Bale. In the eightieth minute, Bale drew a penalty. Time had diminished Bale, but he was still savvy. Walker Zimmerman didn't see Bale sneaking his foot in front of the ball, causing the U.S. defender to kick through him in the American box. Penalty kick. "Clever move," Zimmerman conceded later. Bale converted the penalty kick himself. 1–1. A tie. A single error had cost the Americans two precious points.

In their second game in Qatar, the U.S. faced England, the third such matchup in a World Cup. In 1950, the Americans claimed perhaps the greatest upset in tournament history with a 1–0 victory, and in 2010 the U.S. eked out a 1–1 tie. The odds were stacked as heavily against the USMNT as they had been in those two meetings. The English had reached the semifinals at the last World Cup in 2018 and the final of the European Championship in 2021 and were possibly even stronger this time around. The Three Lions, made up entirely of Premier League stars, mirrored a diverse nation with first names like Raheem, Bukayo, and multiple Harrys. In their tournament opener, England rolled over Iran with a 6–2 win.

Many on the U.S. roster wrestled with complicated emotions about playing England. No fewer than eight Americans played for English clubs; two were born and raised in England but now wore an American uniform; and another represented England at the youth national team level before flipping his allegiance. The Americans would be playing against their league rivals, against their club teammates, against childhood friends. As if to supercharge the must-see event, it fell on Black Friday, the day after Thanksgiving, drawing an American audience of twenty million TV viewers on their day off.

At a minimum, the U.S. matched the English, even controlling the run of play for long stretches. Christian Pulisic snapped a shot off England's crossbar. While the contest played on the big screen in Times

Square, the American fans were once again represented well, this time in Al Khor, at the Al Bayt Stadium styled like a Bedouin tent, standing at the end of a dead-straight drive through the desert from Doha. For a spell, those American fans launched into a cheeky chant, taunting their more talented opponents.

"It's called soc-cer," the giddy U.S. supporters sang for several refrains, mocking the English for their dogmatic insistence on calling the sport "football."

It's called soc-cer.

It's called soc-cer.

Whatever the sport was to be called, neither team scored. 0–0. In a beer garden in London, England fans tossed their drinks in the air in disgust. "There's a lot of people that obviously thought we were going to get blown out," Weston McKennie said. "We went into this game as obvious underdogs. But for us, we didn't feel like underdogs at all. We're not really afraid of playing against top-tier teams."

Beating Iran four days later would guarantee the Americans a place among the top two of Group B's four teams, and passage into the tournament's knockout rounds. Gregg Berhalter was blunt with his players in the locker room following the game. "Iran is going to be a difficult game," he spoke. "How do we beat Iran and go to the next round? Then it gets fucking fun, boys."

Not quite four years earlier, in January 2019, about two dozen American players filed into a meeting room at a hotel in Chula Vista, California. Before them, the track-suited Berhalter introduced himself as the new men's national team head coach and laid out the journey the team was about to set out on.

"What are you prepared to do?" he asked the players in front of him. "We're on a mission together. What we're looking to do is change the way the world views American soccer."

Berhalter is the sort of man who structures his introductory chat with his new team through a slideshow. So he pressed the clicker in his hand and the objectives for his reign flashed across the screen: players enjoying the national team environment; coaches developing a clear playing style; everyone nurturing a high-performance culture.

"Sounds great, right?" Berhalter said. "Here's the problem. It's going to take a shitload of sacrifice from you guys. It's going to be difficult."

There was nary a need to point this out. Nobody had forgotten the debacle of 2017. On October 10, the Americans suffered an ugly loss in Trinidad and Tobago. A pair of fluky results in other games—in which Panama and Honduras somehow each came from behind to beat superior opponents—meant that, in 2018, the USA would miss its first World Cup since 1986. A teenage Pulisic crouched in the soggy Trinidadian turf and buried his face in his mud-streaked number 10 jersey. He took so much punishment from his opponents during that game that he struggled to sit on the charter plane home the next day. But just then, the pain was psychological. The tearful nineteen-year-old sensation understood that the men's national team program had just crashed into rock bottom.

The American soccer community questioned everything. An ascent of more than three decades from complete international irrelevance—and a forty-four-year period without a single win at a World Cup, or even a draw—to a regular place on the global stage was supposed to have inoculated the U.S. men's team from failure on this scale. But the national team, once a cohesive and scrappy underdog, had become less than the sum of its parts, riven by factions and incoherent coaching. A gap yawned between the team's past-expiration veterans and its unripe prospects. At last, the assorted difficulties of qualifying for the World

Cup from the North and Central American and Caribbean region had vanquished them. The grueling travel, the games in nearly impossible conditions—lumpy or sodden fields, riotous crowds, vaudevillian referees, airborne bags of urine—tripped them up this time.

National team careers are an odd kind of sideline in that they usually aren't male soccer players' primary source of income, or indeed the main act in their professional lives. Their club teams pay their salaries, arrange health insurance, and take care of their families. Their clubs are where the players spend more than three-quarters of the year. Their club performances and statistics are also primarily what their careers are judged on. Yet what they do for their nations, when called upon to represent them a few times a year as quasi-freelancers, defines the legacies of even the great players.

Lionel Messi's résumé was considered incomplete until he won Argentina the World Cup, just as Cristiano Ronaldo needed to lift the European Championship for Portugal. Never mind that both men had won a salvage yard's worth of silverware with their clubs. The international stage is ultimately where legends are forged.

To Berhalter fell the task to rebuild a national team with a generation of Americans whose club pedigree was unprecedented: Teenagers somehow signed contracts with Europe's most prestigious clubs—FC Barcelona! Bayern Munich! Chelsea! Juventus! Borussia Dortmund! Ajax! Manchester City! AS Roma! They were already helping those teams win the biggest prizes in soccer. A new generation, young and heedless of the baggage of American insecurity and failure at the international level, born after American soccer's Dark Age. The dread that Americans would never quite belong among soccer's French artisans, Brazilian dancers, and Italian maestros did not burden them. It had taken decades for that inferiority complex to slough off.

Now, could they grow into the greatest U.S. men's national team ever? That was the question. But piecing it together would take time—half a decade at least. All those prospects were in their late teens and early twenties, suggesting that they would hit their prime at the 2026 World Cup, not the 2022 edition. But this kind of long-termism is not permitted in soccer. World Cups are too rare to write off. And besides, if this team was so special, an impatient nation demanded to see something from these ballyhooed boys in short order—the American Way demanded it.

Whatever results the American men mustered in previous decades had come through brawn and gumption. Theirs was an unassuming playing style: "agricultural," as an English soccer announcer might describe it, because it betrayed little sophistication or style. The U.S. was rarely blown out, because it defended stoutly and made it a point of pride to run harder and farther than the other team. But there is a low ceiling on moxie alone. Defensive tactics consistently spared the Yanks embarrassment against big soccer countries, but they were also limiting. To be a world power you eventually must beat other world powers, and that's tough when all you're doing is attempting to negate their strengths, rather than betting on your own. So when Berhalter took over in late 2018, he committed not only to rebuilding the team more or less from scratch, but also to reinventing it. His new USMNT broke from a tradition that had served the program rather well and, instead, endeavored to play beautifully by competing on even footing with anyone. The Americans would cower in their own half no longer.

In the summer and fall of 2021, the new national team made a breakthrough. After eight years of failure to beat regional archrivals Mexico in a competitive game, the U.S. did so three times in the span of a few months, and twice in a final. Winning the CONCACAF Nations League and the Gold Cup, the confederation's two regional tournaments, vaulted the American men into the top ten of FIFA's worldwide rankings of national teams for the first time in more than fifteen years, after they sank to thirty-fifth place in 2017. That put the U.S. within reach of the world's eight best teams, a stated objective of the United States Soccer Federation. The U.S. team faced their demons in World Cup qualifying, plodding through a fourteen-game march. They went to the seething cauldrons of Honduras and El Salvador and Mexico and Costa Rica, and learned to cope with gamesmanship that threatened to make real soccer almost impossible. (The Americans, for their part, reciprocated by hosting Honduras in an outdoor game in St. Paul, Minnesota, in early February 2022 with a wind chill of -13 degrees Fahrenheit, reportedly forcing two Honduran players to leave the game at halftime with symptoms of hypothermia.) The Americans clawed and scraped their way to the seven wins and four ties that got them to Qatar. But things were precarious at times, and the U.S. only avoided a play-in game with New Zealand because its ledger of goals scored and conceded was superior to Costa Rica's—it relied on a tiebreaker, in other words.

How the Americans performed in Qatar would not only dictate the legacy of their 2022 campaign, but would also set the agenda for 2026, the second time they would host a World Cup on home soil—sharing the duties with Canada and Mexico this time. "We really do see this as a responsibility," Berhalter said before traveling to Qatar. "We want to get the public behind us. We want to get a ton of momentum going into 2026."

It was a heavy burden for such a young team to bear, even if the late addition to the roster of a pair of thirtysomething veterans pushed its average age to a near-geriatric twenty-five. But then Berhalter believed that his team's power lay partially in its shared youth, which made the players uncommonly close. They went through the shock of World Cup qualifying in CONCACAF together. They were mostly of college age, or only slightly older, but Pulisic, Adams, McKennie, and most of their teammates had missed out on that experience by turning pro before graduating from high school. With the national team, away from their older club teammates in different countries and cultures, the players seemed intent on making up for lost time, living a sort of millionaire dorm life. They embraced national team recruits as new friends rather than rivals. They talked and ate for hours on end. They went out together and played golf together and shopped together. They brought a barber and a barista on the road with them. They watched *Love Island* and played Uno. And when national team training camps ended, they stayed in touch in unruly group chats and a fantasy football league.

The few veterans who remained from previous regimes testified to a marked difference from the previous World Cup cycle. "There definitely was not that feeling of togetherness," said defender Tim Ream, who made his national team debut in 2010. "This cycle, the togetherness has just been incredible."

Midfielder Weston McKennie, a bubbly, boisterous locker room presence, argued that the team's closeness also gave it a competitive edge. "Many of us have been playing with or against each other since we were nine or ten years old," he said. "We know each other so well."

The stakes of the final group-stage match against Iran needed no further amplification. But the lead-up to the game between longtime geopolitical enemies turned into a circus as the U.S. became ensnared in a series of minor diplomatic incidents. First, former U.S. men's head coach Jürgen Klinsmann claimed on the BBC that the Iranian team's supposed penchant for flopping and for bullying referees was "part of their culture." Iranian manager Carlos Queiroz lashed out at Klinsmann on social media. Before Queiroz's press conference on the eve of the game, Iranian journalists gave him a standing ovation.

Then, U.S. Soccer used a promotional graphic for the game on its social media accounts that showed an Iranian flag without its Islamic Republic emblem. It did so to show "support for the women in Iran fighting for basic human rights," according to a spokesman, in the midst of widespread protests against the Iranian regime. The federation went back to using the regular Iranian flag after twenty-four hours and deleted the original post, but the powder keg had already been ignited. A representative of the Iranian federation called on FIFA to kick the United States out of the World Cup for "disrespecting" the Iranian flag. His comments were reported by an Iranian outlet that sported a burning American flag as its own social media avatar.

In their press conference the following day, Berhalter and captain Tyler Adams were grilled by indignant Iranian journalists from regime-sanctioned media outlets. The Iranian soccer media took the opportunity to grandstand in front of their government's nemesis. The questions tended to begin with a criticism of the United States followed by a query that was either unanswerable—"What percentage of the population of the world will be happy because of the win of the national team of Iran, and what percentage of the whole population of the world will be happy if the United States soccer team wins?"—or had nothing to do with soccer. Berhalter and Adams were asked, among other things, about the American fleet in the Persian Gulf, high inflation, and visa reciprocity.

One reporter began his question to Adams by chiding him for mispronouncing Iran—calling it I-ran, rather than Ee-rahn. Then he asked if Adams, the son of a white mother and a black biological father, was "OK to be representing a country that has so much discrimination against black people in its own borders."

Adams, his fingers clasped together, looked at the reporter calmly. He apologized for the mispronunciation and then responded. "There's discrimination everywhere you go," he answered with such poise that the footage of it instantly went viral. "One thing that I've learned from living abroad in the past years and having to fit in in different cultures is that in the U.S., we're continuing to make progress every single day."

While Iran's press corps eagerly carried water for the regime, the Iranian national team's relationship with the soccer-besotted nation it represented had grown fraught. The Iranian soccer federation, like almost everything in the country, was controlled by the conservative Islamic government that had been in power since the revolution in 1979, when it overthrew the U.S.-backed shah. The players, then, were representatives of the government, a symbol of the regime. But they openly sympathized with the thousands of people participating in the months-long women's-rights protests that roiled the country. Iran's presence in Qatar offered visibility to a people's uprising that had at times been buried in so much other global news. A pitch invader at the Portugal–Uruguay game waved a rainbow peace flag and wore a T-shirt reading "Respect for Iranian Women."

It was up to the Iranian players to thread the tiny eye of this needle. Many were eager to show their support for the protests, yet all were aware of the regime's history of punishing even the nation's most famous athletes for perceived disloyalty—in 1984, the national team captain was tortured and killed for his membership in an opposition party. And so, Iranian players staged a silent protest in Qatar by declining to sing their national anthem before the opener against England. It's unlikely that much of Iran saw the protest, because state television censored it and then muted the live feed of the game whenever anti-regime chants broke out. Before their next two games, the players were reportedly threatened and at least moved their lips along when the anthem played. To this backdrop, the U.S. kicked off a must-win game against an opponent that only needed a tie. The Americans played to move on; the Iranians for a movement.

About thirty-eight minutes into the first half, McKennie dropped a delicate ball into the path of onrushing right back Sergiño Dest, who headed it back for Pulisic. The Americans drew up this very play on the whiteboard in preparation for the game, to crowbar their way into the ironclad Iranian defense. Pulisic charged through a crowd of Iranians and threw his body at the ball, poking it into the net as goalkeeper Alireza Beiranvand's knee collided with his groin. 1–0. The goal came at a cost: Pulisic took such a hard knock that he had to leave the game at halftime and go to a hospital because he felt faint. He was diagnosed with a pelvic contusion and would watch the remainder of the game on a cell phone from a hospital bed. "I paid the price for it," Pulisic said sheepishly.

The Americans braced themselves for the inevitable Iranian assault. The U.S., setting its third straight record for the youngest lineup in the tournament, spent most of the second half shoveling away everything that Iran kicked at it. The closer the game crept to the final whistle, the better Iran's scoring chances seemed to become. In the ninety-eighth minute, the Iranian forward Mehdi Taremi slid after a ball headed in front of him. His shot trickled through goalkeeper Matt Turner's legs, but brushed enough of Turner's calf to slow it down. Walker Zimmerman, seemingly the only person whose heart hadn't stopped in horror or hope, loped after the ball to clear it away before it crossed the line. That did it. A seminal American win.

That's how World Cups go. A bounce here. A bump there. A whistle that shrieks or doesn't. A ball that spins or hops or skips.

Queiroz was impressed with the Americans, explaining his defensive approach in the first half: "When you play against a team of Ferraris—they are very fast—the best way to play is to close the highways."

Several U.S. players consoled their weeping opponents on the field after the Iranians slumped to the grass in exhaustion. Left back Antonee Robinson embraced Ramin Rezaeian while the Iranian bawled in his arms. Robinson had seen images of Rezaeian speaking passionately about the protests before the game. "I was thinking, 'Even though I'm celebrating, that was so close to being us,'" Robinson said a few months later. "They nearly scored and if that shot goes in, we're the ones crying, going home." When the Americans returned to the locker room, they had a joyous FaceTime call with Pulisic, who was still in the hospital. Then Robinson broke down and sobbed himself.

PART I

The First World Cups
1930–1982

1 | At the First World Cup

It is said that the Pilgrims, freshly disembarked at Plymouth Rock, found the First Americans playing a game they called *pasuckquakkohowog*, which translates to "They gather to play ball with the foot." It was contested between entire villages on endless fields, kicking around something akin to a ball, just as many other civilizations did. A rudimentary precursor to the game was recorded even earlier, in Virginia, in 1609. Some 250 years later, Bostonian elites started the Oneida Football Club, which played the Boston game, a sporting concoction that was a precursor to soccer, rugby, and gridiron football. And what is now recognized as the first organized American gridiron football game, between what are now Princeton University and Rutgers University on November 6, 1869, more closely resembled soccer, specifically with the rules set in 1863 by England's Football Association; these rules were a major step toward distinguishing soccer from rugby as we know them today. A second matchup looked a lot more like modern gridiron, and this version caught on at the elite college campuses of the Northeast, feeding on an eagerness to develop a distinctly American game. College football quickly took root, but an intercollegiate soccer team was not formed until Haverford College did so in 1902.

Whereas football wove its way into the American spirit, soccer became a regional game. St. Louis was one of its early hotbeds, with a city league kicking off in 1886. There, they merrily Americanized the game by developing their own rules and their own playing style, a more rugged brand of the game. The *St. Louis Globe-Democrat* declared the local take on the game superior: "Any neutral observer who has an opportunity to compare the two systems, must admit that there is more pep, punch and thrill in the American style of play."

In 1894, six owners of National League baseball teams founded the American League of Professional Football. It became the second fully professional soccer league in the world and was only six years younger than England's First Division. The baseball barons thought soccer might fill their ballparks during the long off-season. Most of them decided that coaching a soccer team required no special knowledge and put their baseball managers in charge of their soccer outfits as well, playing under the same name as their baseball brethren in an early stab at brand synergy. There was even talk of the biggest baseball stars participating. When the Baltimore Orioles won all four of their soccer games by a cumulative score of 24–3, the other teams accused them of employing British players illegally, whereupon the immigration authorities became involved. Meanwhile, the American Football Association, which governed the sport, threatened to ban any player involved in the ALPF from its own league, starting a trend of acrimony between rival American soccer leagues that has yet to abate. Attendance sometimes dipped as low as a hundred lonely souls. The ALPF folded after seventeen days. A second such ball-clubs-as-soccer-teams experiment was conducted in the Midwest in 1901 with four major league teams involved; a single friendly drew only three hundred people and then the whole effort caved in.

A new rival federation, the United States Football Association—which would ultimately vanquish the AFA by gaining recognition from global governing body FIFA—saw the same opportunity. In 1913, founding president Gustav Manning, who had also cofounded the German Football Association and acted as its first secretary, told *The New York Times* that his newly founded organization "aims to make soccer the national pastime of the winter in this country."

The difficulty with delivering on this ambition was that the sport, and its federation, had a reputation as an insular club of immigrants reluctant to assimilate, broadcasting their otherness by clinging to their old-world sport. Soccer consisted largely of ethnic clubs that gloried in their European roots. The 1913–14 edition of the National Challenge Cup, for instance, featured teams with names such as Brooklyn Celtic and Clan McKenzie FC. Also: a team called Young Men's Catholic Total Abstinence Society FC.

Nevertheless, soccer thrived. In 1918, twelve thousand spectators showed up to the National Challenge Cup final in St. Louis. Bethlehem Steel, a factory team and juggernaut of its age, toured Scandinavia in 1919 and lost only two of its fourteen games. A second American team, made up mostly of St. Louis players, posted the exact same record the next year. In 1920, Cleveland ran a professional soccer league consisting of two divisions.

By 1916, a men's national team had been formed as well, selecting the top players of U.S. nationality, borrowing them from their club teams in order to compete with other nations. (A squad nominally representing the United States but made up entirely of players from Kearny, New Jersey, another hotbed, lost 1–0 to Canada in 1885, but that game was unsanctioned.) The United States beat Sweden 3–2 in its first recognized international match in Stockholm in front of King Gustav V and fifteen thousand of his subjects. The Americans were criticized by their hosts for their bruising style. "We were outclassed by the Swedish players on straight football," the USFA secretary reported. "It was American grit, pluck, and endurance that won. No great football stars were members of our team, but we had the pluckiest aggregation ever banded together."

After the Americans' rough approach beat a second Swedish team, the club Örgryte, frothing locals attacked the American players. After the game, one home fan climbed into the U.S. federation secretary's car and stole his prized American flag. The secretary pursued the vandal and, having caught him, landed several blows with his cane before the Swedish police, swords drawn, ended the fracas. No word survives on what happened to the flag. The American team lost only one of six games in Sweden and Norway. Along the way, it demonstrated baseball wherever it went, prompting King Gustav to introduce it in Swedish schools.

In a way, England's First Division brought its existential crisis upon itself. There was enough money to pay players fairly, yet the English league nevertheless decided to cap player salaries at four British pounds per week in 1901. At the time, some players were earning double that, meaning that scores of them were forced to take pay cuts. By 1921, the cap had crept up to ten pounds and then been cut to eight pounds again. (It would take until 1963 for a British court to strike down the maximum wage, which was still only twenty pounds per week during the season and seventeen pounds during the summer. Presently, the highest-paid Premier League player earns almost half a million pounds per week.)

Stateside, meanwhile, soccer players were paid as much as $6,000 a year by 1919, a salary approaching those of established major league baseball players. When the American Soccer League rolled out in 1921, it had enough financial backing to begin poaching British players—to the detriment of the American players, whom few teams now bothered to develop. England and Scotland had pulled out of FIFA over a series of grievances, which, as an unforeseen consequence, allowed their players to tear up their unilateral contracts with their teams without fear of a cross-border suspension. A frenzy to sign the best players in the United Kingdom, the self-styled home of the sport, was on. ASL teams signed away players from some of the leading English clubs of their time, and no superstar was deemed untouchable. The Scottish Football Association called a special meeting to work out how to address what the newspapers dubbed "the American Menace."

The ASL absconded not only with dozens of the First Division's best players but also, briefly, with its reputation as the world's strongest league. (Since there is no way of measuring one league against another, consensus tends to coalesce around whoever has the most famous players.) Yet the ASL still struggled to garner much media attention at home, which is why a great deal of its history went unrecorded. And while the money was good, organization was not. Teams came and went in short order, and not a single one played in all thirteen seasons of the league's existence. Visiting clubs sometimes showed up short of the eleven men needed to field a full team or failed to materialize at all. Kickoff times weren't always honored; good referees were in shortage, as were properly laid-out fields. Not once in the league's history did every team play the same number of games by the end of a season. One National Challenge Cup final was decided by forfeit because the players of one team were expected to report for spring training—their soccer club doubled as a baseball team, and practice for the latter evidently took precedence over a championship game for the former.

Still, attendance was often strong for its time. In 1925, a pair of ASL owners brought over Hakoah Vienna, a powerhouse Jewish club from Austria. An astonishing forty-six thousand people flocked to an exhibition match in New York's Polo Grounds. That number stood higher than the attendance of all but three New York Yankees home games that season. Professional soccer was, in fact, regularly outdrawing pro football, and some thought soccer had the better prospects over the long term.

Then, as soccer threatened to cement itself as an American game, administrative bickering ruined everything. In 1928, the ASL and the USFA fell out over the ASL's refusal to allow its clubs to play in the National Challenge Cup, which brought in most of the USFA's money but burdened teams in ASL play. The USFA threw the ASL out of the federation and started its own rival league, forcing the clubs to choose. It wasn't the first or last time that American pro soccer would immolate itself in a dispute over authority and revenue. By the time a peace was brokered and the federation shuttered its rival league, the fight, dubbed the "soccer wars," left the ASL badly wounded. The Great Depression killed it off in 1933.

While the game developed at breakneck speed in the rest of the world, the United States was sidelined. It would take some four decades before the country managed to put together another globally respected national professional soccer league.

In one of its first acts as the self-appointed global governing body for soccer, the Fédération Internationale de Football Association decided in 1904 that FIFA—its better-known acronym—retained the exclusive rights to stage a world championship. This prerogative was bestowed on it by nobody and nothing other than FIFA's own chutzpah, its signature trait to this day.

Yet it took more than a quarter century for FIFA to exercise the right it claimed. It finally acted when it felt the sport had outgrown the Olympics and its constricting insistence on amateurism. Uruguay, the reigning Olympic champion, was chosen by FIFA as host of this first world championship, named the World Cup, over several European countries because it promised to cover every team's costs and to build a stadium in Montevideo just for the occasion—thus maximizing FIFA's potential profit. But many of the leading soccer countries got huffy over the awarding of the tournament to such a faraway nation and didn't show up. There was no need for regional qualifying tournaments, as only thirteen countries bothered to enter the inaugural World Cup in 1930. The United States was among them, although it could afford to go only because of the financial guarantees.

The timing was fortuitous for the United States. While the ASL began to crumble, a great many American players had benefited from playing in a competition that was among the world's best. Still, the USA sailed for Montevideo absent its two best strikers. One of them, Archie Stark, was a World War I veteran and the proud new owner of a garage, which he decided he couldn't abandon for this three-month lark and the paltry pay of $130. But the U.S. had Billy Gonsalves, a crafty player thought capable of starting for any team in the world. And what the Americans lacked in skill beyond their star, they made up for in brawn, a lineup built so powerfully that they would soon be nicknamed the "shot-putters" by the French team.

When the U.S. arrived at the World Cup, they still hadn't been told who they would be playing, let alone when and where. As it turned out, the U.S. opened with Belgium, whose star player had been suspended by the Belgian federation for the moral infraction of opening a café. It had just snowed lightly, turning the field into "a bed of wet, sticky clay with pools of water too numerous to count," according to Wilfred Cummings, the American manager. On July 13, at 3 p.m. local time, the USA played the first-ever World Cup match against Belgium while France and Mexico shared the same history-making distinction in another stadium just two miles to the south. Before 18,346 fans, among them some 80 Americans, Gonsalves hammered a shot off the post and Bart McGhee scored on the rebound to lead the way to a commanding 3–0 victory. They were aided by José Macías, a permissive Argentinian referee who didn't mind the Americans' muscular approach.

Four days later, the U.S. beat a stronger opponent in Paraguay by the same score, before almost exactly the same number of spectators (18,306 this time) and with the same laissez-faire referee. Bert Patenaude scored all three goals, recording the first hat trick in World Cup history and raising his tally for the tournament to four. This result, spectacularly, vaulted the Americans into the tournament's semifinals, where they would face Argentina.

The Estadio Centenario, newly built for the tournament, offered a different kind of challenge than the Estadio Gran Parque Central, where the U.S. had played its first two games. The dimensions of its field were enormous—to this day, soccer has no fixed field size, just a set of parameters, one of the game's quirks akin to baseball's insistence on putting the outfield fence somewhere different in every ballpark. Certainly, the field was far bigger than the Americans were used to. The opposition was also better. The Argentines were more skillful and even more physical than the Americans, who had run themselves ragged battering into Belgium and Paraguay. And this time, the Yanks were the victims of a lenient referee—John Langenus of Belgium, whose nation the Americans had embarrassed just thirteen days earlier. By the time the second half started, the U.S. was not only down a goal but also reduced to eight healthy players. Goalkeeper Jimmy Douglas twisted his knee in the tenth minute and played the rest of the game on one good leg. Raphael Tracey was injured in the first half as well and didn't make it back onto the field for the second. Andy Auld suffered a head injury and played much of the game with a rag in his mouth. Even the American trainer was a casualty of the game. John Coll was supposed to have run onto the field to argue a call with his treatment bag in hand. He dropped a bottle of chloroform, which opened as it fell. The fumes knocked Coll out cold. Argentina ran up a 6–1 score.

A third-place game was never played, but the Americans were awarded the bronze medal because their group-stage record was superior to Yugoslavia's. It was assumed after the fact that the U.S. team had been made up of veteran English and Scottish professionals who defected to the ASL and joined up with the USA's national team. This wasn't true. Only six of the sixteen players in the squad were born in England or Scotland and most of those had come over as teenagers. Just one arrived in the United States with any experience in professional soccer—seven years before migrating, when he appeared in two games in England's Third Division. These were no imported mercenaries. After the tournament, in fact, several American team members would sign with top clubs in Europe, including Manchester United.

This maiden World Cup set a high-water mark that the U.S. has yet to match on the men's side.

2 | Poison to the Game

The Americans would appear in just one more World Cup game before World War II, and how they managed even that remains dubious.

The U.S. Football Association didn't register the team in time for the North American qualifying tournament leading to the 1934 World Cup in Italy. Still, the Americans decided they would quite like to partake anyway. Mexico had already won a World Cup berth by beating Cuba in a three-game series, after the Cubans had vanquished Haiti in a prior round. Somehow, and wholly unfairly, the USA was allowed to bypass those rounds entirely and play Mexico in a winner-take-all game staged in Rome just three days before the World Cup proper was to kick off.

In attendance at the Stadio Nazionale del Partito Nazionale Fascista was Italy's fascist dictator Benito Mussolini. Il Duce would hijack the tournament for propaganda purposes and create a handy blueprint for German chancellor Adolf Hitler and his Nazi Party to follow for their own mega-event two years later, the 1936 Summer Olympics in Berlin. Mexico, playing in only its ninth official international match, took the lead in the twenty-fifth minute, but Aldo Donelli scored twice for the Americans in the next seven minutes and then twice more in the second half for a 4–2 U.S. victory. Donelli had been added to the team at the eleventh hour at the insistence of returning star Billy Gonsalves.

This World Cup would be played in a straight knockout format between the sixteen survivors of the qualification games that whittled down a field of twenty-seven entrants. As an unseeded team, the Americans were guaranteed to face a strong opponent in the first round, but they could hardly have done worse than drawing Italy, the home team destined for the title just two weeks later. With Mussolini attending once again, the Americans had no chance, collapsing in a 7–1 defeat that could have been worse had it not been for America's Swedish-born goalkeeper Julius Hjulian's heroics. Donelli scored the lone American goal, meaning he bagged all five goals the Americans tallied in Italy. Since these two games would be the only times Donelli ever appeared for the USA, he posted a preposterous 2.5 goals-per-game average in international soccer, all of them scored in World Cup competition.

It would be some time before the U.S. was seen on the global soccer stage again. It didn't even try to make it to the 1938 World Cup in France, joining a boycott by Western Hemisphere countries upset that the tournament would be staged in Europe again. When the United States emerged from the Great Depression, the sport's popularity had fallen away and it had begun its long trek through the wilderness.

American soccer never really stopped trying to reclaim whatever prominence it lost following the 1930s. But it is entirely possible that more energy has been spent theorizing why the U.S. brand of soccer wasn't globally competitive than on actually solving the problem. The findings have broken into several schools of thought, expounded upon in books with angsty titles like *What's Wrong with US?*, *Distant Corners:*

American Soccer's History of Missed Opportunities and Lost Causes, What Happened to the USMNT, and *Why the U.S. Men Will Never Win the World Cup.*

In a book called *Offside: Soccer and American Exceptionalism,* two scholars argue that soccer was crowded out. They posit that the sports that became entrenched in American culture between 1870 and 1930 gained an advantage that made them almost immovable. And that no other country has four major sports, therefore rendering it impossible for a fifth to take hold. But this doesn't account for the fact that soccer *was* a major sport in the early twentieth century, in several regions at least, and that plenty of sports faded after soccer did, or have risen since. America is not a monolith, and such blanket explanations tend not to hold up when laid beside regional histories.

There are more practical theories, too. Allen Guttmann, an eminent American sports historian, argues that for decades, immigrant children abandoned soccer in favor of baseball—a game that sold itself as the embodiment of Americanness—to fit in with their new American peers, particularly during the long periods of backlash against immigration from Europe. "Baseball was unquestionably a vehicle for Americanization," Guttmann writes in *A Whole New Ball Game.* "Because it was perceived as the archetypically American game, baseball won the allegiance of immigrants who wished to cast their lot with their new homeland. Indeed, the children of the immigrants, at home in America and eager to demonstrate their loyalty, became the most enthusiastic fans of all."

There were two diametrically opposed strands to this phenomenon. Some immigrants went out of their way to purge themselves of their old country's culture, in which soccer was often central. Others did the opposite and clung to their old ethnicity in the new world. Soccer teams with names such as the Greek-Americans and Celtic became rallying points for all the new Americans from a certain nation or region or religious sect to meet and mix. Examples remain in evidence today. In an over-thirty men's soccer league a few years ago, we, the ragtag Beacon Boys, faced opponents with names like Germania and Czechoslovakia. The latter was named for a nation that hadn't existed in three decades. But sure enough, its players seemed to be Czech or Slovak without exception. If you know where to look, often in urban parks late at night, you can still find entire leagues consisting just of Mexican or El Salvadoran or Honduran immigrants.

Ethnic soccer clubs may have given their members a sense of belonging and community, but they were also exclusive, even if they were theoretically open to outsiders. In the long periods when there was little organized soccer, this hampered the sport's growth. "The migrants may have helped to keep soccer alive during its bleakest decades," argues Dave Wangerin in his seminal history *Soccer in a Football World*, "but the establishment of ethnic clubs and leagues was poison to the game's chances of breaking through into the mainstream of American sports."

Inevitably, exceptionalism entered the discussion. In the context of soccer, the logic of this self-aggrandizing theory suggests that America could never accept a sport that is the standard most everywhere else in the world. But there is some merit to a slight variation to this notion: that the cultures that dominate Western society develop their own sports, or at least personalize them. The English were not the first to have the idea of kicking a ball at a goal, or jostling one over a line, or hitting it with a stick, but they codified soccer, rugby, and cricket and then exported them within their vast sphere of influence. The North Americans, likewise, either invented sports entirely, like basketball, or took the rudiments of cricket and came up with baseball and altered an early form of rugby into gridiron football. But when soccer reappeared on American shores more or less as we know it today, it carried with it a pungent scent of foreignness. That, consciously or not, made it unsuited for Americanization to many. To some, it still does.

The English, in turn, have scorned the American name for the sport that did break through—and that differentiated it from the gridiron kind of football played mostly with body parts that aren't the foot.

A man called Francis Tabor, an English headmaster of St. Bernard's School in New York City, may have unloosed this trivial debate in 1905. "It seems a thousand pities that in reporting Association football matches THE NEW YORK TIMES, in company with all the other newspapers, should persistently call the game 'Socker,'" Tabor wrote in a letter to the editor. "In the first place, there is no such word, and in the second place, it is an exceedingly ugly and undignified one."

While we could quibble about his second charge, Tabor was flatly wrong on the first count. There *was* such a word. Tabor's English countrymen were the first to call it soccer. In the nineteenth century, they needed to distinguish association football from its burlier cousin, rugby football. The well-to-do schoolboys who codified the two footballs possessed a flair for nicknaming. Rugby became "rugger" and association became "assoccer"—they could hardly call it "asser." "Assoccer" begat "socker" and then "soccer." The British invented the word, although they used it mostly as a nickname. It is no Americanism. One of England's most authoritative publications on the sport has been called *World Soccer* since 1960. Until quite recently, some of its leading TV shows on the sport had "soccer" in the name. And the island nation that exported the game all around the world kept calling it soccer—with new zeal following World War II, for some reason—until 1980 or so. Until, that is, the British apparently all got together and decided unanimously that they would standardize "football" as the only acceptable moniker, and, thenceforth, collectively scorn all who would dare call it soccer.

The memo never made it across the Atlantic.

3 | Dark Decades

The United States Soccer Football Federation, as it was now known, attempted to return to the World Cup in 1950, but its recent body of work did not suggest that it would make a mark there. At the 1948 Olympics in London, an American team, supposedly whittled from a list of five thousand aspirants, somehow showed up in England having never even practiced together. A 9–0 loss to Italy was the result, followed by exhibition losses to Norway, 11–0, and Northern Ireland, 5–0. The federation president, however, wrote in a postmortem that he felt good about the fact the U.S. players had all "conducted themselves as gentlemen" and had made many friends in London.

In its zeal to stave off further embarrassment, the federation made a concerted effort to find better players in its warren of regional leagues. Most of its rebuilt national team hailed from St. Louis, American soccer's epicenter at the time. The Americans lost their first qualifying game for the 1950 World Cup in Brazil to Mexico, 6–0. It was a game so lopsided that the Mexicans were said to have missed a penalty on purpose when they were already up 3–0, taking pity. But the U.S. tied Cuba 1–1 and then beat the Cubans 5–2 after another 6–2 loss to Mexico. It was enough to send the U.S. back to the first World Cup held since 1938, the previous two having been canceled on account of

World War II. The federation went all out and not only paid the players a hundred dollars per week at the World Cup—about twice what most of them made as semipros—but even granted them some time to practice together. Still, the squad selection process was chaotic. Benny McLaughlin couldn't travel because his employer in Philadelphia wouldn't let him. Jack Hynes, one of the nation's top players and a survivor of the war's bloody Battle of the Bulge, was kicked off the team because he had lightly criticized the thin-skinned federation by suggesting it "could have fielded a better team" in a postcard to a journalist friend, who saw fit to print the calumnies in the *Brooklyn Eagle.*

Two other World War II veterans did make the team. Goalkeeper Frank Borghi had been a medic on D-Day in Normandy, for which he was decorated—and drove a hearse after the war. Forward Frank Wallace survived a year in a German prisoner of war camp after his tank caught fire at Anzio in the Italian campaign. Three players who weren't U.S. citizens were added to the team late on, without trying out first: defender Joe Maca, who had already played three games for Belgium; Scottish-born midfielder Ed McIlvenny; and Haitian striker Joe Gaetjens, who had twice represented his motherland.

After the tournament, there would be controversy over the three late additions. FIFA left eligibility up to the national federations at the time, and since all three players had signed their "first papers," signaling their intention to become citizens, the United States Soccer Football Association was satisfied. FIFA demanded an explanation but let the matter go once it was reminded of its own rules. As it happened, only Maca eventually became a citizen. Gaetjens might have saved his own life by doing the same.

In a rare and precious pre-tournament practice game, the United States lost 1–0 to an English team led by superstar Stanley Matthews. The Americans quickly understood that they were underdogs in Brazil. Unlike their opponents, none of the Americans played fully professionally. They delivered mail and stripped wallpaper. They taught in schools and worked in mills. But they had fun with their status. His teammates called Borghi, the goalkeeper, the "six-goal wonder" for his capacity to hold opponents to a mere half-dozen goals. And some American players reportedly showed up to their game against England wearing Stetsons and chewing on cigars.

After just a few days together and a thirty-hour, six-airport trip to Brazil, the Americans showed up with a coach, Bill Jeffrey, who had been hired just two weeks earlier. The team had only a few days to prepare before its first game. Any practice time at all, however, constituted a luxury. Usually, the low-budget U.S. teams showed up much closer to their games.

The Americans acquitted themselves reasonably well in their first World Cup game. They lost 3–1 to Spain, but had been ahead after an hour before running out of gas and allowing three Spanish goals in the final ten minutes. Next, the U.S. would face England.

Jeffrey told the press his team had "no chance" against the English, who deigned to grace a World Cup with their presence for the first time and were expected to win it. Before the tournament, England had beaten two-time defending World Cup champions Italy 4–0 and then trounced Portugal 10–0. One English paper suggested that the decent thing to do would be to spot the Americans three goals at kickoff.

The England players were the guests of an English-owned gold mine outside Belo Horizonte, where two thousand Britons were employed. Some of the U.S. players, meanwhile, were said to have been out carousing until the early morning hours before the game. Yet the Americans had several advantages. Their unexpectedly scrappy performance against Spain gave them some confidence, as did the presence of a few hundred U.S. servicemen from a nearby military base. The Brazilian locals, meanwhile, rooted for the American long shots in hopes that they might prevent a showdown between the English and the home country at the business end of the tournament.

At last, the U.S. and England met in the small, tatty Estádio Independência. The English rested Matthews, their star, who had finally joined the team after his North American tour. The American goalie, Borghi, "the six-goal wonder," shut out the dominant English in the first half. Charlie Colombo anchored the American defense. He was an amateur boxer who liked to wear a pair of fingerless gloves on the field, emphasizing his bruising, spitting, swearing presence. "If his mother was on the other team, he probably would have kicked her, too," defender Harry Keough recalled decades later. "He played very well in that game. He was stepping over the line a few times, but he got away with it most of the time."

Before halftime, American midfielder Walter Bahr attempted a long shot to the far post. Out of nowhere, Gaetjens laid out for the ball, dinking it into the goal with a clever, glancing header that wrong-footed England goalkeeper Bert Williams. Unimaginably, the Americans were ahead.

As the sensational scoreline held in the face of an English onslaught, the crowd of ten thousand swelled to as many as forty thousand according to some reports. They had come to witness what was surely the greatest upset in the sport to that point—and perhaps since. When the final whistle trilled, the fans set off firecrackers and built bonfires in the stands. Others rushed the field and carried Gaetjens and Borghi away. "Colombo took off his mittens," Keough remembered. "And the first thing I heard him say in that raspy voice of his was, 'It's about time we beat these bastards.'"

English World Cup chronicler Brian Glanville would record England's calamity as "the formality that turned out a fiasco." Several newspapers around the world mistakenly printed the score as 10–1 to the English, assuming that the 0–1 reported on the newswires was a typo. In the wake of England's shocking loss, a lot of English newspapers, magazines, and books spent years attempting to explain away the debacle in Belo Horizonte. They landed on the assertion that the American team had been recruited on Ellis Island. The players were supposedly picked out of the immigration line and moved from one boat right onto another, headed for Brazil. Perhaps this fable made the loss more palatable somehow. The other excuse was that the Gaetjens goal had been a fluke, which beaten goalkeeper Bert Williams insisted on all his life. But every American on that team who was ever asked swore up and down that Gaetjens's header was intentional and a signature play of his.

"I don't mind saying we were almost sorry to beat the English team that day in Belo Horizonte," Keough later told the *St. Louis Post-Dispatch*'s Dent McSkimming, who was the only American reporter present in Brazil that day, having followed the team around on his vacation. "We felt it was going to be a terrible blow to them, and we knew we were not yet strong enough to win the championship. But we beat them and in the last five minutes came close to making it 3–0 instead of 1–0."

The Americans had one more group-stage game to play and an outside chance of becoming the lone team to advance to the next stage from the group. They went behind two goals to Chile, fought back to tie the game, and then stumbled to a 5–2 defeat. It didn't matter. Spain beat England, eliminating the U.S. regardless of its own result.

Hardly anyone came to meet the U.S. team at the airport when it returned from Brazil; the players took three different flights to save money. Bahr's wife picked him up in New York so they could hurry to the Adirondacks, where they would make some extra money working a summer camp. "A St. Louis guy's wife had come to the airport too," Bahr recalled. "Just to scold him for being back late."

After a few fruitless years in the French leagues, Joe Gaetjens, the scion of a wealthy and powerful family, returned to Haiti. He disappeared a decade later, most likely murdered by the François "Papa Doc" Duvalier regime in a political purge. Had Gaetjens followed through and become a U.S. citizen, it's unlikely that Papa Doc would have dared to have him killed.

In the 1954 World Cup qualifying cycle, the U.S. lost both its games hopelessly to Mexico by a combined score of 7–1. Four years later, the U.S. not only lost to Mexico, 6–0 and 7–2, but also managed to lose a pair of games by a combined score of 8–3 to a Canadian team that hadn't played an official game in thirty years. For the last of those games, the Americans didn't even employ a coach. From mid-1950 through 1964, the Americans played only nineteen games and lost sixteen times—including an eleven-year winless streak. During this dire time, England avenged its 1950 World Cup defeat to the U.S. with 8–1 and 10–0 romps in friendlies. The U.S. even lost to Iceland, which had won only three previous games in its entire history. In the qualifying cycle for the 1966 edition of the World Cup, the American campaign was so poorly organized that two coaches simultaneously claimed to be in charge of the USA. Meanwhile, the players were left to find their own transportation in Honduras, winding up in a painter's truck.

These were sorry efforts at returning to the world stage, contested by players memorable only for their unlikely names: Walter Schmotolocha, Siggy Stritzl, Miro Rys, Juli Veee. Even when Mexico qualified automatically in 1970 as the World Cup host, leaving the CONCACAF region's spot wide open to everybody else, the U.S. could not pull it off. More than once, the Americans lost their coach in the middle of the qualifying cycle. Dettmar Cramer left after only two games. The federation threatened to sue Cramer for $10 million for breaching his contract only to realize that it had forgotten to make him sign anything when it appointed him.

American teams tended to be assembled just days before key games, getting in a few practice sessions if they were lucky. Sometimes they flew in the day *of* the game. Tension forever simmered between the underpaid players and the penniless federation. Some players declined national team invitations altogether. Before a late game in the long-lost 1974 World Cup qualifying effort, the U.S. team recruited a player from the stands to make up the numbers. This failed campaign was nonetheless followed by an inexplicable eighteen-game, eight-country European tour, in which the U.S. used sixty-one different and largely foreign-born players and lost most of its games heavily. During these dark decades, it was hard to make out which indignity weighed heavier. Perhaps the twelve-game losing streak, despite only playing a few games in most years. Or the 10–0 loss to Italy in a match that, mercifully, was never made official. Or maybe the time its Mexican hosts played the German national anthem, rather than "The Star-Spangled Banner," before beating their guests 4–0.

The Making of a National Team: Tyler Adams

The people kept on coming, wanting pictures, wanting autographs, wanting to chat. Every time the pack thinned out a little and he became visible again at the center of it, more people realized, *Holy shit, that's Tyler Adams!*

His mother, Melissa, stood off to the side, deputized to handing out Sharpies and holding people's things as they posed with her son. She'd gotten used to the kids wanting to be near him, for him to touch something of theirs and to provide proof that they had met the United States men's national team pillar, the English Premier League player, the youngest captain at the 2022 World Cup at age twenty-three. The kids wanted to text the evidence to their friends and post it to social media. This made sense to Melissa. But she would probably never get used to middle-aged men beset by the same giddiness as all those preteens, just as eager to stand next to her boy.

On a drizzly summer night, Adams signed and signed. A girls' soccer team decided that they all ought to have *two* Tyler Adams autographs *on each shoe*—four apiece!—and he didn't flinch at their excessive demands, he just kept on signing. He stood along the soccer field at Mount Saint Mary College in Newburgh, New York, where the minor league Hudson Valley Hammers team that he co-owns with his parents was about to play. The Mount Saint Mary campus sits on a bluff overlooking the Hudson Valley. The Hudson River sprawled behind Adams. From a few steps down the hill, the river snaked up toward Poughkeepsie, where Adams and his mom started out in a little apartment. Downstream, the river runs past Wappingers Falls, where their family tripled in size, and then alongside New Jersey, where Adams lived out his dream as a professional soccer player. And back up here, to Newburgh, where he hoped to repay the region that made him with the game that gave him everything. He signed jerseys and cleats and phone cases. He caught up with old family friends, with extended-family members. He took a picture with the referees at halftime.

Tyler Adams was twenty-one years old when he and his parents started the Hammers in their backyard as a developmental minor league team. Five years into his own professional career, Adams was already fretting about how he might leave the game behind for the next generation of local prospects. The family had discussed doing something like this for years until one day Darryl, Adams's stepfather whom he refers to and thinks of as his dad, just went ahead and started it. "People think this was a well-thought-out plan for how we can develop soccer in the area," Adams said. "And although we'd talked about it a million times, us starting this was not in-depth at all. We jumped in the deep end and learned how to swim. We needed to figure it out because the impact I'm able to have, especially while I'm still playing, won't last forever. And I want to share my experiences with the people in the community who helped raise me."

The whole thing is quintessentially Tyler—concerned with the greater good, ambitious, a bit impatient, and looked after by a sprawling web of family and friends. Although the Hammers play in the fourth tier, draw perhaps a hundred people to their home games, and are made up largely of unpaid collegians, their conditions belie their station. That's Tyler, too: standards. "It's not some hillbilly thing," he said. "It's giving players opportunities to play at a level they maybe didn't think they'd be able to play at. Without having a contract for £100,000 a week, it's a professional environment. You'll be coached by good people. You'll have food and uniforms and all these things that not everyone at that level can provide."

Adams and his parents want to open a pathway that didn't exist when Adams was a prospect. "As parents, we were exhausted driving to Jersey for Tyler and Dylan every day," Melissa recalled—Dylan is one of Tyler's three stepbrothers, who, like Tyler, came up through the New York Red Bulls Academy in northern New Jersey. They want local kids to be able to play at the highest level without forcing their families to waste so much of their lives traveling to the nearest professional academy. "The whole thing is very personal to us and to our boys," Melissa said. "There are a lot of kids who don't make it because they don't have the means to even get to a team like that."

After all, the U.S. men's national team has never really looked like America. Historically, it looked more like America's upper-middle class: disproportionately wealthy and white. For every player who scraps his way up from the hinterlands on talent and guile, a dozen emerge from the pipeline at least in part because their parents could afford the pricey pay-for-play system in some tony suburb.

The path into elite soccer leads almost exclusively through the travel soccer scene, which typically costs each player's family thousands of dollars a year. The only alternative is the youth academies of MLS teams, which tend to be free but offer only so many spots in so many towns and usually don't take players on until they are teenagers—past some crucial development years. For everyone else, youth soccer costs a great deal of money. Many families are priced out before anybody has had a chance to find out if their child might be any good. A 2020 study by *Yahoo! Sports* found that the 161 elite soccer clubs affiliated with the nation's top youth circuit were contained in zip codes with a median household income of almost $100,000, far higher than the national average. If you don't live in an affluent zip code, chances are that there is no high-level youth soccer club in your vicinity. Such clubs are not just financially inaccessible to many Americans, but physically inaccessible as well—it's tricky getting out to the suburbs if you live in a city and don't have a car.

Good thing Tyler Adams's mom had a car.

Melissa Russo got pregnant right after finishing community college. She put off her bachelor's degree to take care of the newborn in her arms. She was twenty-three and a single mother to an energetic, outgoing, headstrong boy. In day care, Tyler had an unusual gift for getting the other kids to follow his lead, to play what he was playing, and to do it the way he thought it should be done. "He was no different than he is now," Melissa marveled some twenty years later. "He seriously was the same."

They lived in a small apartment in Poughkeepsie. Adams's biological father was around sporadically at first. "He didn't come from a great background, family-wise," Melissa said. "I just don't think he had the tools to understand how to be a parent." Soon enough, he got mixed up with drugs, wound up in jail, and then wasn't around at all.

"My mom was that father figure for me early on that I didn't have," Adams said. "She invested a lot of time into me and not a lot of time into herself."

Melissa and Tyler didn't have much. But they had structure. Routines and chores. Adams liked to help his mom. And when he'd done all that he had to, and sometimes more, he could go kick his soccer ball against a wall in a nearby park or buy his beloved bacon, egg, and cheese sandwich from the Italian deli on the corner with his allowance. "He was the kind of kid where you see the devil and the angel at the same time," Melissa said. "He knows what's right and pushes as many buttons as he can on the other side."

By the time he was eleven, Adams's talent was apparent and the burdens of elite youth soccer—all the money and all the travel—created new exigencies for Melissa, who took extra work shifts just to afford it all. Yet when Adams tried out for the New York Red Bulls Academy team, whose players were all at least a year older than he was, nobody ever called him back.

In the seventh grade, Adams met a boy in technology class named Darryl Sullivan Jr. They played on the same soccer team and grew close. Little did they know that Darryl's father and Tyler's mother had known each other in high school and were reconnecting on the sidelines. It was Darryl Jr. who, a few weeks into the school year, invoked the possibility that their parents might be dating. Adams dismissed this notion out of hand, with no small amount of hostility. "I always figured growing up with a single mother that there's nothing going on in their personal life," said Adams.

As Melissa's relationship with Darryl Sr. blossomed, Tyler's own introduction to him was rocky. Darryl loves to tell this story, and Tyler gives a salty eye roll whenever it comes up, but it goes something like this: When Darryl came over for the first time, he watched Tyler beat his mother at the *FIFA* video game. Darryl pretended to be a novice and challenged Tyler to a match, even promising him a new pair of cleats if Tyler won. "He was like, 'Oh, I've never played this game. Let me play,'" Adams recalled. "And he'd played it a million times, obviously, and he killed me. He brings it up to this day anytime we talk about anything in life. It could be about literally anything and he's like, 'Remember that time I beat you in *FIFA*?'"

Darryl picked up the story from there. "He goes crying to his room, so pissed off," he said. "So I needed to let him know what the deal was. I told him to come back out and play me again. I beat him worse; back into the room again." Each time Tyler stormed off, Darryl coaxed him back for another game before beating him yet again. There was a lesson in there. Tyler got his new cleats anyway. "I didn't think when I was mad about losing at *FIFA* that it would have such a big impact on my life as it has, but without him I wouldn't be where I am," Adams said.

Tyler and Darryl built a deep connection. They had their own traditions and routines, even their own language. They applied a similar pragmatism to their lives, taking the long view of things, thinking strategically, making a game of outmaneuvering one another in anything at all—like shopping for groceries most efficiently. "Tyler and Darryl don't share any genetic material, but they're soulmates," said Melissa.

"My dad did a really good job of truly acting like his father and not just some guy," said Darryl Jr. "My dad definitely is not easy on us, but he made us all better people. I think that changed Tyler the most."

Darryl Sr. had been a college soccer player himself and coached at the college level after leading a high school girls' team to two New York State titles. In Tyler, he saw a player whose technique was lacking and who didn't have much of a knack for goal scoring—unlike most promising players at that age—but whose vision and attitude and work ethic nevertheless made him special. Adams tried out for the Red Bulls again in 2012. This time, he not only made the under-13 Red Bulls team, but a scout for his age group's U.S. national team happened to be at the tryout. Just like that, he was in a professional academy *and* the youth national team program.

But Adams had a habit of fixating on his mistakes. On the soccer field, Darryl noticed that a single bad pass could ruin Tyler's entire game, because he dwelled on it and then his performance spiraled. One night, Tyler was writing a paper for school in his immaculate handwriting and made a mistake. It was late but he wanted to rewrite the entire page. "I said, 'No, just put a line through it and write above it,'" remembered Darryl, who was a schoolteacher himself. "He goes, 'I don't know if I can do that.'" Darryl took the paper away and sent Tyler to bed. Tyler learned to move on from his errors. Not every page had to be perfect.

Every year, the teachers in Tyler's elementary school asked the pupils in the class to raise their hand if they had a sibling, and then raise them again if they had a pet at home. Every year, Tyler would come home crying because he didn't get to raise his hand either time. "And it's Tyler, so it's always dramatic," Melissa said. "Then we merged the families, he got three brothers, and he got a pet. All the boxes were checked."

Gradually, Melissa and Tyler moved into Darryl's home in Wappingers Falls and formed a new family with Darryl's three sons and dog. Darryl Jr. was only two months younger than Tyler, Dylan was two years behind him, and Donovan the youngest by another year. Darryl Jr. and Tyler became inseparable. All four boys had sleepovers in the same bedroom, chattering away deep into the night. But the transition was hardly smooth. Tyler and Dylan were ferociously competitive. The first time they met, at Tyler's grandmother's house to watch the Super Bowl, a driveway basketball game between the four boys came to blows. "Tyler threw a punch at me and I just met the kid—what the heck," Dylan recalled with a chuckle. "We used to call him Punk Tyler when he'd get like that. He'd be a sore loser. Granted, he rarely lost things."

His parents' divorce left Darryl Jr. with more responsibility for the care of his younger brothers. Tyler's arrival lightened that load, since Darryl Sr. expected him to take care of his new stepbrothers as well. It was a role Tyler came to relish. "It's like it was puzzle pieces that came together, all of us," said Darryl Sr. "Tyler's kind of the glue with the boys."

Moving into the Sullivan home at thirteen is perhaps when Adams became a team captain. "I've always been vocal, wanted to lead by example," he said. "But without having brothers, I'm not sure I would be as relatable or as patient as I am today."

Darryl took an active role in Tyler's soccer career, using his contacts and his experience in the sport to guide Tyler to the right coaches, the right teams at the right age level, and helped Melissa afford the mounting costs. Adams had always played up in age, but Darryl insisted he spend a season with his peers to learn to take control of a game, to build up his confidence and leadership. When Adams joined the Red Bulls Academy, Darryl Sr. took on some of the endless drives down to New Jersey, which devoured afternoons and energy and whatever time he and Melissa hoped to have for themselves.

Adams, for his part, grew into an uncommon maturity. If they had to leave the house at 6 a.m. for practice or a game, he would be standing at the door, dressed and packed, right when he was supposed to. If they got home at midnight, he would be on time for school early the next morning, without complaint. "I didn't want to let anybody down for the opportunity," Adams said. "I knew that getting any little one percent over the kids in my age group was going to be important."

Before joining the Red Bulls Academy, Adams had attended a soccer camp at a Red Bull development affiliate. There were perhaps fifty players there. As a group, the boys were asked by the coaches how many of them the kids thought might go pro. After they discussed this for a while, they landed on a consensus of ten or so. The coaches said that the camp would have been a success if it helped to produce a single professional. More likely, they said, it would yield none. Adams took note. "I remember thinking to myself, 'Well, if there's going to be one, it's going to be me,'" he said. He decided there and then that he would never give anybody anything to hold against him. So he would always be ready, always on time, always at his best. "The last thing you want to be called in this game is unprofessional," he said.

The first invitation to move into the under-17 U.S. national team residency in Bradenton, Florida, arrived before Adams's freshman year of high school. He was too young, his parents decided. There was only so much of his childhood they were willing to sacrifice at the altar of his budding soccer career. As a compromise, he would parachute into camp for a week at a time, every month or so. His sophomore year, he went full-time. He liked it there, immersed in soccer, doing and thinking of little else. He forged close friendships with two other residents, Christian Pulisic and Weston McKennie. But he also felt like the place could be suffocating. "As soon as you pick up everything and you go to Bradenton, you're staying with only your teammates in school," Adams recalled. "There's no interacting with other people. It's the same teachers for everything. You lose a lot of social life and having fun." Besides, he felt like he wasn't developing any quicker than he would at the Red Bulls Academy. He came home after just a year.

By the time he turned sixteen, it was apparent that Adams would, at 5 foot 8, be undersized in his best position as a central midfielder. His growth spurt came on early but leveled off just as quickly, and soon, all the players around him caught up to him and then got bigger.

If he was going to compete, Adams would have to get smarter. His size forced him to think more deeply about the game, to see it better, to predict where the ball would go before everybody else did, and then beat them there. "I was never the most technical player," he said. "My understanding of the game has always been my best trait on the field—reading plays, anticipating plays. My IQ definitely needed to improve at a younger age because I wasn't the biggest player anymore." These soft skills, as it turned out, would set him apart from the dime-a-dozen prospects who packed more brawn but had a weak grasp of how soccer games are actually won. Soccer is, at its core, a game of spatial problem-solving. A teenage Tyler Adams solved the problems quickly and efficiently.

The New York Red Bulls, part of a global conglomerate of energy drink–powered soccer teams that were analytically savvy before most of their competitors, recognized Adams's understated talent. Weeks after his sixteenth birthday, the club offered him his first professional contract. Melissa and Darryl worried endlessly about the decision—Tyler was too young to sign without his mother's consent. Signing professionally meant closing the door to a scholarship at one of the many colleges that would soon be vying for his soccer services. So the family negotiated tuition money for an online college into Adams's deal with the Red Bulls, whereupon Melissa extracted a promise from her son that he would, at some point, earn a degree.

After a spell with the club's minor league development team, Adams made his senior team debut in the summer of 2015 in an exhibition against Premier League giants Chelsea. He scored a goal on a header. By the 2017 season, he was a regular starter. That spring, he excelled at the U-20 World Cup. "He was two years younger than everybody else, but he just had that demeanor from the beginning," said U.S. under-20 head coach Tab Ramos. "He came in and he took over. He outworked everybody. He was younger, but he was a step above."

Later that year, Adams would also make his senior national team debut against Portugal, the first match the U.S. played after its failure to qualify for the 2018 World Cup. Along the way, Adams received his high school diploma in a special ceremony hours before his classmates, so that he could make it to New Jersey in time to play against crosstown rivals New York City FC.

Darryl Sr. built a tight circle of advisers around Tyler, turning to relatives and family friends who were all successful in their respective fields and wanted only to support him. That circle did not include Tyler's biological father, who had been out of jail for several years. While Melissa and Darryl encouraged Tyler to rebuild a relationship with him, he found his biological father to be unreliable and cut him out of his life. "For me, it was never, 'Aw, man. I hate this guy. He left us. He went to jail for drugs,'" said Adams. "Shit, that's life. Everyone goes through something. Everyone has their own story."

It's just that Adams resented him for making his mom's life harder, for all the extra work she had to do, for all the effort she had to make to finish college, to provide as a single parent. Adams didn't like how his biological father assumed he could walk right back into his life after his release. Adams also felt a deep loyalty to his mother and appreciated all that his stepfather and his stepbrothers had done to fit him into their lives, to embrace him as one of theirs. He decided that his biological father would have to earn his way back into the equation, and he never put in the work.

The New York Red Bulls' head coach, Jesse Marsch, had warned some of the team's veterans that a promising teenager with a big personality would be joining the senior team. Sure enough, Adams quickly made his mark. "When I was a rookie, I would never say shit. I would never talk to the old guys," said Sacha Kljestan, a veteran on that team.

"Tyler's first couple of training sessions, he was tackling people hard. He didn't say sorry, he was just like 'This is me.' It was like, 'Fuck this little kid. Who does he think he is, coming in here and not having respect for the older players?' But within three months you could see this kid was the real deal. He had this crazy mentality about him. You could see he was going to go far."

Felipe Martins, a Brazilian midfielder and one of the Red Bulls' key players, was merciless on the young rookie, tweaking Adams day after day. "Felipe always picked on him, like a big brother but also in a threatened kind of way," said Kljestan. One day, Adams, who was almost a decade younger than Felipe, ended the abuse. "I just picked him up and dropped him and stood over him and was like, 'You've gotta stop doing that. I'm not a little kid,'" Adams remembered. "I don't think he understood my mentality and who I was. I never took shit from anyone; I didn't really care who it was. From that day on out, he definitely stopped. That was a turning point in the way people looked at me."

At nineteen, Adams moved to RB Leipzig—the German Bundesliga club atop the pyramid of Red Bulls' global system of sister clubs. Melissa was supposed to help Tyler settle into his new home. But she broke her ankle and Darryl Sr. wound up taking him instead. "It was just like dropping a kid off at college," Darryl said. "It just happens to be in a foreign country." Darryl barely slept on the flight, turning over in his head all the things that had to get done while Tyler snoozed blissfully. Scurrying from the airport to the club's practice facility for Adams to undergo his medical exam before the deal could be completed; getting out a pile of cash from a German bank to put down a deposit on an apartment; handling the endless little things that had to be arranged.

The medical exam included a fitness test. Adams put on his headphones and began pumping his legs on a treadmill. He didn't stop until Darryl told him to ease off, reminding Adams of the nagging injuries he had been dealing with, and that he had practice the next day. When he finally stopped, Adams had very nearly broken the club's fitness test record—even though he'd walked right off an intercontinental night flight. "I'm gonna break that fucking record next time," Tyler told Darryl, and he did. The next day, Darryl's stress subsided when he watched Adams practice with his new teammates, palling around with them. Darryl flew home, his mind at ease.

Adams was an RB Leipzig regular before long, and in August 2020, he scored the goal that advanced Leipzig to the semifinals of the UEFA Champions League, the club's best-ever performance. In three and a half seasons, he helped RB Leipzig to four top-four finishes in the stacked Bundesliga. But Adams felt himself plateauing. He could have stayed at the club another decade; he was sure of it. In the summer of 2022, having turned twenty-three and been reduced to a diminished role under a new coach, Adams pushed for a move to the English Premier League, where he had hoped to end up all along. He was sold to Leeds United and went to play for Jesse Marsch for a third time—Marsch had also managed Leipzig for a short spell.

An injury cut short Adams's first EPL season and marred most of his second, with AFC Bournemouth after Leeds was relegated to a second-tier league. Yet when he was on the field, Adams established himself as one of the best young defensive midfielders in Europe.

In 2018, the year he turned nineteen, Adams made eight appearances for the national team. By the 2022 World Cup, he was a load-bearing pillar and the team's emotional leader with his fanatical devotion to the team he'd rooted for since he was a boy. He was its most consistent player, too, thriving at the World Cup and managing to stand out in an unglamorous position. He defended so much terrain in front of the back line that it freed his fellow midfielders to charge forward without concern for the space they were vacating. He won more tackles than any other player in Qatar, whose team hadn't made it past the round of 16.

Adams had arrived. But Darryl never stopped coaching him. While Adams played for the Red Bulls, they created a system of hand signals for Darryl to pass along his observations from the stands. When Adams started playing abroad, Darryl texted him his scouting reports at halftime. Now, on days when Darryl is in the stadium, Adams will make eye contact with him as he heads to the locker room, holding his thumb and his pinkie to his ear, just to make sure his dad remembers to do his duty. "He sees everything," Adams said recently. "I don't think people understand his knowledge of the game. He dissects the game better than ninety percent of the analysts and coaches I've had. He sees a lot of little details, especially because he's watching *me*." Darryl will tell Tyler to get into his team's defensive shape quicker, or to close down a certain player on his left foot on the inside, or what spaces to defend or push into. "It's good to get the perception from someone watching from a bird's-eye view," he said. "In my position, that makes all the difference. Me winning a ball is the difference between a team scoring and not scoring."

Every now and again, Punk Tyler slips his reins.

On a rare family trip in the sliver of free time between soccer seasons, Melissa, Tyler's partner Sarah, and Sarah's mother organized a lawn game competition for everyone, replete with team T-shirts and prizes. They got to just the third of eight events—egg-and-spoon races, cornhole, and the like—when they had to call the whole thing off. Tyler was screaming at his mother to run faster, and things got so heated between him and his brothers that they agreed to end the competition in order to salvage the rest of the vacation.

Adams learned to harness his roaring competitiveness, the elite athlete's superpower, and managed to deploy Punk Tyler only when he was useful. "Part of that person still sticks with me, just in appropriate settings, whereas before it would be as more of an attention-seeking teenager," he explained. "My dad put me in my place fairly quickly."

Melissa calls Tyler an old soul. "He's very content being a homebody and now thinks he's a wine connoisseur," Melissa said. "He's always acted older than he is." Adams rarely has fun going out for a drink with friends unless Darryl Jr.—who played college football as an offensive lineman—comes along to scare strangers away. He doesn't go clubbing. "I was never scared of partying, but when I decided that soccer was the path that I wanted to take, that would just slow down the trajectory of what I was trying to achieve," Adams explained. "You put yourself in bad situations, bad things are going to happen. So I always try to limit who I'm around. When you have so much to lose, there's a very small amount of people you can trust. A lot of athletes fall into the trap of getting recognized and taking advantage of it. There's so many perks to being an athlete, but those aren't the perks that I choose to use."

Even though he was a millionaire several times over before he was old enough to rent a car, Adams's money is mostly saved. He splurges only on travel and sneakers—and before long, he changed his mind about the value of a large sneaker collection. With a goal of building generational wealth, Adams and his financial team have created a portfolio of careful investments. He hates losing money. "The value of money doesn't change just because you have more of it," he said. He remembers where he and his mom started out. "Those beginnings often humble me. Because I'll think back to those small rooms. It wasn't in a great neighborhood. Fortunately, now me and my girlfriend have a big house in Bournemouth and we live close to the beach and we have all these things you would never dream of having when you're in that one-bedroom apartment." Becoming a father at the age of twenty-four only crystallized the contrast for Adams. "With a kid now, I look at things with a completely different perspective. I have luxuries that my mom didn't have raising me." Luxuries like helping to pay for a new soccer field in Poughkeepsie, close to that little apartment, for the kids who live in that area now.

Rather than enjoy the spoils of all his toil, Adams prefers to go in for extra training on days off and to take classes online, working toward a degree in psychology, which he thinks he might want to apply to sports when he's done playing. He doesn't feel any need to be the center of attention. Adams isn't on social media beyond the bare minimum required for personal branding. He sneaked into his younger brothers' high school graduations, careful to go unnoticed lest he steal their thunder, just to witness their big day.

Jesse Marsch considered making Adams the New York Red Bulls captain when he was only seventeen. Tab Ramos put the captain's armband on Adams in the second half of his very first scrimmage with the under-20 national team. For the first few years of the U.S. national team's rebuilding project after the failure to reach the 2018 World Cup, head coach Gregg Berhalter didn't appoint a full-time captain, a symbolically charged role in international soccer. "We gave these guys space to grow," he explained. "We didn't put pressure on them. We used the time we had to develop strong leaders." Instead of a captain, the team elected a leadership council of seven players: Tyler Adams, Christian Pulisic, Weston McKennie, Aaron Long, Walker Zimmerman, Sean Johnson, and DeAndre Yedlin. The captain's armband rotated among them. By the summer of 2022, however, FIFA's rules demanded a permanent captain be appointed ahead of the World Cup. Berhalter proposed a workaround. Johnson was a reserve goalkeeper and unlikely to play. If Johnson became captain, they could still hand the armband to somebody different for every game, since the captain had to be on the field.

Out there between the lines, it was clear who the team's leader really was. Antonee Robinson has played alongside Adams for many of his national team games. He found Adams impossible to ignore in all of them. "He's loud as fuck," Robinson said. "He knows the game, knows where everyone needs to be, and he demands everything. He's not afraid to speak to anyone. If we'd have had really experienced players, if they weren't doing the right thing, he'd have been screaming at them, too. But he also leads by example. He's running the most on the pitch, he's throwing himself into tackles, and he's really, really passionate. So he's easy to get behind."

The team made this sentiment official by voting overwhelmingly to make Adams their captain. In spite of being only twenty-three and the youngest captain at the World Cup, he was undaunted. "I wouldn't say there are many things out there that intimidate me," Adams said in Qatar. "Other than spiders."

PART II

The Reawakening

1983–1989

4 | Team America

When North American Soccer League President Howard Samuels called Robert Lifton to ask if he wanted to bankroll a new team, Lifton's inclination was to hang up the phone. "I was very skeptical of the whole idea," recalled Lifton, a successful entrepreneur with no previous connection to soccer.

By 1983, the NASL was in free fall. It had been six years since Pelé left the New York Cosmos and the hype around the league died down. The other superstars of their age—Johan Cruyff and Franz Beckenbauer, George Best and all the rest—were either gone or in obvious decline. In just the past three years, the league had shriveled from twenty-four teams to twelve and ABC no longer cared to broadcast it—nor did anyone else. There were rumors of a work stoppage. The league was said to be losing $25 million a year.

The U.S. men's national team, meanwhile, had played just one game in 1982 and none at all in 1981. "The national team was bankrupt," recalled Alan Merrick, an NASL veteran from Birmingham, England, who had just become a U.S. citizen and therefore eligible for its national team. "The United States Soccer Federation was disheveled."

One of the many issues afflicting the national team was that few NASL coaches trusted their domestic players. The global stigma against

American soccer would linger into the twenty-first century. The nation simply had no track record of producing players who could compete with foreign opponents. And so most coaches didn't bother with them. The league had to institute a rule requiring at least two, and then three, North American players on the field at all times. Most coaches sidestepped this quota by fielding a few token Americans in lesser positions, or, better yet, by getting green cards for foreigners.

Ahead of the 1983 season, Samuels dreamed up a cockamamie plan "in the nationalistic interest." It would, he promised, revive his league and solve the federation's woes all at once. Together, they would pander to the patriotic zeitgeist of the Cold War by fielding an all-American squad, turning the national team into a professional club and entering it into the league. This would present commercial opportunities and improve the moribund national team all at once, by giving it meaningful time to practice and play together.

Samuels, who had worked in the administrations of three U.S. presidents but had no apparent soccer background, had taken over the NASL's presidency just months earlier. He diagnosed the league as being overly foreign and drew up a plan for "Americanization." The new franchise would be named Team America in an unsubtle play for jingoism. St. Louis was dismissed as its home in favor of Washington, DC—never mind that three separate NASL teams had already gone under in Washington, two of them as recently as 1980 and 1981. Samuels managed to convince Lifton, a fellow soccer neophyte, to take on the team. "We're going to show the rest of the world that America can play the world's game as well, if not better, than the rest of the world," Lifton proclaimed.

The idea of impounding a national team was not without merit or precedent. National teams in soccer tend to benefit when the bulk of their players represent just a few club teams. Herb Brooks brought his U.S. Olympic hockey team together five months before the 1980 Winter Games and played sixty-one preparatory games, laying the groundwork for the team's unlikely gold medal. U.S. Soccer, in fact, had already attempted a version of the gambit, albeit with little success, fielding national teams composed entirely of players from a single club several times in the 1940s and '50s.

Team America's media guide attempted to explain the project while drizzling its special sauce of soccer nationalism over the whole deal.

America's Cream!
Washington's Team!
Look out world, here comes Team America. A star-spangled soccer sensation about to hit the North American Soccer League. Think of it. Right here in Washington. All the excitement of NASL soccer with something extra—*The best American soccer players all on one team.*

Team America declared that it expected an average attendance of as many as thirty thousand at RFK Stadium, for which it signed an eight-year lease. That would be double the crowd most other NASL teams were drawing, and about equal to the number pulled in by the globally famous Cosmos. It also announced a free Beach Boys concert after the June 12 game against the Fort Lauderdale Strikers, with two more to follow.

"We're talking fun, fun, fun," Beach Boys lead singer Mike Love promised at a press conference. "We're talking good vibrations. We're talking Team America soccer."

Alketas Panagoulias loved three things deeply: soccer, smoking, and the United States of America. His announcement as the first head coach of Team America in 1983 meant that Alkis, as everybody called him, could devote himself to all three at once.

To the few people listening, he proclaimed that the United States was a "sleeping giant in soccer" and that he, of course, would be the one to rouse it.

Panagoulias was born in Thessaloniki and lived through the Nazi occupation of Greece and the subsequent civil war. The four years of hunger during World War II marked him, as did staring down the barrels of the retreating Nazis' machine guns, which cut down his uncle but spared Panagoulias. After playing several seasons for Aris, one of Greece's biggest soccer clubs, he left for the United States in 1961. As a twenty-seven-year-old, he somehow wound up studying at and playing for Orange County Community College, in New York's Hudson Valley. From there he transferred to Upsala College in New Jersey. "The first day, I bent over to tie my shoelaces so that I could see how the other players kicked the ball," he later recalled to the *Los Angeles Times*. "I said, 'If I'm not the king, I'll be the prince.' Twenty-four hours later, my picture was on the front page of the newspaper."

He married an American; they had two children and settled in Brooklyn. Panagoulias became a U.S. citizen. In New York, he starred for and then coached the New York Greek American Atlas Astoria Soccer Club, to give it its full due, back when the best soccer was likely played in the ethnic leagues teeming with former professionals from Europe. While working in real estate and earning a postgraduate certificate in international relations, Alkis led the Greek Americans to three straight U.S. Open Cup titles from 1967 through 1969. Somehow, he parlayed this success into a job as an assistant coach, and then head coach, of the Greek national team—a baffling leap up the coaching ladder. Panagoulias guided Greece to qualification for its first major tournament, the 1980 European Championship. In his next job, he won a Greek championship with league powerhouse Olympiacos.

In Panagoulias, Team America hired a big name and a bigger personality. The chain-smoker, who did not let games interrupt his cravings, had a gift for covering up deficiencies in his teams. He was less successful at shoring up his personal appearance. He sported an Olympic comb-over, sprouting just above his left ear and soaring across his still obviously bald head.

For his abundant idiosyncrasies, the strangest idea rattling around in Alkis Panagoulias's mind was that he believed the United States could be good at soccer. "This isn't some underdeveloped, underprivileged country," he told *Sports Illustrated*. "Even now as we talk, somewhere—in Harlem, in Tampa, in LA, I don't know where—there are Pelés growing up. There was no compulsion for me to leave a comfortable career in Greece and come here. But I believe that American soccer has a tremendous potential for success."

In December 1982, before a single player had been invited to Team America's preseason training camp, Rick Davis, the most famous American player of his time and a mainstay with the Cosmos, eviscerated the experiment with an opinion piece in *The New York Times* titled "Team America: Not the Way for Soccer."

He noted that if you took the best American players out of their clubs, they might actually wind up with less aggregate playing time. Only eleven of them could be on the field at once for Team America, while more than that were starting for their current teams—which offered better competition in practice to boot. Besides, Davis said, picking a national team for the next three years was impractical. By the end of that period, a lineup of the eleven best American players could look entirely different, yet there would be no flexibility to upgrade to a new cycle of talent. Why not, Davis proposed, set aside the money earmarked for Team America and instead stage an extensive national team tour after the NASL season? That way, the players got high-level soccer *and* time together with the national team. Nobody of consequence paid Ricky Davis's pleas any mind, no matter how much sense he made. But he was hardly alone in harboring reservations. "The only players who have made up their minds are the ones who don't know all the issues," Cosmos goalkeeper David Brcic told *The Washington Post*.

The first person to turn down Team America was not an American but a Dutchman, Rinus Michels. The most influential coach of his time wanted nothing to do with the job. A rumor made the rounds that somebody asked Michels how long it would take to develop better American soccer players. "Five years," he had supposedly answered. "Because that's how long it takes for a foreigner to become an American citizen."

Invitations for the training camp in Tampa went out. But haggling for players with cash-strapped teams took longer than expected and the camp was delayed by a week. Some teams, like the Seattle Sounders, argued that since they took American players seriously, they weren't a part of the problem Team America was designed to address and therefore shouldn't have to give up the players they developed. When camp finally opened on February 8, only twenty-two of the thirty-nine players who had been invited showed up.

And not all who materialized stayed on. Several established players quit and returned to their original teams. Ricky Davis went through camp in spite of his misgivings. Alkis called him "the all-America boy who belongs with Team America," but Davis decided otherwise. "I didn't feel that Team America was the way to do it, and it created a lot of animosity with a lot of people," Davis recalled decades later.

Team America had missed out on most of the national team's pool of forwards and creators. So many national teamers declined to join, in fact, that Team America scrambled to find warm bodies who could fill out the roster. The new team was shaping up to be something like a national team tribute band, rather than the real deal.

To fill in the many gaps on its roster, the new franchise turned to a class of foreign-born NASL players who had recently become citizens but never represented the U.S. before. Alan Merrick had been a regular for West Bromwich Albion in England before moving to the NASL in 1976. A U.S. citizen for all of six months, he answered Team America's plea for players. Joining him were naturalized players who had been born in Yugoslavia, Italy, Ecuador, Cape Verde, Costa Rica, and Trinidad and Tobago. Three players had not yet been naturalized, meaning they could play for Team America but not the actual national team—rather defeating the point of the whole thing.

A bitterness lingered toward the bona fide national teamers who had opted out of the project. At times, Team America's season devolved into the Ricky Davis Revenge Tour. The star was cast as a scapegoat for the many ills that would come to ail the team in his absence. "We didn't like Ricky for a long time," said Merrick, who sought Davis out on the field whenever Team America played the Cosmos so he could kick him anytime he got the chance.

Before the season even began, the narrative surrounding Team America shifted from a powerhouse expansion club coming to save the league to an underdog story. "The team took on a different tenor in the sense that if Rick Davis is not here, it's not really the national team," said Jim Henderson, the team's vice president of public relations.

Panagoulias understood that all the defections had made his task immeasurably harder. "Right now, we look like the three hundred Spartans against the Persians, but I have faith in these boys," he said.

So did Leonidas. The Spartans all died anyway.

In early April, Team America played its first four games on a tour of Haiti and Colombia, exhibitions to get them ready for the NASL season. In Port-au-Prince, they won a scrimmage against a local team 1–0. Then, on April 8, the USA descended again from its mountain hotel, where electricity was sporadic, to play the full Haitian national team in a hostile stadium with fans banging on the locker room walls. Even more fans climbed over the stadium's walls to witness the event. This was no friendly match for the home team, which made it an extremely physical affair on a bad field. The U.S. won 2–0 on goals by Chico Borja and Jeff Durgan, but Sonny Askew was so badly hurt that he had to go to a hospital, where he was, according to several players on the team, "treated" by a witch doctor.

It was the only sanctioned national team game that Team America would ever play, although it took a few phone calls before kickoff to get it recognized as such. The U.S. national team would not officially play again for more than a year.

When Team America kicked off its NASL season against the Seattle Sounders on April 23, the fault lines that would cause its collapse were already showing. Panagoulias had only twelve players available, two of whom were goalkeepers. He could make no substitutions unless a goalie got hurt. Some players were still tied up with their indoor teams at that point, but at no time during the season would the roster count more than sixteen players—a desperately thin squad for a team about to embark on a thirty-game schedule with a few extra exhibition matches crammed into less than five months, much of it in the summer heat. All year, the players labored through injuries. "There were games where three players on the field should not have been on the field," Merrick remembered.

Nevertheless, Team America beat the Sounders in the tie-breaking shootout after a scoreless game. To compensate for its shortcomings, the new team had employed a bruising, conservative, scrappy style. But it made no apologies when criticism ensued. "We had twenty-eight fouls, and they had eight," Durgan, who had been named captain, told *The Washington Post*. "If they want to call us dirty, they want to say we're hackers—whatever they say, it doesn't matter. Just look at the scoreboard."

Panagoulias went further still, dismissing a distaste for defensive soccer as national naïveté. "In America, you have a very wrong idea about soccer," he declared. "You think that soccer is attacking. But there is beautiful football in defensive play."

A month later, after another quarrelsome match, San Diego Sockers President Jack Haley called Durgan "just another hatchet man for those butchers" before rechristening Team America as "Team Animal." Team America, or Animal, had just beaten the Sockers 2–1. And it wasn't bothered by the nickname.

Later in the season, Cosmos manager Julio Mazzei would tell *Sports Illustrated*, "I don't blame Alkis for playing defensively," before doing just that. "But I don't like to think this is the emerging American national style. This is not soccer. This is anti-soccer."

The defensive style papered over the absence of qualified forwards. The team's only real striker was Tony Crescitelli, who grew up in a town outside of Naples so poor that he couldn't afford a soccer ball until the family immigrated to Long Island when he was eleven. Crescitelli set an NCAA Division III scoring record at North Adams State College—an astounding 123 goals in sixty-two games. And then, in 1980, he found himself playing on the Washington Diplomats with Johan Cruyff, the sport's biggest star of the prior decade. Once the exacting Cruyff had rearranged the team to his liking, Crescitelli discovered that his job of scoring goals had become a great deal easier. "I don't even know how," he remembered. "I would look up and the ball is right there at your feet." He scored fifteen goals in the last eighteen games of that season, but the Dips folded and Crescitelli never replicated that scoring streak. In twenty-three appearances with Team America in 1983, he wouldn't score a single goal from the run of play.

Jim Henderson, meanwhile, had a terrible time getting the media to show up. When he worked for the Tampa Bay Rowdies, he put on a luncheon for the press before each season that was always well attended. Henderson figured he'd do the same thing in DC. "It just bombed," he said. "I think we had one TV station there."

Soon, a bigger problem emerged: Panagoulias himself.

For all of Alketas Panagoulias's zingy one-liners and natural media savvy, he made no impression whatsoever on his team as a coach. Which is to say that he didn't coach. This was problematic inasmuch as the entire pretext for Team America was to improve America's team. Yet it had a coach who apparently viewed himself more as a kind of human resources manager than a person whose job it was to school his players on the finer points of the game. He didn't have an assistant coach to do the actual coaching, either.

"He wasn't a big-time technician," Jeff Durgan said. "He didn't sit down with the team a lot and talk about the style of play and 'Here's what we want to do.' He was more about putting us out there and turning us loose, to go compete."

Alan Merrick, who turned thirty-three during the season and was the team's oldest player by several years, wasn't impressed either. At seventeen, Merrick had taken coaching courses in England. He played under Michels with the Los Angeles Aztecs, picking his famous coach's brain whenever he could. "I liked him," Merrick said of Alkis. "I just didn't have an enormous amount of respect for his soccer knowledge and acumen."

Panagoulias neglected the basics of team organization, and he did not seem to even understand the shootouts used to decide tied NASL games. Instead, he endlessly ran a head-throw-catch drill, a heading exercise where the whole team would run up and down the field as a pack, lobbing the ball in the air with their hands for someone else to head. It was a children's drill with little benefit at the professional level. "We were probably the best head-throw-catch team in the world," said Crescitelli.

After practice, the players would sit down and work out what was missing. Then, after Panagoulias left, they'd go back out to the practice field to fill in the tactical gaps. Informally, Merrick organized the team until an irate Panagoulias found out and put a stop to it.

If Panagoulias didn't have a plan to win, he did have strong feelings on how his players should experience defeat. "I tell them if they lose an international match, they should cry," he told *The New York Times*. "The way players from Honduras and El Salvador and Greece cry when their team loses."

Midfielder Perry Van der Beck recalled this emotional disconnect between the coach and his players. "He'd come in after a game if we lost and he'd be really upset and go, 'In Europe, you wouldn't be allowed to go out.' And we'd go, 'Alkis, come on. We've been in this two months. We've really never played together.'"

The ways of Alkis were often inscrutable. To this day, Durgan couldn't tell you how he came to be the Team America captain at age twenty-one when Merrick was the team's emotional leader. Midfielder Sonny Askew wasn't playing much at the start of the year and got into a screaming match with Panagoulias about it. Askew called his wife to tell her he planned to quit the team and return home to Baltimore. "He was very condescending," Askew said of his former coach. "He had very, very sarcastic, cruel remarks." But by late July, Panagoulias got upset with another midfielder, national team mainstay Boris

Bandov, for not running out the clock late in a game. Panagoulias turned to Askew ahead of a high-profile friendly with Italian juggernaut Juventus, which featured stars such as Marco Tardelli. "He said to me, 'Tomorrow night, you're going to mark Tardelli,'" Askew remembered. "And I said, 'Fuck him. I'm not fucking marking anybody. If anybody is going to be marking, Tardelli is going to fucking mark *me*.' That changed the whole season for me. Because he *loved* that attitude. It went real well after that comment."

Usually, you have to win something before your team gets to meet the president of the United States. Team America had done nothing of the sort, but team owner Robert Lifton, who had been a Jimmy Carter supporter, pulled some strings and arranged a meeting with President Ronald Reagan in the White House on May 4. The hope was that the glow of the presidency would reflect onto Team America and give it some patriotic sparkle. "I met with President Reagan in the Oval Office ahead of time, just the two of us, chatting, and I tried to make sure he understood that this was a soccer team and not some baseball team," Lifton recalled years later.

Reagan walked out to the Rose Garden and went down the line shaking the hand of every player, a multitude of mullets and perms and mustaches, making small talk as he went along. Then he gave a short speech. "It's a great pleasure to greet this team here, this all-star team, the Team America," he spoke. "And it marks quite a few firsts and we hope one yet to be, and that is the first appearance in a World Cup series of an American team." Close enough.

Reagan joked that the Rose Garden was too small for soccer and that the South Lawn sprinklers had been turned on to keep the players off. Then he told a story faintly related to soccer about Knute Rockne, the longtime gridiron football coach at Notre Dame. Lifton handed Reagan a ball signed by all the players and a Team America tracksuit. "When we win the World Cup, we'd like you to hold on to that," Lifton said of the signed ball, as the president posed for a picture with the team. Reagan, the former B-movie actor, did an unconvincing job of feigning delight at the gifts.

Then the players clustered around Reagan and handed him passes to a game. "I think I even told him if he ever needed tickets to give me a call," defender Rudy Glenn remembered.

"That was a glorious moment for all of us," Lifton said. "I'm pretty sure it was probably the highlight of the history of Team America."

Perhaps not.

On June 12, Team America beat the Fort Lauderdale Strikers after a shootout in front of 50,108 at RFK, far and away the biggest crowd the team would ever draw. Because of the free Beach Boys concert after the game, of course. The win improved Team America's record to 6–4, which led the weak Southern Division for a spell. They posted a series of credible results in mid-season exhibitions as well, tying Watford—the Elton John–owned runners-up in England's First Division—and played to further draws with Soviet champions Dinamo Minsk and a Juventus team that powered Italy to the 1982 World Cup gold.

After stunning the half-hearted Juventus players with their signature brutality, Team America nevertheless partied with their guests at Juve's hotel following the 1–1 result. That was another thing Team America did well: have a good time after games. "Those boys knew how to party," midfielder Rob Olson remembered. "All them boys, they didn't have any problems with the ladies."

Team America's cigarette sponsor didn't exactly entice clean living either, placing a fresh carton in each player's locker before every home game and leaving stacks more on the training table. The gifts were eagerly consumed.

But Team America came unstuck in the middle of the summer and suffered an eight-game losing streak. They would win just twice and lose fifteen games the rest of the way, sagging to last place in the entire league. Their paltry thirty-three goals scored in thirty games were the fewest in the league by fifteen. Not a single Team America player was named to any of the three All-Star teams. Ricky Davis was.

The victory over the Strikers months earlier turned out to be a microcosm of Team America's season: a strong start through stout defense, issues when they were down on manpower, a steep decline when they ran out of gas, and a nice party afterward. The two other planned Beach Boys concerts never happened.

When a team collapses, there is usually more than one cause. Team America was undermanned, underpowered, underfunded, and undercoached. It's a small wonder that it led its division until the middle of the season.

As the summer heat and the jam-packed schedule ran Team America ragged—it played twice in three days five times, and on back-to-back days twice—chemistry among the exhausted players broke down. "In the beginning of the season we were like a band of brothers, could not see enough of each other, loved each other," Crescitelli remembered. "And then when stuff started getting sour, we hated each other, we couldn't wait to get out of Washington." There was a lot of name-calling—much of it emanating from their coach. "It was horrible, horrible, horrible."

Frustration mounted and Panagoulias lashed out. After a mid-August game against the Tulsa Roughnecks, which Team America lost after a goal was disallowed for offside—wrongly, in the coach's view—Panagoulias fixed his ire on the referees. "I don't understand how these owners can spend all this money for players and not get good referees," he told *The Washington Post*. "When I told him what he missed, he said I was right. But they would not change the call. The referees in this league have no personality. All they do is give out yellow cards—a sign of weakness."

Panagoulias also complained about the federation. He liked to claim that Albania, Greece's Stalinist neighbor, treated its national team better than U.S. did Team America. He hollered at waiters in the team dining room. He yelled at stadium staff once because loud music was playing in the stadium before a game, something that wasn't customary in Europe.

But there were fewer and fewer people there to see Alkis's antics. After 31,112 fans came to a home game against the Cosmos on June 17, just five days after the Beach Boys bonanza, Team America played nine more home games. The attendance for only two of those matches cracked five figures. In the last three games at RFK, an average of just 5,335 people showed up to the cavernous stadium.

"We thought we could overcome the hurdle with an exciting team, with a team that could feature scorers that would capture the imagination of the press, that might get people to come to the game, and then that might entice advertisers to participate; each thing would follow the other," Lifton would later say. "The problem was, it was the other way around. The lack of scorers, the lack of excitement, the lack of press coverage of any real substance, it all resulted in no great support for the team. There was just no excitement that was being generated. Nobody wanted to come out to see the team."

Actually, Lifton's team didn't do so badly in the media or at the gate when compared to its peers. *The Washington Post* covered the team in depth, *The New York Times* paid it frequent attention as well, and even *Sports Illustrated* wrote about it. The only teams in the league that posted a higher average attendance than Team America's 13,754 were the Cosmos and the Vancouver Whitecaps. It may just be that Lifton, the newcomer, badly misjudged the upside of his investment in soccer and gave too much credence to the promises and projections of desperate men trying to save their league.

Lifton complained to anybody who would hear it that the U.S. Soccer Federation was reneging on its promise to schedule a lucrative postseason tour of international friendlies for Team America and back it with hundreds of thousands of dollars' worth of marketing, helping to offset the $750,000 in losses he was running. Several league executives dismissed his carping in an article in *The Washington Post* that pointed out that only the Whitecaps had "a chance to make money in 1983," while several more teams seemed destined for bankruptcy. "If a team, any team, lost just $750,000 in its first year, then I'd say they had done an exceptional job. Most teams dream of losing that little," a Chicago Sting executive said.

"I have very little sympathy with Mr. Lifton's position," echoed the general manager of the Fort Lauderdale Strikers. "With his losses, he's got the best deal in the league."

On the final day of that season, Lifton and Alkis expressed confidence that the team would return the next year. Certainly, Lifton said, he wouldn't be moving the team. A month later, he changed his mind and announced that he wanted to relocate to New York. It didn't matter. Team America had played its final game. Lifton pulled the plug, whereupon he was offered the chance to buy the Cosmos. "They figured that I was a shmuck with a fountain pen," he remembered.

At the 1984 Summer Olympics, just three Team America alumni—Chico Borja, Jeff Durgan, and Bruce Savage—even made the U.S. national team, which was still coached by Panagoulias. Less than two months later, the national team began the qualification process for the 1986 World Cup with a shameful 0–0 tie on a dirt field in Willemstad against the Netherlands Antilles, perhaps CONCACAF's worst team. The Americans won the return game 4–1 in St. Louis, but it helped that the Antilleans were reduced to eight men after three ejections. All of six Team America players featured in those games.

Even though the Montreal Manic announced that they would play the 1984 NASL season as Team Canada—but went bust before they got the chance—Team America was, in the end, an unparalleled failure. It did nothing to meaningfully improve the United States men's national team and it didn't save the North American Soccer League, which would lumber on for one more season before crumbling under the weight of its own dysfunction.

Everybody involved with Team America reflected on the wacky endeavor as a missed opportunity. The three-year project was cut short after only nine months. "That was crazy," Alan Merrick said. "It disappointed me that it was able to fold so quickly and there was no legacy, no footprint left from Team America. Done. Boom."

"They wouldn't even let us take the jerseys," Sonny Askew recalled.

The national team still played in noticeably cheap jerseys. It still stayed at seedy motels. Its games were still hastily and poorly organized. And when the team fell short of the 1986 World Cup, extending its drought to at least forty years, things looked especially bleak. "I thought at that time that U.S. Soccer was really going to struggle to survive," said Jim Henderson, who went to work in the federation's communications department after the NASL collapsed. "If you had told me in 1985 that nine years later we would draw three and a half million people to a World Cup in our country, I would have said there's no chance that could happen. Zero."

Yet in another way, Team America's fleeting life was useful. It represented a spark of ambition. It signaled, if nothing else, that American soccer was committed to fielding a proper national team.

Somehow, the Team America debacle didn't hurt Alketas Panagoulias's remarkable managerial career. He declared that the 1983 season had been a success and stayed on as U.S. national team coach. At the 1984 Olympics, for which the U.S. qualified automatically, the Americans hammered Costa Rica 3–0 only to lose to Italy and tie Egypt, missing out on a place in the quarterfinals.

Panagoulias's record in official games with the U.S. was six wins, five losses, and seven ties. Satisfied, he went back to Greece, where he coached Olympiacos to another championship and twice managed Aris Thessaloniki—which would later make him its club president. In a second spell as the Greek national team head coach, he led his side to its first World Cup appearance in 1994—in the United States, of all places. "People in Greece would say, 'Only Alkis Panagoulias can do it,'" Alkis boasted to *The Washington Post*. He made sure to point out that he was the only American head coach at that tournament, although his team would place dead last with zero goals scored and ten surrendered in just three games.

Still, the cigar-waving, motor-mouthed Panagoulias retained his celebrity status in both the country of his birth and across its diaspora. Wherever Team America went, the local Greek community had feted him. He couldn't walk around Athens without drawing a crowd. Traffic cops apologized to him when they pulled him over for speeding. One of Greece's conservative political parties put him on the ticket for Thessaloniki's city council elections and he won.

In 2006, when the U.S. men were between head coaches, Panagoulias restated his belief that the American national team was underperforming. “The U.S. should be the No. 1 power in soccer, I still believe that,” he told *The New York Times*. “Only an American can really represent the U.S.A., not a foreign coach. But if they can disregard my age, I can do the job tomorrow.”

The seventy-two-year-old Alkis never got his old gig back.

5 | A Series of Miracles

Following the demise of Team America, the U.S. national team spent the mid-'80s loafing around in its own irrelevance. But two events in the summer of 1988 ignited a spark. First, on July 4—Independence Day, no less—FIFA's executive committee awarded hosting rights for the 1994 World Cup to the United States. The U.S. had lost out on the 1986 edition in Mexico, which presented a much thinner bid but was considered a safe pair of hands after hosting in 1970. But the hundred-thousand-plus crowds for the two men's soccer medal games in the Rose Bowl at the 1984 Olympics in Los Angeles, along with a sturdier bid supported by President Reagan, finally swayed FIFA.

Failing to reach the 1990 World Cup before staging the subsequent edition would embarrass U.S. Soccer. A baseless rumor made the rounds that missing out in 1990 could retroactively cost the U.S. its right to host in '94. Besides, the Americans wouldn't want to contest a home World Cup with a totally inexperienced team. Qualifying for the first time since 1950, then, was paramount.

Twenty days after being chosen as host for 1994, the U.S. achieved another breakthrough. The national team managed to hold Jamaica to a 0–0 tie in the heat and humidity of Kingston, and on a horrid field. On August 13, 1988, the Americans played Jamaica in the St. Louis

Soccer Park, a bleacher-lined field that seated just 6,100 people that day. The game was knotted at a goal apiece for an hour until the U.S. finally strung together four more goals to make it to the final stage of qualifying for the 1990 World Cup.

Archrival Mexico had been suspended for two years for fielding overage players in a youth tournament—a deception discovered when the Mexican federation's yearbook accidentally listed the players' real birthdays. Canada, meanwhile, which had taken up the other CONCACAF slot at the previous World Cup, hadn't made the final round either. The competition for the region's two berths in the World Cup was wide open for the five teams left standing.

U.S. Soccer president Werner Fricker had a lot to do. Of the eleven starters who had beaten Jamaica in the return game, five had no club team to play for. The Major Indoor Soccer League, the only professional soccer league left after the NASL's collapse in 1984, was crumbling as well. Two outdoor coastal leagues had joined up to become the American Professional Soccer League, only for thirteen of twenty-two clubs to fold immediately. The national team didn't offer a living either, with its $5 per diem. Sometimes, the players were asked to forgo this bonanza so that the federation might afford to extend camp by a single day.

Hours after the U.S. beat Jamaica, the federation announced it would be signing its national teamers to full-time contracts so that they might better prepare for the final round of qualifying. Only a handful of regulars were on the books with professional teams in Europe, and by the time the 1990 World Cup kicked off, Peter Vermes—under contract in Hungary, where his father had also been a pro and played alongside superstar Ferenc Puskás—would be the only player on the USA roster not signed directly with the federation. The rest of the squad careened from one underfunded semipro team to another, chasing payments of a few hundred dollars per game. Mike

Windischmann, a defender who would soon be named the national team captain, lived in his parents' basement. That was hardly unusual.

In 1989, the federation's base national team salaries ranged from $20,000 to $34,000, climbing as high as $40,000 by the next year. The salary increase was life-changing for a lot of players. "That was a big turning point," remembered defender Brian Bliss. "It gave us a little bit of security. We didn't have to go overseas. We didn't have to bounce around the leagues to make a living."

The onset of professionalism brought a new seriousness to a national team. "It was a very competitive environment because you could actually afford to make a living," said striker Bruce Murray, who had briefly played in the Swiss league before returning home. "It wasn't a great living, but it was good enough. It drove the competition. There were so many guys competing for spots, it made me hypercompetitive."

The national team would get a full-time head coach as well. The incumbent, Lothar Osiander, didn't want to leave his job as a maître d' in a restaurant in San Francisco, having worked his way up from waiter. Osiander had been coaching the national team on his vacation days. The organization was so amateurish, after all, that Osiander once had to buy his team an entire set of new uniforms out of his own pocket before a game in Honduras. So, in January 1989, Bob Gansler was named the head coach of the outdoor national team. The next month, Gansler would lead the under-20 national team to fourth place at the FIFA World Youth Championship (where it had taken the place of the banned Mexicans), still that team's best performance ever.

At last, the national team would have time to train before the final round of World Cup qualifiers. Rather than a day or three before a game, it convened at least a week ahead of time. But that still didn't amount to a fully professional workload. The national teamers had to scrounge around for playing time, if no longer for paychecks. They were left to their own devices for weeks or even months between national team camps, freelance footballers. “We still needed to play for the New Jersey Eagles and Albany Capitals, trying to find a way to play a game and stay fit and sharp,” said midfielder John Harkes. “A lot of it was left to you to figure out, to do what you can to scrap to be a better player.”

When Gansler said goodbye to his players, he had to trust that they would stay in shape. “You gave them homework,” he said. “You said, ‘Please work on this, work on that.’ You’ve got to be a tough motor-scooter in order to do that without playing.”

Yet this arrangement was still preferable to the old plight of the nation’s most talented players. Many had been stuck in college, where their development was often stunted, for lack of a viable alternative. Tab Ramos became a starter on the under-20 national team as a fifteen-year-old, just three years after emigrating from Uruguay. He had cursed his father, a former pro himself, for moving the family to the one country in the world that didn’t seem to play soccer. But then they wound up in Kearny, New Jersey, the unlikely soccer hotbed where Ramos, Harkes, and the rest of their crew of future national teamers broke into an elementary school through a window during the summer to play soccer in its gym. Ramos’s U.S. citizenship was fast-tracked when his talent became apparent. As a high schooler, he was the last player cut from the national team for the 1984 Olympics. The New York Cosmos drafted Ramos while he was still in prep school, but went bust before he could make his debut. So Ramos enrolled at North Carolina State University as a seventeen-year-old. He believes he regressed there, if anything. “In college you could go two months without having real training sessions that make you better,” Ramos said. “When you’re seventeen to nineteen, that can’t be good for your development.”

But at least his career had some structure in college. When Ramos left NC State, he was thrown into the void, bouncing between teams. He was on trial with a club in Spain when he got a call from the U.S. federation to return home and sign full-time.

Bob Gansler was, at his core, a college coach. Before taking on the senior national team, he had been the University of Wisconsin–Milwaukee's men's soccer coach and in charge of the under-19 and under-20 U.S. national teams, coaching college-age players. It was unsurprising, then, that Gansler dumped most of the players from the ignominious 1986 qualifying cycle and decided to rebuild more or less directly from the college game, with young talent he could mold.

In the absence of sufficient time or staff, it was impossible for the new head coach to trawl the country's distant soccer pockets for the best players. But America's soccer coaches formed a small and tight fraternity. Gansler could rely on his coaching network to feed him honest assessments of the players he was considering for the national team, and to flag new prospects.

One such player was goalkeeper Tony Meola, a three-sport star in Kearny. Meola's father, an immigrant barber from Italy, urged him to stick with the sport of their homeland even though Tony also took to baseball. Meola had become a goalkeeper as a six-year-old because, as he later told *The New York Times*, "I was a fat little kid who couldn't do the running." In high school, Meola, no longer fat, was still only a part-time goalkeeper for his team. He was hardly a blue-chip talent—cut from New Jersey's Olympic development team; the under-17, under-19, and under-20 national teams; and then the 1988 Olympic team. But Meola pressed ahead with his goalkeeping career even though the New York Yankees wanted him to play baseball and offered him $4,000 to sign after high school—a staggering sum of money to young Tony. The day after turning down the Yankees, he went to the under-19

World Cup in Chile, having finally made the team. Then he accepted a dual scholarship for the soccer and baseball teams at the University of Virginia. Having finally come into his own as a goalkeeper, Meola broke into the senior national team just before his freshman year of college. When he starred in a scrimmage against Portuguese powerhouse Benfica, he knew he had picked the right sport. Others noticed him, too. "Get ready, Europe," *Sports Illustrated* wrote not much later. "Here comes Tony Meola, the gifted goalie who promises to be the U.S.'s first world-class soccer star."

Midfielder John Harkes, another Kearny and UVA product and a former Cosmos ball boy, leapt at the federation's full-time offer. Eric Wynalda disappointed his father not only with his indifferent approach to his studies at San Diego State University but also by leaving college early for a chance with the national team. In March 1990 he signed on for $22,000 per year and only then learned what the term *prorated* meant.

To fully understand Bob Gansler, you first need to hear his war story. Or, rather, the story of how World War II changed his life. Gansler was born in 1941 in Mucsi, a farming town near the Yugoslavian border that was physically in Hungary but ethnically and culturally German, the upshot of a wave of migration in the eighteenth century. Gansler's father was conscripted into the Hungarian army, which fought on the side of Nazi Germany. "Reluctantly," Bob Gansler insisted. "But when you're put in the army, they point you in the direction you're supposed to shoot, and you go from there." His father was captured by the Russians on the Eastern front; two of his uncles were killed in the Battle of Stalingrad. When the war ended, the Germans, who made up about 95 percent of Mucsi's two thousand residents, suffered the same fate as many ethnic Germans all over Eastern Europe and were expelled into West Germany. The Ganslers had been fairly successful farmers. Now they were ruined, squeezed onto a freight train that took two weeks to reach its destination.

In Germany, the Gansler family was reunited with Bob's father, finally released from a prisoner of war camp. Bob discovered soccer, playing it every spare minute. After six years the Ganslers moved to Milwaukee, where much of their old village had settled. There were no youth soccer programs in the area, so Bob took up baseball and before long was offered a minor league contract with the Milwaukee Braves. He turned it down and went to college at Marquette and played soccer for the Milwaukee Bavarians, a regional power. He made the U.S. national team in 1963 and became its captain the following year. And then Bob Gansler managed another rare feat in his time: He figured out how to cobble together a career as a soccer coach.

Gansler had a quick wit and held on to the perspective his turbulent childhood had brought him. He was also a disciplinarian, precise—running practice sessions that went *exactly* two hours. "When I first met him, I was terrified of him because he has an aura about him," Eric Wynalda said. "He needed to protect this hard-ass exterior that he would project at all times. You wouldn't know that he was on your side until you had a private meeting and he would open up."

The inexperience of Gansler's young players meant that they would give mercurial performances. But he allowed them room to fail. "Bob would stick with you," said Bruce Murray, who scored just twice in Gansler's first year in charge but repaid his coach's faith with eight goals in 1990. "He would literally say, 'You're my guy. I believe in you. I know it's a tough time, you'll get through it.' And then he'd tap you on the face. You would run through a wall for Bob Gansler."

Gansler's unseasoned charges understood that he and his tough methods represented their best chance of getting better, of making it to the World Cup. "It was a game-changer when he took over," Tab

Ramos said. "We all liked Lothar a lot, but I'm not sure that Osiander would have gotten us to the promised land."

In order to qualify for the 1990 World Cup out of the CONCACAF region, the United States had to withstand the following: hostile crowds both at home and on the road; inconvenient, cut-rate travel; obviously partial referees; low-stakes sabotage; inexperience; and, of course, opponents steeped in the dark arts of soccer gamesmanship.

Getting to Italy meant gathering enough points to place among the two top teams out of the five CONCACAF nations left standing. Over the course of eight months, the U.S. would play each team twice—once at home and once on the road. And every last minute of it would be difficult. "We played a game against Guatemala, it rained and the field we played on was absolute slop—it was just mud, the conditions were horrible," Peter Vermes said. "In Jamaica, we had a band playing the entire night outside our hotel to keep us awake. We went to El Salvador and it just so happened that ten or eleven of us got in an elevator for a pre-game meeting and the power in the hotel went out. We were in the elevator between floors and we were stuck in there for thirty minutes. This is hours before the game. If you were the guy that took the corner kick, they would throw bags of piss at you. They would throw batteries and you could hear them bouncing off the crossbar."

There seemed to be no bounds to the ingenuity of the home fans laying siege to the USA's hotel, scheming to keep the Americans awake. Loud parties. Banging on pots and pans. Fireworks. Trucks circling and laying on their horns. The local bus driver hired to ferry the team from the airport delivering them to the wrong hotel. And when the Americans made it to the right hotel, the rooms never seemed to be ready. When they finally were, those rooms were somehow always on the noisier lower floors. The food served would be nothing like what the coaching staff ordered. The buses would take miles-long detours to the stadiums. Their hosts would do anything to make the U.S. team as uncomfortable as possible. All was fair in love and CONCACAF World Cup qualifying.

"Politically, all of Central America hated the U.S. anyway," Tab Ramos recalled. "You knew everything was against you when you'd step onto the field."

Things weren't a whole lot better at games in the U.S., where fans of the visiting team always seemed to greatly outnumber the U.S. fans. Sometimes even the halftime entertainment suggested that the Americans were actually playing a road game—Mike Windischmann recalls a mariachi band playing during a game in Texas. In St. Louis, the Costa Rican fans were so much louder that the public announcer implored the home fans to "remind the players what country the game is being played in."

Yet in the face of all this, the young Americans were getting results—sometimes in comical flukes, like when they beat a Costa Rica team that missed a penalty, saw two goals disallowed, and was denied another goal when Steve Trittschuh cleared a ball with his arm. A tie with Trinidad. A win over Guatemala. A win against El Salvador. These were hardly commanding performances. "We could've lost every game," Tab Ramos said. "That's how close it was. It wasn't ever like, 'OK, we're coming home to play T&T. At least we can get those points.' It was never like that against anyone."

Meola, still enrolled at UVA, had been pressed into service as the starting goalkeeper by injuries to the two other, more experienced goalies. The U.S. leaned heavily on the twenty-year-old, who posted shutouts in Guatemala and at home against El Salvador. "Had he given up a goal in any of those games, we would not have qualified," said Dr. Joe Machnik, the assistant coach in charge of goalkeepers. The trouble was, the Americans didn't score many goals either, wasting a chance to sew up qualification in the latter match. El Salvador had already been eliminated and its federation subsequently disbanded the national team, sending a glorified club team to play the USA, which arrived the night before the game following a fifteen-hour trip. "We threw up on ourselves in the El Salvador game," Bruce Murray remembered, still annoyed about the 0–0 tie decades later. "That was a half-assed El Salvador team; they brought a bunch of young kids. And we couldn't beat them that day."

A series of little miracles enabled the big one. Traveling to Port of Spain for its final game, the U.S. needed a win to reach the World Cup, whereas Trinidad and Tobago would make it to Italy with a mere tie. The stakes were existential. "We realized that if we don't win, there's going to be no soccer," said Mike Windischmann. "The national team might not play for two or three years. How are you going to make a living? Those were the choices."

Trinidadian confidence was absolute, even though their Soca Warriors had never reached the World Cup in six attempts since the country gained its independence from the United Kingdom in 1962. (Their qualifying failure for the 1974 World Cup came with an asterisk, though, since no fewer than five Trinidadian goals were disallowed in a pivotal 2–1 loss to Haiti, after which the referee and a linesman were banned for life.) Still, this trifling formality with the Americans would surely be navigated without incident.

The American federation found the money to put on a ten-day training camp in Florida, where the weather somewhat resembled Trinidad's, and even flew in the national team of Bermuda as a sparring partner. Stiff with tension, the U.S. looked hapless against Bermuda, and routine plays in practice provoked scuffles. In a final indignity, the national team was announced as the "Miami Soccer Club" over the PA system at the Miami airport as it left for Port of Spain. Pessimism was warranted.

In Trinidad, preparations were underway as well. The government whipped the population of 1.2 million into a frenzy in the week preceding the big game, assigning a theme for each day during "Winners Week." One day, citizens were instructed to wear red, the national color—some went further and painted their entire houses red. Another day, they were to pray for the national team. T-shirts preemptively celebrating qualification sold everywhere. Travel agents were already selling packages to Italy. The Monday following the game was declared a national holiday to accommodate the inevitable celebrations. Calypso bands wrote and performed songs feting the team's coach and celebrating their most important goal in qualifying. "We're going to beat them like bongos," one song promised. The Americans flew to Trinidad three days before the game on a plane called Destiny. As it made its approach, the pilot announced that thousands of fans had come to the airport to welcome the U.S. At about 10 p.m., the team walked into a sea of red, a mob chanting, "No way, USA!" Thousands more thronged the road to the team hotel, banging on the sides of the bus. At the hotel, the players' rooms were—where else?—at street level. Music boomed through the night, every night. The players had to disconnect the phones in their rooms to stop them from ringing all night.

The field was bumpy and surrounded by people milling about. At 9 a.m. on game day, the stadium was already packed for the afternoon kickoff. Jack Warner, a crooked Trinidadian administrator destined for a starring role in several FIFA scandals decades later, could not resist selling far more tickets—35,000 by some estimates; 45,000 by others—than the 28,500 the National Stadium could hold, creating dangerous overcrowding. Warner had also handed the American delegation a plaque ahead of the match that read: "With the Compliments of Trinidad & Tobago World Cup Team 1989." The crush of people pushed onto the track ringing the field; some fainted. Defying the gasping heat and humidity, tens of thousands more flooded into the park next to the stadium, where the game would be shown on a big screen. The U.S. team's bus couldn't reach the stadium for the crowds, forcing the players to get out and push through the mob to get to their locker room. Out on the field, calypso bands sang about the World Cup.

About 130 American fans traveled to the game as well, perhaps unaware that their team had not won a World Cup qualifier on the road in more than twenty-one years—the win over El Salvador had come in Honduras, a neutral site. But if all these portents seemed ominous, Peter Vermes spotted something that filled him with confidence. "They only needed to tie, and I knew before the match that we were going to win," he said. "You know when the two teams enter the tunnel to go out to the game? I was looking at all the faces of the Trinidad and Tobago players, and I've never seen a group of guys more nervous. I think what happened was that the national holiday backfired. I think it put an incredible amount of pressure on the players."

The contest itself was not pretty—qualifiers seldom are. Within two minutes, the Americans were spared a credible penalty that would probably have put the World Cup out of reach. Instead, the arc of the modern U.S. men's national team history bent the other way around the half-hour mark. Paul Caligiuri, a surprise inclusion in Gansler's lineup, dinked the ball past an opponent and unloosed a long left-footed half volley. Lost in the afternoon sun, the ball dipped awkwardly and soared past goalkeeper Michael Maurice and into the net. It was Caligiuri's first national team goal in more than four years, yet one he had been preparing for all his life—the kind of long shot he practiced against his family's battered garage door growing up in Diamond Bar, California. It was the USA's first goal in 239 straight minutes of action and the only one of the unsightly match.

Before the game, Caligiuri had mused to his roommate Tony Meola that the newspaper headlines would note that he got the goal and Meola the shutout. And that's how it transpired. Caligiuri's goal was dubbed the "shot heard round the world" in American soccer lore, although it's doubtful the rest of the world paid it much mind—even most Americans weren't aware of it. After the game, the Trinidadian federation donated its stash of chilled champagne to the Americans, because Gansler had been too superstitious to buy any. When the U.S. got back to the hotel, the victory party was muted by exhaustion and relief. The players mostly just sat by the pool, too tired to paint the town.

The Making of a National Team: Matt Turner

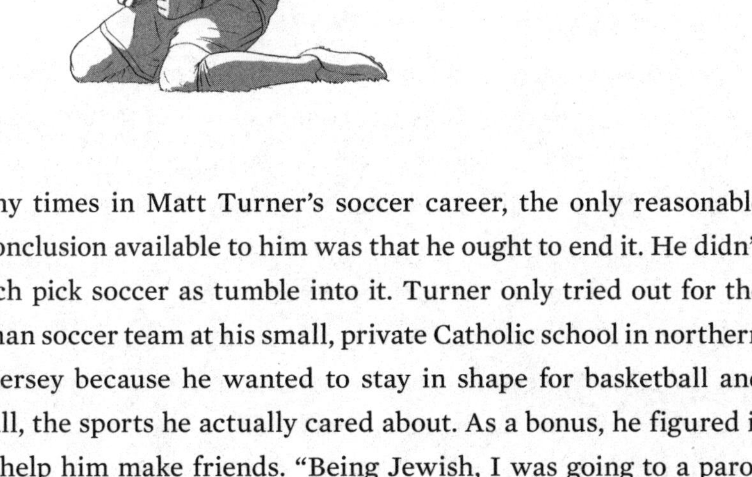

Many times in Matt Turner's soccer career, the only reasonable conclusion available to him was that he ought to end it. He didn't so much pick soccer as tumble into it. Turner only tried out for the freshman soccer team at his small, private Catholic school in northern New Jersey because he wanted to stay in shape for basketball and baseball, the sports he actually cared about. As a bonus, he figured it might help him make friends. "Being Jewish, I was going to a parochial school," Turner recalled. "Soccer was to get comfortable with people around me because I was going to be a little bit different than everybody else."

He started out as a field player. The first day of tryouts went so badly that his parents had to talk him into going back for the second day. That's when the goalkeeper of the freshman team got injured.

Turner happened to have some old goalie gloves in his bag. He sometimes played in goal at his two older sisters' soccer practices, primarily because it afforded him the chance to flirt with the other girls on the team. That, it turned out, was sufficient qualification to become the freshman team's goalkeeper by default, never mind that Turner stood a mere 5 foot 3.

It wasn't until his junior year of high school, when he was sixteen, the age when the elite prospects tend to sign their first professional contracts, that it even occurred to Turner to take soccer seriously. Watching Tim Howard play in goal at the 2010 World Cup gave Turner the unlikely idea that he ought to follow in the footsteps of his fellow New Jerseyan. After finally making the varsity soccer team, Turner quit basketball and baseball and joined a club soccer team in search of better competition. Soccer would be his game, he decided, his ticket into college sports.

The early results would have discouraged a more reasonable teenager. Turner, now a foot taller, sent out hundreds of letters and dozens of highlight tapes. It wasn't much of a tape. Set to techno and then rock, the low-resolution video showed him making a few routine saves, catching a few lazy crosses, punting the ball upfield. While he had turned a bad high school team into a competitive one with his endless saves, there was nothing at all in the grainy images to suggest that the boy at the center of them was a future World Cup goalkeeper. It didn't even convince anybody that he might make for a serviceable goalkeeper at the college level. No school, playing at any level, showed the slightest interest in Turner as a soccer player. Never mind that he was a student with a 95 percent grade average from a family wealthy enough to pay for his full tuition. No scholarship money needed. All he needed was a roster spot as a walk-on. But even at a price point of zero, there was no market for Turner's goalkeeping services. Eventually, his father emailed the head coach at Fairfield University and convinced him to give his son a look at a tournament the coaching staff already planned to attend to scout a different player.

Fairfield's goalkeeping coach Javier Decima saw in Turner something like a starter kit for a Division I college goalkeeper, albeit one that nobody had bothered to assemble. "He had the athleticism," he recalled. "He looked like the prototype of a goalkeeper: long arms, long limbs, athletic. But his technical ability with his hands was not there. And his feet were a challenge." To see a promising goalkeeper in Matt Turner, all you had to do was look past his hands and feet.

Turner had been accepted by Fairfield as a student and was invited to the soccer team's showcase for prospective players. "He didn't put a foot wrong," Decima said. "He made the routine saves and was able to make a big-time save." The coaches figured Turner might, at some point down the line, develop into something useful. There wasn't much to lose. "Can you turn an athlete into a goalkeeper? I believed so," said Decima, who became Turner's first actual goalkeeping coach even though at eighteen he was long past soccer's prime development years. "He was able to get behind the ball so fast—I think baseball was the reason. He was quick. And his wingspan was incredible."

Turner was offered a spot as a backup goalkeeper, provided he walk onto the team with no soccer scholarship. Yet for all the effort he had made just to get himself into college soccer, he harbored doubts about whether the opportunity Fairfield was offering him was worth giving up the place his grades had earned him at his dream school, the University of Richmond. Fairfield was hardly known as a powerhouse in collegiate soccer. The Stags had won just one NCAA Tournament game in their history and produced only a handful of pros, none of whom made much of an impact. Still, something compelled Turner to commit to Fairfield, to soccer.

He got his first opportunity in a competitive game as a sophomore. After months of fighting for a chance to play, he got a break at halftime of a game against Iona University. The struggling freshman starter, who had leapfrogged Turner upon his arrival from England on a full scholarship, was pulled. Turner, the walk-on, made a sturdy impression until, some twenty minutes into his debut, an Iona player took a long shot that arced onto the crossbar and caromed straight into the sky. A freak shot. Turner, recognizing that the ball was still in play, settled underneath it. An experienced goalkeeper would have punched the ball over his crossbar and out of play, conceding the corner kick but foreclosing on any further risk of giving up a goal. Turner, however, was not experienced. He attempted to catch the ball and bobbled it. As it skipped into his own net, he sank to his knees and fell onto his stomach, covering his face with his gloves. An own goal. It was the first time that the wider world would hear the name Matt Turner: Footage of the play went viral and made SportsCenter's Not Top 10 blooper reel on ESPN, where it was replayed for months. "This isn't for me," Turner told himself. "Maybe it's better for me to focus on school and having a good time." While he could have started the next game, he asked not to play anymore that season.

He thought about transferring to another school. The trouble was that interest in Turner hadn't exactly picked up. He couldn't even get himself onto a summer league team. He was cut from four different Premier Development League teams, the circuit where any semi-serious college player extended his season. Turner again considered quitting the game. But the summer before his junior year of college, he finally hooked on with a PDL team. The Jersey Express wasn't particularly high on him either, it's just that it needed a backup to the backup goalkeeper. And Turner kept asking. Decima pushed the Express head coach, a friend of his, to give him a chance. Turner had, after all, toiled through three rounds of tryouts, paying the team fifty dollars each time just for the privilege of participating. The Express relented and gave him a spot.

Before a game early in the season, the starting goalkeeper took a freak fall running on a track while peering at his phone, tearing his ankle ligaments and ending his campaign. Now Turner was the backup goalkeeper. Then the other goalkeeper hurt his hip in an odd injury caused by a bad field. And so it came to pass that Matt Turner—who spent the rest of that summer working a job setting up bouncy castles and blow-up slides—became the starting goalkeeper for the Jersey Express.

It was a lucky break—two of them, maybe; or perhaps three. With Turner surrounded by a much better standard of players and coaches, who soon developed a higher opinion of him than anyone he had yet encountered, his confidence swelled and he excelled. In the fall, he returned to Fairfield looking like a real prospect. He wrested the starting job back and managed to hang on to it, posting the best save percentage of any college goalkeeper in the country as a junior—not that anybody noticed. By the end of his senior year, he had assembled an enormous twenty shutouts in just thirty-nine appearances while conceding a puny 0.77 goals per game. He also made the All-MAAC second team that year, as the second-best goalkeeper in his conference. Even so, he didn't seem to be counting on a professional career. In a video recorded his junior year, Turner said that he saw himself working as an investment banker within five years.

The professional soccer ranks agreed. Matt Turner wasn't invited to Major League Soccer's draft combine—a tryout for prospective professionals—and he attracted no interest from his local teams, New York City FC and the New York Red Bulls, whose games he had regularly gone to as a teenager. A tryout with the Philadelphia Union, which he paid several hundred dollars just to attend, proved a waste of time—he never made it onto the field inside the Union stadium where the coaching staff was actually watching. Banished to the auxiliary fields, he might have wondered whether a tryout really happened if nobody was there to see it. (Turner had by now spent hundreds of dollars on tryouts for teams that never signed him, when the whole idea was that somebody would pay *him* to play soccer.)

In college, Turner double-majored in math and finance and maintained a 3.9 GPA. He was the kind of student who tutored his teammates to make sure they stayed academically eligible to play. Years later, he still had dozens of old alarms stored in his phone to remind some teammate or other to go to class or do his coursework. General Electric offered Turner a job in its financial management program upon graduation. It was a ticket to the upper-middle class with a starting salary of $75,000, the kind of shortcut nobody had ever offered him in soccer.

But the soccer gods weren't done with Matt Turner. The New England Revolution brought him in for preseason training because, like the Jersey Express several years earlier, the team needed another warm body in goal. Turner managed to parlay a ten-day trial into a $51,500 rookie contract for the 2016 season. But he arrived in the pros wholly unprepared for the job he had finally landed. By now, his hands could do what was expected of them; his feet still could not. His shot-stopping was prodigious, but he was incapable of consistently and accurately hitting short passes. He had immense trouble hitting a lateral one-touch pass as little as ten yards. It was an alarming deficiency in his game, akin to a basketball player who swishes one three-point shot after another but can't make a layup. Turner was more or less self-taught as a goalie until he got to college. He had learned things primarily by enlisting his analytical mind to reverse engineer goalkeeping. "I really had to teach myself the mechanics of kicking the ball," he said. "Nobody had ever taught me that. No one had ever taught me what it's supposed to look like when you catch a ball. Or how I should be set when somebody is about to shoot the ball. I just sort of picked that up from watching a YouTube video and then I'd text my two best friends to go down to the field and try it."

In college, Turner still wore cleats that, at size fifteen, were much too big because he simply didn't know they ought to fit snugly. He didn't even take his own goal kicks in high school, unable to strike the ball far enough up the field to avoid an immediate counterattack by the opposing team.

Still, the Revs were sufficiently enamored of Turner, or badly enough in need of a backup to their backup goalkeeper. He had such a knack for the core goalkeeping competence of blocking shots that the team was willing to overlook his shortcomings. Only one goalkeeper can play, after all, and third-string goalies might not see the field for years at a time. Turner spent his first two seasons as a professional shuttling back and forth between Foxborough, where the Revs played and practiced, and the Richmond Kickers, the minor league team in Virginia that he was farmed out to as a kind of finishing school. When he didn't have a game on the weekend, Turner went home to New Jersey. He and his sister crossed the river into Manhattan on Saturday mornings to watch Premier League games at one of the soccer bars teeming with fans of every foreign club you might have heard of, or haven't. He didn't think he was all that different from those fans. He was barely a professional player himself, after all, clinging on to the margins of the game.

Turner watched the men's national team's fateful 2017 loss in Trinidad and Tobago, dooming them to a summer without a World Cup, on a couch at the house he shared with several other young teammates in Massachusetts. "I didn't think to myself right then and there, 'The door is open. I'm gonna work so hard and get to the national team,'" he said. "I'm worried about my contract for the next season; I'm not worried about making it to the national team."

He did get a contract for the 2018 season. And he had a new manager in Brad Friedel, one of the best goalkeepers the nation had ever produced. Friedel spent seventeen seasons in the Premier League and set a record for appearances in consecutive games, at 310. Friedel was sympathetic to a homegrown goalkeeper with an unusual path into the professional game, just as his own had been. Turner wrote out a list of goals for himself for the upcoming season, like he always had and still does. Ambitiously, he aimed not only to get on the field but also to play in eight Revs games. He wound up appearing in twenty-seven.

"You couldn't score on him," Friedel said. "There's two attributes a goalkeeper has to have to play at the highest level that you can't coach. One, the goalkeeper has to be brave. And two, he has to be athletic. Turner has both of those in abundance. There was a lot of work that needed to be done, especially with his feet. But his shot-stopping ability is superb, really top quality."

But no sooner did Turner establish himself as a bona fide starting goalkeeper, carving out a place for himself in the professional game at last, than Friedel was fired early in the 2019 season. In Turner's first game under the new manager, Bruce Arena, he got himself a red card for crashing into D.C. United star Wayne Rooney. "I would be lying to you if I said that we felt we had a real good one in Matt Turner when I moved in," Arena told NBC later.

Yet they did have a good one in Matt Turner. In his first season as a starter, he saved one more goal for his team over the course of the season than the advanced metrics would have expected an average goalkeeper to. Turner was, at minimum, competent. In 2019, after he reclaimed the starting job under Arena, he saved his team 5.7 goals over what an average netminder might have been expected to allow, according to FiveThirtyEight.com. By 2020, that number would soar to 8.2 goals prevented. And by the middle of 2021, he had, over the span of three seasons and change, contributed more net goals to his team's cause—by preventing them—than any other player in the league, at *any* position. His 25.6 goals contributed eclipsed that of the next player in the rankings, Seattle Sounders goalkeeper Stefan Frei, by more than 50 percent, while international stars Carlos Vela and Zlatan Ibrahimovic lagged further back.

National team head coach Gregg Berhalter took notice. "What really struck me was he was outperforming his expected goals like crazy, making big save after big save," said Berhalter, adding that the arc of Turner's career suggested a strong mentality. "This was a guy worth looking at."

In late 2019, Berhalter called Turner up for the national team camp for the first time. In 2020, Turner was voted the runner-up for MLS's Goalkeeper of the Year award and won the Revs' Player of the Year. In 2021, he made not only his national team debut but also appeared in thirteen matches for his country, posting nine shutouts and benefiting from an injury to the incumbent goalkeeper, Zack Steffen. By the end of the year, Turner had won the regional Gold Cup championship with the USA as the starter, the Supporters Shield for the best regular season record in MLS with the Revs, the MLS Goalkeeper of the Year award, the MLS All-Star Game MVP, and the Gold Cup Golden Glove for its best goalkeeper. These were the first prizes or awards he had ever won in soccer. He also became the national team's undisputed trivia champion, the benefit of his nightly appointments with *Jeopardy!* and *Wheel of Fortune* and four years spent in college with the expectation that he would be putting his education to use in short order.

On the national team, Turner quickly developed into something of a cult figure to hardcore fans. He inspired a comedy Twitter account, Matt Turner's Rebellion, which casts him as a kind of Civil War captain. "Dearest Gregg, I fret the ink may desiccate on the quill, as I toil to strike the apt verbiage to express my chagrin" reads one such spoof tweet, after Turner missed out on a national team camp with injury. "I long to scrap beside the men, yearning for glory in a foreign land . . . alas, I must convalesce my wound. Swiftly share my regards; deliver them Hell."

In the summer of 2022, the Revs sold Turner to Premier League powerhouse Arsenal. A few months later, he was named the starter of the U.S. national team at the 2022 World Cup and performed without fault in four games. He cut an imposing figure between the goalposts, standing tall, bellowing instructions to organize his defense, smothering attacks, parrying all shots within his reach—and some slightly beyond it. In their first three games in Qatar, their opponents scored 2.1 fewer goals than expected, largely to their goalkeeper's credit.

At the outset, Matt Turner is suspicious of the suggestion that his unlikely story elucidates anything beyond its own unlikelihood. "I think I'm an outlier," he said. "I don't think it's very common for somebody to pick things up the way I do."

Whether he likes it or not, the very fact of Turner's career gives a damning account of the system that produced him. Because that system tried very hard to discard him along the way, and in so doing illustrated a problem with American soccer's talent development.

Again and again, the sport took the measure of Matt Turner—6 foot 3 and quick as a cat—and found him lacking and unworthy of a place even in college soccer, which had long since lost the battle for the nation's best talent to the professional academies. Whatever it is that made Matt Turner special, whatever made up the particular blend of talent and circumstance and development that fashioned him into one of the nation's best goalkeepers, nobody recognized it but him.

Turner only got his chances because a series of injuries to others allowed him to make good on his uncommon resolve. "No one would have looked at a list of names on a sheet of a paper and been like, 'Yeah, you'd better watch out for *that* guy.' It never happened to me my whole life," Turner said. "I never won anything. I wasn't on the top-100 list of goalkeepers coming out of college. I didn't ever have that differentiating factor."

It was only stubbornness and an incomprehensible faith in his own abilities that kept him in the sport. He would record more shutouts—fourteen—in his first twenty USA games than anyone in history.

"I didn't go from the age of five thinking, 'I'm going to be on the U.S. national team,'" Turner said. "I really do feel like I am a fan as well; I lived that life. I went to the bar to watch games. That's why I feel I'm the self-proclaimed people's 'keeper."

PART III

Back at the World Cup

1990–1994

6 | Galumphing, Cornfed College Boys

U.S. Soccer remained broke, with its payday still months away. Federation president Werner Fricker took out a loan against his construction company in Philadelphia just to bankroll preparations for the 1990 World Cup. Meanwhile, the players' contracts expired at the end of qualifying and they expected to get raises now that the federation would get a bigger slice of the FIFA pie. They were sorely disappointed.

After they had qualified for Italy, the players were marched through a hotel room in the Waldorf Astoria one by one, without their agents present, and told what they would be making, take it or leave it. The numbers were more or less the same as before. "They got what we could afford," said administrator Sunil Gulati. Some players balked. Things quickly got acrimonious, setting the tone for years of labor strife between the players and the federation. In the short run, it sparked a curious dispute on the eve of the 1990 World Cup over a shoe deal some players signed with Puma that conflicted with the federation's apparel deal with Adidas, resulting in a brief standoff at a practice session and a lawsuit that went nowhere.

"It was a really difficult atmosphere to be in for a brand-new guy," said Eric Wynalda, who had joined the team in early 1990. "I didn't know what the hell was going on, but I understood these guys hated the federation for the way they'd been treated and were going to make a stand. And I was expected to stand in solidarity."

The Puma brouhaha was just one of the attempts by the national teamers to make some money on the side. It was something of a fad just then for famous athletes to record songs, and a half-dozen team members decided they would try their hand at it. Rapper Def Jef and DJ Eric Vaughn were enlisted to write a song. An established music video director signed on. And before long, "Victory" was recorded, set to a video of a bunch of shirtless national teamers dancing on a beach, interspersed with footage of other athletes—OJ Simpson! Marcus Allen! Luc Robitaille!—dropping into the studio for cameos and singing along.

Respect yourself, as well as others, love your sisters and
love your brothers . . .
Stay off drugs, keep your mind clear, so you can see when
victory is near . . .
Togetherness and unity means victory in Italy . . .

"Victory" quickly fell out of rotation on MTV.

All the while, Bob Gansler was at work on the more serious task of constructing his final World Cup roster. He decided that it was his duty to tee up the program for the long term, even if it meant being less competitive in the present, and, controversially, left veterans Rick Davis, Frank Klopas, and Hugo Perez off his roster. "I was thinking not only for '90, but I was thinking about the nineties," Gansler said. "The only way you can prepare for a World Cup more than adequately is by having been in a World Cup."

Picking a team with an average age of just twenty-three—including three members who were still effectively college players—was a selfless thing to do. Gansler, like all coaches, would be judged on immediate results, rather than the team's long-term prospects. He would pay a price for that decision—he was not retained for the 1994 cycle, though he expected to be. "There were likely better players out there that were older than us," said Tony Meola, whose roommates at UVA put a sign on his door, GONE TO THE WORLD CUP. "But Bob Gansler made a decision that he was going to build something. He hasn't gotten enough credit for that. He was forward-thinking in a lot of ways." Sure enough, six members of that 1990 team were still around at the 1998 World Cup in France and played major roles for the U.S.

At 500–1 odds, the Americans' chances of winning the 1990 World Cup may have been priced generously. From February 2 through June 2, the USA lost to Costa Rica, the Soviet Union, Hungary, East Germany, Switzerland, and Colombia. It did beat Bermuda, Finland, Iceland, Malta, and Liechtenstein, but those teams were non-factors in the global game, and most of those victories had been close.

Even before the World Cup kicked off, things had soured in the American camp. The team began its final preparations in Switzerland, in beautiful facilities. The plan was to make base camp at Coverciano, the Italian federation's gloriously appointed training center on the outskirts of Florence. But when the draw assigned the USA to the same group as Italy, the Americans were no longer welcome at the home of their hosts. U.S. Soccer was assured that the alternative accommodations—Olympic facilities of some kind in Tirrenia, on the Tuscan coast—were every bit as nice. The federation didn't have the money to send somebody to go check.

"We went from this posh, lavish training setup, and then we got to these army barracks," said Tony Meola, who recalled barbed wire and armed guards at an isolated compound, windows covered by steel shutters at night, the only cafeteria in Italy that served bad food, and beds that were "maybe a step above cots." Several players said their college dorms had been nicer.

"It was like being in a jail," said Mike Windischmann. "Same food every day, nothing to do. We couldn't see relatives or anything. Everybody was getting on each other's nerves." A lot of players had family that traveled to Italy, but Gansler decided that his team should stay sequestered. Rather than focusing his players—who gnashed their teeth at their TVs as they watched other teams emerge from fancy hotels—the isolation only worsened morale.

"We were wound up way too tight," Wynalda said. "We were just angry the whole time. It was really hard to enjoy the World Cup."

Gansler maintained years later that his players fussed too much over the facilities. "A lot of the guys should have been happy with going to the World Cup," he said. "Maybe they were thinking more about Taj Mahal accommodations. This was less—perhaps not five-star, but it was more than adequate."

The Americans were a curiosity at the World Cup, vaguely remembered for their upset of England in 1950 and still more faintly recalled for doing quite well in 1930. Ahead of the U.S. team's opening game against a strong Czechoslovakia side, an Austrian journalist refused to believe what Bob Gansler had just told him in a press conference. It simply could not be, the scribe reckoned, that the United States had no domestic professional outdoor soccer league and had made it to Italy anyway. Gansler switched into German and told the reporter he would be happy to repeat in his native language what he had just said in English. "It was almost like he was insulted that we had the gonads to be in the tournament," Gansler remembered.

Gansler was bullish about his team's chances, but his players were awed. "I remember that it felt almost like we were tourists there," Tab Ramos said. "We couldn't believe that we were playing against some of the best players in the world. We really were not even professionals."

Italy was perhaps the best team in the world and the Austrians were in good form. So the points would have to come against Czechoslovakia. The American coaching staff convinced itself that they could win that game. Before the tournament, Gansler flew over to England to watch Czechoslovakia play—the only opponent he'd had an opportunity to scout in person. He told his players that they would be the bigger team. But when they stood side by side with the Czechs in the player tunnel before the game, the U.S. players quickly discovered that they had been misinformed. "I'm 6 foot 3 and I'm looking up at six or seven guys at least," Bruce Murray said. "We got completely outmuscled in that game."

Yet somehow, the USA was the more dangerous team for the first twenty-five minutes or so, until naïveté sunk the young Yanks. Czechoslovakian striker Tomáš Skuhravý was granted the run of just about the entire American penalty area when the whole defensive line chased after a different man. Skuhravý thanked them for their kindness and put the Czechs ahead in the twenty-sixth minute. Before halftime, Mike Windischmann gave up a boneheaded penalty, and a bad defensive lapse just after the break made it 3–0. "We were so unprepared and it showed," defender Marcelo Balboa said. "It wasn't a true representation of who we were, but it was that day."

And then things fell apart altogether. The mulleted Eric Wynalda shoved Ľubomír Moravčík, who had been baiting him all game long by stomping on Wynalda's feet. The young Californian was sent off with a straight red card, reducing his team to ten men. "In our inexperience, we thought we needed to get out there and get more physical—shit, I went to war," Wynalda remembered. "I should have been red-carded three times prior to that. We didn't know how to address the Czechs' physicality. Because we were kids, we weren't pros. We were right in the middle of our learning process."

The U.S. lost 5–1. A harsh lesson in World Cup soccer. The Americans hadn't been four goals worse than Czechoslovakia. For flashes of the game, they had matched their bigger, faster opponents. But the Czechs converted most of their scoring chances and largely avoided mistakes in the back; the Americans did the opposite.

"You can prepare and you can talk about it," added Bob Gansler. "But my World Cup background was nonexistent. Once you get there, the awe factor needs to be overcome."

The foreign press dismissed the team. The famed English World Cup chronicler Brian Glanville called the U.S. "a galumphing side of cornfed college boys," while *The Times* reported that the Americans had been "utterly exposed by such Bronze Age devices as an overlapping full-back."

Perhaps the outburst was inevitable. The Americans were young, frustrated, and in over their heads, cooped up and embarrassed. Some players who had been regulars in qualifying were benched and wondering whether they might have done better. "Trainings were heated," said defender Brian Bliss, one of the players benched. "It got more tense because we got thumped in that first game. People started blaming each other. There was more than one altercation among teammates."

The USA's strength, such as it was, issued from its closeness, from its chemistry. The players held one another accountable. Now they took to wearing their metal, screw-in studs on their cleats in practice. Those were usually saved for games, because they were likelier to injure an opponent. The tension built from one acrimonious practice session to another. Things finally came to a head when Eric Eichmann went after his old Clemson teammate, Bruce Murray. "He was chasing me around the field, two-foot tackling me," remembered Murray. "I warned him. The third time he came in, he just went over the ball and I grabbed him and we went at it. It was a fistfight. It was crazy. We ended up in the net. There were guys everywhere, trying to pull us apart. We're still best friends today, we laugh about it now."

The fight opened a release valve for all that frustration. Everybody got along better after that. "It seems odd to say that a fight would loosen things up a little bit," said Tony Meola. "The bubble was burst, and we could take a deep breath."

They would need every gasp of oxygen for their next game against the hosts, Italy. The U.S. had lost to Italy by ten the last time they'd played, in Rome in an unofficial game in 1975. The foreign reporters were back to torment Gansler with their questions. "Mr. Gansler," a German journalist asked him, "what would be an acceptable number of goals to lose by? Five goals? Six goals?" The Italian fans were harsher still. Along the bus route leading the American team to Rome's cavernous Olympic Stadium, which would be crammed with more than 73,000 fans, locals held up both hands with all ten fingers splayed when the U.S. passed by. The players thought all those people were greeting them. The team interpreter explained that those friendly seeming fans were predicting a 10–0 Italian victory.

To an inexperienced team playing just its second World Cup match, facing the host country was daunting enough. Italy, however, was a favorite to win a record fourth World Cup. "It was a who's who roster and it was so intimidating," Bruce Murray said. Sure enough, those stars sliced through the American lines at will and needed just twelve minutes to go ahead. Gianluca Vialli dummied the ball, flummoxing the U.S. defense and freeing up Giuseppe Giannini to beat Tony Meola. Just then, those ten goals looked entirely plausible. But the U.S. settled down. A second Italian goal never quite came off, and in the middle of the first half, the Americans strung so many passes together that the home fans began whistling at their own players in dismay. Italy missed a penalty and the Americans, though utterly dominated, almost equalized in the seventieth minute when Peter Vermes's close-range shot was slowed as it snuck through goalkeeper Walter Zenga's legs and cleared off the line. But the 1–0 loss was just. "At the end of the day, they were so much better than us," Vermes said. "We didn't deserve to get a result that game."

Yet losing so narrowly was a kind of upset in its own right, even if it meant the U.S. was practically eliminated with a game left to play. Gansler felt like his team had earned some respect with its grit. "We showed that we could hang in there," he recalled. "It was a score that you could say, 'Yeah, OK, we earned that.'"

The Italians would be heavily criticized by the press for not beating the U.S. more convincingly, but several of Italy's stars nevertheless went to the American locker room after the game to congratulate their opponents on a hard-fought contest. They traded jerseys and shared beers. "I'm sitting there with Paolo Maldini and then I have Franco Baresi telling me what a great job I did holding him off the ball," Murray said. "And I'm thinking to myself, 'I can't believe this is happening.'"

On the bus ride back to Tirrenia the next day, people waved at the American bus again. This time, they didn't hold up ten fingers. Instead, they clapped or gave a thumbs-up. In the town itself, locals flew American flags next to their Italian ones.

Improbably, there was still a scenario whereby the Americans could make it to the second round of the World Cup. They would need to beat Austria by five goals in their final group-stage game. Also, West

Germany and Brazil needed to beat Colombia and Scotland, respectively, while Sweden had to win against Costa Rica, but by no more than a goal, and South Korea and Uruguay could only tie. Oh, and England–Egypt and Ireland–Netherlands had to produce winners, not ties.

Only if those seven results shook out exactly as prescribed would the U.S. advance. It didn't happen. They lost 2–1 to Austria in a chaotic and frightfully physical game. But they looked savvier, like a team that had figured out how to play at a World Cup. "Even though we lost tonight, I think we ended on a high note," Ramos said after the game.

Federation president Werner Fricker disagreed. He summoned the players and staff into a room at the team hotel. "It was so damn hot in this room," Meola remembered. "We'd just played three games in a World Cup and we're sitting in a sauna. And Werner Fricker came in and he just absolutely tore us apart. 'This was an embarrassment. This can't happen again. This won't happen in 1994. You guys need to do a better job.' I walked out of there thinking, 'Aw, shit, man. I thought this was great. I just played in a World Cup.' It was such a weird night."

When the tournament was over, a gaggle of theretofore unknown Americans signed with professional teams in Europe. Tab Ramos went to Figueres in Spain, John Harkes to Sheffield Wednesday in England. Others went to Sweden, Germany, and Czechoslovakia. The World Cup had found them worthy on a global stage. And they understood that if the U.S. men's national team was going to get anywhere, they needed to test themselves. "We all said, 'I want more,'" Eric Wynalda recalled. "The second that the 1990 World Cup was over, we were thinking about '94. The question was, how do I prepare myself over the course of the next three years and 350 days to never let that happen again?"

7 | Bora Ball

FIFA had no obvious front-runner when it came time in 1988 to pick a host country for the 1994 World Cup. Japan and South Korea hinted at a joint bid that FIFA ruled out—too complicated. Brazil's bid lacked the all-important support of its own government, and its stadiums would need a great deal of renovation. Morocco had trouble convincing FIFA that it would actually build nine brand-new stadiums, as it vowed to. The U.S. didn't need to build or renovate anything, just to take temporary residence in nine cavernous National Football League stadiums. And its bid assuaged some of FIFA's concerns by promising to launch a new professional league in the wake of the tournament. Still, the United States and soccer? Tough sell.

FIFA would be entrusting its signature event, its world-stopping money-spinner, to just about the only nation in the world that was apathetic to the sport and had no pro outdoor league. When the United States House of Representatives debated a resolution in support of the American bid for the 1994 World Cup, Republican Congressman Jack Kemp rose to speak in opposition. Kemp had quarterbacked the Buffalo Bills to two AFL championships and went on to become the Republican vice-presidential nominee in 1996. "I think it is important for all those young out there, who someday hope to play real football, where you throw it and kick it and run with it and put it in your hands," Kemp said, "[that] a distinction should be made that football is democratic capitalism, whereas soccer is a European socialist sport." Among prominent American sportswriters and broadcasters, poking fun at soccer was cliché, the thing they resorted to when they had nothing else to write or say. Franklin Foer, in his book *How Soccer Explains the World*, argued that soccer reflected the split between progressive and conservative America—one side yearned for the worldliness the sport conferred while the other side rejected it for exactly that reason.

When the final FIFA vote was conducted in 1988, the U.S. beat Morocco by ten votes to seven. By 1990, however, nervousness about the risky choice set in. FIFA turned to Alan Rothenberg, a successful lawyer and a onetime investor in the North American Soccer League. He had overseen the Olympic soccer tournament in 1984, which drew 1.4 million spectators, contributing substantially to the Summer Games' $200 million surplus even though ABC gave Olympic soccer little TV exposure. This was the tournament that showed FIFA the only thing it cared to see: dollar signs. "FIFA were not happy with what they perceived to be the lack of preparations for the '94 World Cup," Rothenberg recalled. Through intermediaries, he was asked if he was interested in taking it over. He could only do this by also becoming president of U.S. Soccer, of which he was not even a member. "I had never been a part of the soccer federation and, frankly, didn't have a lot of respect for them." Still, he agreed. Incumbent federation president Werner Fricker turned out to be vulnerable among the sport's voting rank and file. Rothenberg engineered a comfortable victory.

U.S. Soccer aimed to put on the greatest World Cup ever played. These were lofty aspirations, considering the many roadblocks. "Your chances of success are minimal," recalled Hank Steinbrecher, then the federation's general secretary. "You have no pro league. Your players are a bunch of amateurs and college kids. You don't have any real infrastructure within your organization. The list of things we were going to fail at was very long."

Also on that list were concerns about terrorism, visa issues, and the hooligan battles that beset the 1990 World Cup in Italy. The latter problem resolved itself when England failed to qualify, ridding the tournament of its biggest hooligan threat. The foreign press was skeptical, too, howling about the indignity of cheerleaders at a soccer match—even though there was never any talk of that. There was, however, a short-lived suggestion to make the goals bigger to induce more scoring.

The World Cup organizers reenlisted an unlikely ringer to address these many obstacles: former Secretary of State Henry Kissinger. In his youth in the interwar Weimar Republic, Kissinger aspired to becoming the goalkeeper of the German national team. Instead, he settled for a career as a diplomat and one of America's most notorious war hawks. But when he wasn't busy orchestrating the bombing of Cambodia or backing a military coup against a democratically elected government in Chile, Kissinger played a role in the growth of American soccer. It was Kissinger who convinced the Brazilian regime to allow Pelé to play abroad for the first time in his career and sign with the New York Cosmos in 1975. Until then, Pelé had officially been designated a national treasure by the Brazilian junta and therefore ineligible to be exported.

Kissinger helped to solve a lot of the quotidian issues attendant to putting on a mega-event like the World Cup, opening doors and lending credibility to the effort. But he couldn't help but marvel at the sport's messy governance. "The politics of soccer," he said, "make me nostalgic for the politics of the Middle East."

No World Cup host had ever failed to survive the tournament's first round. Bob Gansler expected to be kept on for a second cycle, but his performance in Italy had not convinced his new bosses that he was up to the task. Once Werner Fricker tumbled as federation president, Gansler's days were numbered as well. "I felt like we needed to have somebody with international experience," Rothenberg said of Gansler. "As good as he was, he was a college coach. I thought that's not going to do it for us."

Rothenberg approached Rinus Michels, one of the world's premier coaches, who had worked for him when Rothenberg owned the Los Angeles Aztecs of the NASL. The Dutchman demurred, just as he had turned down Team America in 1983. Steinbrecher interviewed Sven-Göran Eriksson, who had just coached Portuguese club Benfica to the final of what would become the UEFA Champions League, but the Swede proved much too expensive and took the high-profile Sampdoria job in Italy. The U.S. also spoke to Carlos Alberto Parreira, who would coach his home country of Brazil to the '94 World Cup title instead. Rothenberg did reach a handshake agreement with German former all-world defender and New York Cosmos alumnus Franz Beckenbauer, who had just managed West Germany to the 1990 World Cup title. Der Kaiser, as he was nicknamed, had only recently become the manager of Olympique de Marseille. Rothenberg met him in Germany, where they came to terms. But before Rothenberg could fly home, Beckenbauer got a phone call from the south of France, whereupon he reneged on taking the American job. "I guess Marseille sweetened his deal," Rothenberg said.

Other U.S. Soccer executives were relieved the Beckenbauer deal fell through. Rothenberg had not consulted them on hiring the onetime Studio 54 regular and they had serious misgivings. "My intuition told me that Franz would probably come over and play a lot of golf," Steinbrecher said. The job was not to bring down your handicap. The job was to fashion a ragtag band of unemployed young players into one of the sixteen second-round teams at the World Cup.

Velibor Milutinović, or Bora to both friend and foe, was born in Yugoslavia and orphaned by World War II. After a childhood spent kicking an inflated pig's bladder around in the streets, he and his two brothers made the national team. He signed with clubs in Switzerland and France before winding up in Mexico. He became a successful coach there and then managed the Mexican national team. With an unconventional approach, he brought a moribund team to an improbable quarterfinal on its home soil at the 1986 World Cup, making him a Mexican hero. He was hired by Costa Rica just two months before the 1990 World Cup, dumped half a dozen of the team's stars, and made it the first Central American nation to reach the World Cup's second round. He was a certified miracle worker.

He was also, somehow, available to the United States at a salary in the very low six figures—which was to be paid to an offshore company that then "loaned" the federation Milutinović's services, according to Rothenberg—a fraction of what the other candidates commanded. Milutinović had other job offers. Certainly more traditional ones than this strange gig sculpting a respectable national team out of players most of whom had no club team. But he thought of his life as an adventure. Milutinović wanted to live in Southern California and believed there was untapped potential in the team's young core. Their mentality appealed to him. They would shut up and do whatever they were told.

In March 1991, Milutinović and his signature mop of early-Beatles-style hair signed on to coach the American men through the 1994 World Cup. "It was an incredibly good challenge to do something special in a special country," he remembered. Milutinović was famous in Mexico, but stateside he was, as he put it to *The New York Times*, known only to the cooks and the gardeners—"This is enough." Rothenberg hoped that Milutinović's star status would help the national team make inroads with the country's swelling Hispanic population: "He was God in that community," said the federation president.

It didn't take long for one of Milutinović's myriad quirks to reveal itself: his use of language as a weapon. When Steinbrecher met with Milutinović in Mexico City, he was told the coach spoke no English. Since Steinbrecher had no command of Spanish, Milutinović brought his personal translator. "I had a distinct feeling that Bora knew absolutely everything I was saying," Steinbrecher remembered. So he decided to lay a trap. After Milutinović was hired, he came to the federation's then-headquarters in Colorado Springs and, this time, Steinbrecher made sure to supply the translator himself. Then Steinbrecher instructed the latter not to translate what he said simultaneously, but to wait until he finished talking. In English, Steinbrecher welcomed Milutinović and then, with a straight face, announced that he and not Milutinović would be the one to set the lineups for the team—an unthinkable incursion on the coach's authority. "Before the translator could open his mouth," Steinbrecher recalled, "Bora goes, 'No, no, no, no, no, *señor*!' Gotcha."

Milutinović, for his part, maintained decades later that he really was heedless of the language. "What was my problem was I don't speak English, only Spanish," he said, in English.

Rothenberg wanted Milutinović to at least speak English when he addressed English-language media. Milutinović did his entire introductory press conference in Spanish. Years later, when Milutinović had taken a job with a different federation, Rothenberg couldn't help but note that the coach gave his first press conference in English.

Ask his former players about Milutinović and they'll wonder out loud how they could possibly begin to describe a man so enigmatic yet so charming.

Alexi Lalas, a young and obscure defender who would grow into one of Milutinović's stars, still couldn't quite define his old mentor three decades after last working together. "Bora is a strange mix of Yogi Berra, Yoda, and Yogi Bear," Lalas said. "He speaks five languages and none of them well. He is the most frustrating coach and person that I've ever met, and also the most illuminating. In a strange way, he's the best coach I ever had."

"He was a mystical, magical character," Steinbrecher said. "A genius. Don't ask Bora why he did something tactically; you don't ask Picasso why he had a flick of the wrist. Bora was not a scientific coach, he was an artistic one who felt the game, breathed and lived the game. Our players needed that."

At Milutinović's first camp, he informed the stunned players that they would not be stretching before the day's practice. At first, he wouldn't let his players drink water during breaks from his grueling workouts either, in the belief that it would toughen them up—a team doctor had to intervene. The American player, Milutinović thought, was coddled by his cushy circumstances. There was no desperation in their game because success wasn't a condition for their survival. "This is the problem with these people: They don't have a problem," Milutinović told journalist Simon Kuper in his book *Soccer Against the Enemy*. Then again, Milutinović admitted that he liked working in the U.S. because he got to live in Southern California and there was virtually no pressure on him.

Milutinović rarely explained anything and barely talked to anyone but the team's few Spanish speakers. Instead, he paced the field and demonstrated. When he did speak, it was hard to make sense of his message, which was typically delivered in fragments of several different languages. Sometimes Milutinović's pregame instructions were so bewildering that the team worked out its own tactics. "The players would get together and say, 'Bora's lost his mind. Let's just play,'" Bruce Murray remembered. "So we'd play and do the complete opposite of what he'd asked us and he'd be like, 'This is the perfect game.'"

No detail was too small to escape Milutinović's attention. He once substituted Eric Wynalda out of a game right after scoring a goal because the coach felt that the striker should have shot the ball with his left foot rather than his right. Shooting pool was banned because Milutinović worried the players might hurt their hamstrings leaning over the table. He told them how to tie their shoes, shifting the knot of their laces off to the side of their cleats in order to create a flatter surface to strike the ball with. Mike Lapper's cleats had a long tongue, which concerned the coach. "So he literally bent down and cut the guy's shoes," Tony Meola said. "And we're like, 'This guy's a maniac. What's wrong with him? He's like a mad scientist.'" He even told the players how to eat their spaghetti. They were to twirl up their pasta with a spoon, rather than on their plates. "He had a lot of lessons," Marcelo Balboa said. "I'm not sure if he was doing it to fuck with us, but you always learned something from Bora."

Beneath all the eccentricity, Milutinović was a sound coach who filled the many gaps in his players' techniques, and an astute tactician who did his best work at halftime of games, recalibrating his team to the rhythm of the match. Milutinović got the players to believe. Within months of his hiring, he had led the U.S. to victory at the Gold Cup, the first significant trophy in the program's history. The Americans beat Mexico 2–0 in the semifinal, their first competitive victory over their neighbors since the 1934 World Cup play-in game. "He seemed at times to be a scatterbrain," Lalas said. "But there was absolutely a method to his madness. When you're in it, it was very difficult to see."

In the wake of the 1990 World Cup, a scant few national teamers had earned fully professional contracts in Europe or elsewhere in the Americas. John Harkes was in England. Peter Vermes and Tab Ramos had made it to Spain. Eric Wynalda and Brian Bliss played in Germany. Cle Kooiman was with Cruz Azul in Mexico. Desmond Armstrong had somehow caught on with Santos in Brazil for a season. Steve Trittschuh joined Sparta Prague in Czechoslovakia, where he discovered that the availability of food wasn't always a given behind the Iron Curtain. Paul Caligiuri learned much the same in East Germany with Hansa Rostock, which took ten weeks to get him and his wife into an apartment sparsely appointed with old Russian furniture.

European soccer clubs tend to follow convention, preferring players from the fashionable footballing nations. That left the rest of the U.S. national team pool stuck somewhere in limbo, floating between the meager full-time national team contracts still being offered and various ill-fated flings with European teams. Lalas, who had gone to the 1990 World Cup as a fan, his face painted with the Stars and Stripes under strands of his long red curls, had a trial with London powerhouse Arsenal but didn't stick. Brad Friedel saw moves to Nottingham Forest in England and Celtic in Scotland fall through and was commuting to national team matches between classes and Pac-10 games at UCLA. A string of would-be contracts in France didn't work out for Meola and he didn't last long in England.

Absent a robust market for the services of *all* the national team, the federation still had to close the gap in playing time with camps and games. But there were only so many of those to be had. It didn't amount to the critical mass of practice time a young team needed to avoid losing all its games at the World Cup again. Going the Team America route wasn't an option, since there was no credible league to enter the national team into. So U.S. Soccer concocted a third way: a full-time, live-in national team camp that would open at the start of 1993 and run all the way through the World Cup, which kicked off on June 17, 1994.

It was a bold and unprecedented plan, a training camp running for a year and a half—modeled, like Team America, on the 1980 U.S. Olympic hockey team. "We were going to have to do something different, because we weren't going to be as good as other teams," said Sunil Gulati, then the director of national teams.

The locker rooms and facilities that the city of Mission Viejo, California, promised to build in its winning bid to host the marathon training camp weren't finished by the time practices started. During those early days, the players had to get changed in an empty storefront the federation rented out in a strip mall next to a schnitzel restaurant, and then sprint across a busy road to their field. "If the stars had aligned in the most evil sense," Alexi Lalas said, "a truck could have taken down an entire generation of American soccer players." The field, meanwhile, was flooded by heavy rains generated by El Niño, forcing the team to run on the beach for weeks instead. "We became like *Baywatch*," said defender Dominic Kinnear.

National team general manager Bill Nuttall, meanwhile, had to figure out how to pay for it all. Milutinović wanted to play a game every ten days or so, and since there would be no qualifiers for the World Cup hosts, whose berth was automatic, those would all have to be friendly matches. The fifty-odd games leading up to the World Cup had to cover costs, and payroll as well. The formula Nuttall settled on was to play a handful of big opponents every year, drawing a big crowd, and use the profits to pay for all the unappealing games and the running cost of camp. This involved a lot of guesswork. Young fringe players, Nuttall recalled, made as little as $1,800 a month; established core players as much as $80,000 per year. "We didn't have a budget," said Nuttall. "How many games are you going to play? How much money are you going to make?"

The roster was a revolving door. The team had about twenty players under contract at any given time, but Milutinović tried out two or three new players a week. He might like the look of an opponent his team faced and invite him to camp a few weeks later. By the rough estimates of several longtime campers, about a hundred players passed through Mission Viejo between January 1993 and the World Cup roster announcement on June 2, 1994. Some of them showed up uninvited, hoping for a spontaneous tryout. But to make it onto the field, any newcomer first had to beat the crafty Milutinović at a game of soccer tennis. If they stuck, Milutinović would at first refer to them by their hometown or state. Those who survived eventually earned a rolling monthly contract and an apartment—and the honor of Milutinović learning their actual names. Players could be cut at any time, but the federation held their rights indefinitely, planning to farm them out to a new American professional league that was supposed to kick off sometime in 1995. Most of the players, however, weren't worried about free agency. They were just trying to keep their jobs.

"It was one of the hardest times of my life," said defender Jeff Agoos. "Not just the taxing physical demands put on you, but the emotional and mental side."

Nevertheless, the full-time camp represented a lifeline for a lot of the players there. "I headed out there because I had nothing," Lalas said. "I had no options except for maybe playing indoor, and certainly no pathways to Europe. So this was the answer to my prayers. I showed up into what nowadays would be looked at as a reality-TV, *Survivor*-esque type of environment. It was just a constant churning of players."

Lalas, then, didn't much mind that he was only making $2,500 a month. "I was single, I had a bed, I had some money in my pocket, and I was training to be on the World Cup team," he said. "I was in heaven."

Brad Friedel, for his part, trained and lived with the team but refused to sign a contract, the better to keep his options open in Europe. Instead, he lived off the $35 per diem, the meager appearance and win bonuses, and his Reebok endorsement deal. But not everybody was so agreeable. The federation had always taken a hardball approach in labor negotiations with its players—sign or somebody else will. Some veteran players expected more from a federation that no longer teetered on the edge of ruin, as it had for decades. "They had just gotten some money pouring in from these advertisers, and the money didn't filter down to the players," Bruce Murray said. "As a player-rep type of guy, who was involved with a lot of this stuff, I knew for a fact we were getting stiffed."

The real payoff promised to come once you made the World Cup roster, which came with a $20,000 bonus. At the World Cup proper, meanwhile, there were tens of thousands of dollars more to be made, depending on their performances.

When the team wasn't on the road playing games, Milutinović ran two training sessions a day in Mission Viejo. But that wasn't all. There were hours-long lectures on tactics and endless games of soccer tennis; during their lunch break on days with UEFA Champions League action, the players were expected to join Milutinović at a local restaurant to watch the games. The whiteboard tactical sessions were vexing. Milutinović would draw up a problem, quiz everyone in the room, and then give the one answer nobody had come up with. "I think, for Bora, the two-a-days were more of a mental thing than him thinking we needed to train twice a day—just to see who would hold up," said Meola.

Practice sessions were monotonous and included stretches of the dreaded "one player, one ball" drill that could run as long as half an hour. Milutinović would give no instruction other than for each player to grab a ball. From there, they were on their own. "It was one of the most mundane, unproductive exercises I've encountered as a professional soccer player," Dominic Kinnear said. "I think he thought, technically, we were not that great and so the more touches we got on the ball, the better we would be. Some people would shoot the ball over the goal on purpose just to kind of skip the exercise for a good fifteen to twenty seconds."

"Many times, they tell you, 'Hey, we don't train nothing,'" Milutinović said decades later. "But at the same time, we're training everything."

Milutinović's methods were hard to parse. He would announce that a scrimmage would last five more minutes but not blow his whistle to end it for another twenty-five. When he refereed during practice, he made bad calls on purpose, just to see how his players would react. "It made you pull your hair out," said Lalas. "It made you question everything that you had known about soccer. And some players, honestly, ultimately it was their demise."

One day, Renato Capobianco, the team administrator, went up to Lalas and informed him that Milutinović wanted him to cut his long red hair. After protesting vigorously, Lalas got a haircut. The next day, Milutinović walked in, glanced at Lalas, nodded, and said nothing. From that day, Lalas grew his hair out longer and wilder than before, adding in a bushy goatee for good measure—the iconic look that would make him famous at the World Cup. Milutinović never bothered him about his hair again; Lalas had passed his test.

The players who spoke no Spanish had a hard time communicating with their coach. Yet Milutinović had other ways of making himself understood. One day, some players got into one of the team vans and waited for Milutinović. With some time to kill, they got onto one of their favorite subjects, complaining about their coach. "We're waiting and we're waiting and next thing you know, Bora pops out from underneath the backseat," Balboa recalled. "'Everywhere you go,' I remember him telling us one day, 'just remember, if you think you can get away with something, you won't. Remember, I am Bora. I know the people that work here. I know the cooks, the cleaning lady, the people behind the front desk. They will tell me if they see you leaving the hotel. They will tell me if you're ordering food at eleven o'clock at night. They will tell me.'"

When the 1994 World Cup finally neared, Milutinović's work was essentially done. His eighteen-month indoctrination camp had turned out a team that had grown close and developed a tactical coherence. They'd traveled the world over several times and experienced just about anything a World Cup game could throw at them. If his methods were maddening, Milutinović also seemed to have delivered on his mandate. The Americans were competitive.

8 | A Nation Changed

A few weeks before playing in the 1994 World Cup to a global TV audience of a billion people, Alexi Lalas sat on a plane. Economy. Middle seat. Of course. He got to talking to the woman seated next to him, and no matter how he tried to explain it to her, she simply could not conceive of the notion that he played soccer for a living. She was hardly alone in being heedless of the upcoming tournament. Thomas Dooley, a veteran of the German Bundesliga where soccer players were swarmed wherever they went, marveled that nobody paid the U.S. team bus any mind. A poll showed that, on the eve of the 1994 World Cup, a mere fifth of Americans knew what it was and that it was about to kick off in their own country.

Still, the pressure on the tournament's organizers was mammoth. The stakes were no longer existential for the federation. Soccer in the United States would survive regardless of how the World Cup did commercially. But this mega-event promised to be an inflection point, when the nation would either embrace soccer at last or recommit to its apathy. When Tab Ramos returned stateside from his Spanish season with Real Betis, things were finally beginning to shift. He noticed that World Cup preparations were being covered on the major TV networks. Milutinović even starred in a beer commercial on Spanish-language U.S. TV, going against American convention and possibly even federal regulations, since head coaches in the four major sports leagues were barred at the time from promoting alcoholic drinks. The *Los Angeles Times* asked the beer-peddling coach about the hubbub. "I don't drink beer," answered Milutinović. "I don't like it."

This newfound attention also dialed up the strain on the players, who remained fearful of becoming the first World Cup hosts not to survive the opening round. They understood that they weren't just playing for themselves or the team or even their nation, but also for an unprecedented opportunity to supercharge the sport. The team talked about its fears a lot. Meanwhile, Milutinović culled his roster to the final twenty-two. Bruce Murray, the program's all-time leading scorer, was cut before the turn of the year. Peter Vermes, who had been the team captain for most of Milutinović's time in charge, was cut in the middle of April. "I was not told in a very professional manner," Vermes recalled. "I wasn't really told. Bora never really said it to me." Murray and Vermes were both labor leaders on the team and wondered, decades later, whether that played a role.

General manager Bill Nuttall insists that every player got a sit-down meeting and an explanation after being cut, but the players dispute this. Sometimes, several of them said, a player would be told that he was cut in a note handed to him by a secretary. "There were cuts after runs on the beach," said Agoos. "So you literally would run to your car because you didn't want to get the tap on the shoulder." Desmond Armstrong apparently didn't run fast enough and was cut in the parking lot. Agoos never even made it off the beach before getting cut. He'd been in camp for its entirety, almost a year and a half. When he got home, he threw his training gear into the garbage. Then, feeling that he'd let his team-issued outfit off too easy, he burned it in the fireplace.

Dominic Kinnear wasn't cut until June 1, the day before the final roster was announced. He was asked to meet Milutinović at the practice facility in Mission Viejo. "When I drove up, the parking lot was empty and I knew right there," he recalled. "Aw, shit."

The survivors were never actually told that they had made the team. They were on a bus to a promotional event when it dawned on them that there were only twenty-two of them left and that, therefore, they had made it.

Their exuberance could not be diminished even by the realization that they would take the field in some of the strangest uniforms ever designed. Adidas made a big show of coming out to California to present the national team with the jerseys and shorts they would be wearing for this seismic event. Two executives started the unveiling, giving a talk about America and its flag and its culture and ideals. They spoke about the American West and the nation's fabric. Then they revealed a jersey in faux blue denim, made to look like a jean jacket with white stars woven through it. The shorts matched. It was a design unlike anything anyone had ever seen. The players were horrified. The silence finally broke when they started to laugh uproariously. Only when the laughter subsided did it dawn on them that they were not, in fact, being pranked.

There wasn't any time to be upset over jerseys—besides, Adidas gave each player a $10,000 bonus for making the team, which smoothed things over. The Americans capped their eighteen-game World Cup preparations, stretching back to mid-January 1994, with a showdown against archrivals Mexico at the Rose Bowl in Pasadena on June 4, just two weeks before their World Cup opener.

The year had started inauspiciously, with a three-month winless stretch that included a loss to lowly Iceland. The Americans had won just a quarter of their games that year. And doubts lingered about Milutinović's grand experiment in his Mission Viejo lab. Those who followed Mexico and Costa Rica closely before they went to a World Cup with Milutinović at the helm had also been nervous about his methods and whether they would deliver. The U.S. federation was no different in '94. "Has he panned out? If you look at the win-loss record, the answer has to be no," Steinbrecher said of the coach on the eve of the tournament. "If you look at where we were three years ago—stylistically, lack of competition, credibility—the answer has to be yes."

Under Milutinović, the Americans played endless games, barnstorming the world. In 1992 alone, Tony Meola counted 250 days on the road. In 1993, the Americans played in three summer tournaments and an unheard-of thirty-four games in all, traveling to Japan and Saudi Arabia and Ecuador and Iceland and everywhere in between. One day, they might play England in a packed NFL stadium, and in their next game face the Cayman Islands in front of just a few thousand. Yet after all those games, Milutinović still didn't appear to have settled on a lineup. Scrutiny swelled. Rather than a handful of reporters, more than fifty of them now followed the team around every day. In the Rose Bowl, a crowd that overwhelmingly favored the visiting team booed the U.S. That was fine—the players expected it. Then the Americans beat Mexico 1–0. "It was proof of concept," Alexi Lalas said.

Several years of living in the United States rubbed off on Milutinović. He discovered and eagerly adopted those motivational posters with eagles on them that you're supposed to hang in your office to remind employees to work as a team. His favorite read "carpe diem," but he got the English translation slightly wrong and was forever urging his players to "size the day."

The night before they were to play their World Cup opener against Switzerland, Milutinović brought his players to Michigan's Pontiac Silverdome. They stood on the field and watched a highlight reel of themselves in action on the big screen. "We showed them a beautiful film," Milutinović later recalled. "They were ready to do something great." He had done the same thing with Mexico and Costa Rica. And while the players weren't big on the choice of music—Queen's "I Want It All" and Van Halen's "Right Now"—the eleven-minute video made its point: They belonged at the World Cup.

That same day, Oprah Winfrey had fallen off the stage while emceeing the World Cup's opening ceremony, where Diana Ross performed "I'm Coming Out." Ross took a shot at a goal as part of her act, but she missed from just a few yards out, rather ruining the intended effect of the goal splitting in half as the ball hit the net. That night, OJ Simpson led the LAPD on a low-speed police chase after he failed to report for questioning in connection with the murder of his ex-wife and her friend. Tony Meola was riveted by the TV coverage and refused to go to bed, irritating his roommate, John Harkes. The goalkeeper showed up exhausted for the team's pregame preparation at 6:30 a.m. for the 11:30 a.m. kickoff.

The unusual morning kickoff didn't make it any cooler in the Silverdome, which was about to host the first World Cup game ever held indoors. It had been ninety-nine degrees in Michigan the day before and the weather promised to push past ninety again. The Silverdome, however, had no air-conditioning system but instead relied on an array of fans. It was a gridiron football stadium, after all, designed for the Michigan winter and thus to keep heat in, not out. Dooley recalls that several of the cooling fans weren't working. As the sun beat down on the dome, the temperature inside climbed to 106 degrees. A grass field had been laid over the Silverdome's artificial turf and watered zealously, making the field soggy and the air unbearably humid, slowly poaching everybody inside the stadium. "I hope the temperature is 300 degrees and the humidity is 2,000 percent," Milutinović told reporters before the game. He assumed that the Swiss would be less resistant to such conditions than the unpampered Americans. Milutinović told

Dooley that he'd turned off a few of the working fans—Dooley wasn't sure whether he was kidding.

Milutinović got his wish. "It was the hottest game that I ever played in my life," said Tab Ramos, adding that even afternoon games in Dallas in the dead of summer weren't quite so oppressive. "We were boiling in there. They were carrying people out from the upper deck; fans were passing out."

The Americans, however, were used to playing in suboptimal circumstances. "We were fit," remembered forward Earnie Stewart, crediting Milutinović for their conditioning work. "I don't think anybody was as fit as we were, and we needed to be. Because of the heat, and because we weren't as good as the other teams, we needed at least to be able to outrun them."

The home team, clad in its hateful denim uniforms, had another thing working in its favor: a literally fevered home crowd. The stadium was packed with 73,425 fans who screamed for the USA—the rare occasion when the U.S. had a solidly home crowd in a major stadium. The Americans would need to win one of their group-stage games if they were going to make it to the second round. Switzerland represented the best chance to bag those crucial points.

Alas, Thomas Dooley made a reckless tackle from behind on Alain Sutter in the thirty-ninth minute, and Georges Bregy put the Swiss ahead with a beautiful free kick. Just before halftime, however, the Americans were awarded a free kick that seemed too far off to threaten the goal. Eric Wynalda had arranged for a bag of balls to join the team on the trip to the Silverdome the night before, when Milutinović showed the highlight reel. Against Milutinović's wishes, and to the coach's subsequent ire when he found out, Wynalda had taken a dozen or so free kicks to test the air in the dome. Now he settled behind the ball and told the teammates who were also angling for a shooting opportunity to get lost. And then he deposited the ball into the net, off the underside of the bar, about as well as you can place a free kick. 1–1. There were no more goals.

It was the first American point at a World Cup in forty-four years. Still, they would need to beat either Colombia or Romania, both better teams on paper than the Swiss.

The pressure felt by the American players at the 1994 World Cup, while immense, was nothing like what the Colombians suffered. Their country was still in the grip of drug cartels. Colombian soccer, on the other hand, was living through something of a golden age because the nation's drug lords flooded the sport with money as another means of competing with one another. The soccer-besotted narcos, who tended to wager heavily on the games, had such a degree of control over the sport that jailed cocaine kingpin Pablo Escobar summoned half a dozen professional players to his personal prison, La Catedral, to play against him and his guards. Escobar even hosted superstar Diego Maradona there while the Argentine was, sort of fittingly, suspended from soccer for using cocaine in 1991. Escobar escaped from "prison" in 1992 and was killed in 1993. But by the 1994 World Cup, the narcos' threat to soccer remained implicitly or, just as often, explicitly.

Los Cafeteros were both very good and very scared of what the drug lords might do if they didn't win. They placed third at the 1993 Copa América, the continental championship, and might well have won that tournament with a little more luck. Pelé announced that he believed Colombia to be the World Cup favorite, which probably didn't help matters any. Neither did losing their opener to Romania, 3–1. Colombia's manager, Pacho Maturana, returned to his hotel room to find that his TV displayed not its usual welcome message but a death threat. If he put midfielder Gabriel Gomez in the game against the U.S., the entire team would be killed. (Gomez didn't play.) The Americans, for their part, had only a vague sense of the danger felt by their opponents.

These were not the only matters weighing on the Colombians' minds. The team's uniforms were stolen before the tournament. Star goalkeeper René Higuita was imprisoned for brokering the release of a girl kidnapped by the Medellín cartel—delivering the ransom money and pocketing a cut of $64,000—and was left off the World Cup team. Striker Faustino Asprilla was forever crashing his car in Italy, where he played for Parma. He was possibly even more dangerous while parked, once leaving his BMW in the middle of a busy intersection for two days. Defender Luis Herrera learned during the World Cup that his brother had been killed in a car crash.

When the tournament's draw dropped the Colombians into the same group as the U.S., it had been a blow to the hosts, a bad bit of luck. But Milutinović's policy of playing as many opponents as possible to mitigate the awe factor paid off. The U.S. had played Colombia in 1992 and 1993—and twice in 1990 as well—and lost each game by only one goal. "In a lot of ways, we didn't have any business being on the field with those guys," Meola said. "But Bora constantly drilled into your head, 'You can compete with them.'"

Milutinović knew Colombia inside and out. He understood how their strengths could be negated and their weaknesses exploited. His opposite number, Maturana, was just as much of an oddball as Milutinović was. Maturana, a dentist by trade, thought he needed to blend players from the mountains, to provide the hard work, with players from the coast, to inject creativity. He encouraged his players to read poetry books in the belief that personal growth would help their soccer.

On a ninety-degree day, the Rose Bowl heaved with 93,868 fans, many of them Colombian. The U.S. survived some sketchy defending early on when Mike Sorber almost bundled the ball into his own goal, which instead pinged off the post and was cleared off the American goal line. Around the half-hour mark, Wynalda hit a shot off the far post. A few minutes later, Harkes sent a low cross into the path of the fleet-footed Earnie Stewart. Colombian defender Andrés Escobar had to choose between letting the ball roll to the wide-open Stewart and making a difficult clearance that risked an own goal. He gambled on the latter and slid the ball into the Colombian net. The home team was ahead against one of the tournament favorites.

After halftime, Alexi Lalas was wrongly denied a goal for offside, given that the ball had caromed into his path off a defender. Lalas had rammed the ball into the net off the underside of the bar—the "shot of a life," according to the announcer. Instead of a goal, he was presented with a yellow card for playing after the whistle, which was also a wrong decision. Video replay was decades away.

In the fifty-second minute, the U.S. doubled its lead anyway. Ramos chipped a lovely ball into space for Stewart, who caught goalkeeper Óscar Córdoba in no-man's-land and dinked the ball slowly into the net off the near post, making it 2–0.

"I take real pleasure in saying that I can think of a few journalists who are going to have to stop the soccer bashing for a while in this country with this kind of performance today," ESPN's analyst Seamus Malin gloated. The celebrations were no less rambunctious for Colombia's Adolfo Valencia's ninetieth-minute goal, which tightened the score to 2–1.

When the final whistle blew, Tony Meola pumped his arms in ecstasy. The Americans had practically guaranteed themselves a place in the second round. They had beaten their toughest opponents and with a game to spare, no less. The players ran around the Rose Bowl waving American flags. The Colombians skulked off.

"We played Colombia so many games and it was always 1–0, 1–0, 1–0 for Colombia," Milutinović remembered later. "But the way they played, we were not inferior. Tactically, we made some adjustments. Everything was perfect."

The game exacted a toll from the Americans. A dehydrated Marcelo Balboa needed more than four hours before he could muster a urine sample for his random drug test after the game. Then heatstroke kept him up all night, vomiting. He didn't train for two days. Andrés Escobar, author of the Colombian own goal, fared much worse. Ten days after the loss to the U.S., which eliminated the Colombians, he was killed outside of a bar in Medellín, reportedly on the orders of a drug lord who had lost a big bet. The murder was the nadir of the Colombian national team's history. The American team, meanwhile, became a national sensation.

Until this week, they were mere shadows on the American sporting scene," Jim McKay spoke as the U.S.–Romania broadcast began on ABC's *Wide World of Sports*. "Lonely figures traveling the world, trying to make their mark on the world's most popular sport, but a sport that receives little notice in their home country. They are the American national soccer team."

In the spring of 1993, the U.S. tied the Romanians 1–1 in Santa Barbara, prompting the Romanian coach, Cornel Dinu, to declare that the Americans "are very nicely dressed." "They'll need a hundred years to play soccer," Dinu continued. "The Americans only scare us if they bring aircraft carriers." This was quite a statement, given that the U.S. had beaten Romania 2–0 on the road in 1991. Dinu was fired well before the World Cup began.

Dinu's successor, Anghel Iordănescu, joined Milutinović for a game of chess in the latter's hotel room late on the night before the game. Milutinović loved chess. But the next day, he would not outmaneuver Iordănescu the way he had Pacho Maturana. It was 101 degrees in

Pasadena and 120 on the field in the Rose Bowl. Another sellout crowd showed up anyway, and many American fans arrived wearing red wigs and fake goatees, adopting the Lalas look—who would be shown at halftime of the TV broadcast singing and playing his guitar. The American players had indeed emerged from the shadows.

But in the seventeenth minute, Dan Petrescu finished a well-worked Romanian attack by overlapping on the right and beating Meola. The U.S. had chances but lost its first game at the World Cup. It had also dropped into third place in the group on goal difference—eked out by the Swiss—meaning they would have to wait through two agonizing days for certainty that they had made the next round. When they did, the loss to Romania consigned the Americans to a date with Brazil in the round of 16, rather than a much more manageable matchup with Argentina or Spain.

It was a missed opportunity that the Americans still lamented many years later. They expected to need all three games to secure the four points most likely required to advance. When they got them in just two games, they let the Romania match slip away.

The Brazilian people were delighted that their national team should face such a lightweight opponent as the United States in the first knockout round. *The Washington Post* interviewed some in Rio de Janeiro, who assumed their team's passage to the quarterfinals was a formality. "Americans want to dominate the world through imperialism," a Brazilian architect told the paper. "We want to dominate the world, too, but through soccer."

The Brazilian players were not so confident. Sometime after the game, Marcelo Balboa made a commercial appearance with Bebeto, one of Brazil's star strikers. Bebeto confessed that out of all the opponents the Brazilians faced at the '94 World Cup, the Americans had made them the most nervous. "Because they didn't know any of us, had no clue, had no footage because none of us were playing in any sort of league where they could keep up on us," Balboa said. "And they knew it was Independence Day in the United States." The Brazilians also knew that the U.S. had beaten Colombia and that with their objective already reached, the Americans had nothing to lose.

More than eighty-four thousand spectators at Stanford Stadium witnessed the kind of game only soccer can produce: One team overwhelmed the other, yet the score remained deadlocked, slowly dialing up a frustrated tension. Before halftime, Brazil's Leonardo clobbered Tab Ramos in the face with an elbow. Leonardo was sent off with a red card, but the foul rattled the Americans. His teammates were worried for Ramos's well-being in the locker room. He was clearly in a bad way, confused, and, it turned out, coping with a concussion and a cracked skull. (Leonardo, who would be suspended for the rest of the tournament, came to see Ramos in the hospital after the game, apologized, and broke down and cried. The two were friends thereafter.) The American players did not discuss the game itself before they went out for the second half.

In the seventy-fourth minute, Bebeto put the Brazilians ahead at last, threading the needle between Lalas's legs, Meola's reaching hand, and the inside of the far post. The Americans, who had a man sent off as well—Fernando Clavijo, in the eighty-fifth minute—kept the score close, even if the run of play had been a slaughter.

The Americans' World Cup was over. Millions of their fellow citizens had just watched them play Brazil to a near draw. The U.S. national team's most recognizable players—Alexi Lalas, Cobi Jones, Tony Meola—had become stars overnight. Still, the players weren't quite sure how to compute what they had just lived through. There was no celebration. After their final game, many of them went out to dinner, joined by Robin Williams. The comedian had befriended the team after helping to conduct the World Cup draw and making merciless fun of FIFA bigwig Sepp Blatter onstage.

As the organizers had hoped, the 1994 World Cup elevated American soccer. The sport went mainstream. Before the tournament, John Harkes was named one of *People* magazine's fifty most beautiful people, although it took three phone calls before he accepted that he wasn't being pranked. Alexi Lalas and Cobi Jones, with their striking appearances, became celebrities in their own right—Lalas for bringing a dash of rock and roll to the team and Jones as the heartthrob. The players were constantly on MTV and started signing endorsement deals with major companies. Tony Meola tried out as a kicker for the NFL's New York Jets and acted on Broadway. The players went on late-night talk shows, too, and soon enough, Lalas was partying with Metallica. "The landscape changed fundamentally in one month," Lalas said. "America had changed relative to soccer, and it didn't go back. I milked it for all it was worth, don't regret a second of it, and remember some of it."

The sport writ large benefited as well. More than 3.5 million people attended the World Cup (including Jack Kemp, the gridiron-loving congressman), over a million more than any previous edition. This record still stood through the 2022 tournament in Qatar, even though every subsequent World Cup counted eight more participants and twelve more games. Meanwhile, an expected $20 million profit turned out to be $50 million. Rothenberg was awarded a $7 million bonus by an organizing committee he had appointed himself. What was left served as seed money for the launch of Major League Soccer in 1996.

"The criteria for success were for the team not to embarrass themselves—and they didn't," Sunil Gulati said. "Two was to make some real money for the sport, and we did. Three was to increase the popularity of the game, increase players and registration, and launch a league. The fourth one was developing human capital." Hundreds of people who helped stage the 1994 World Cup went on to become important figures in the sport behind the scenes, running Major League Soccer teams, taking key posts in the federation, or becoming promoters and agents.

Milutinović's contract was up at the end of 1994. He said the day after the U.S. was eliminated that he wanted to stay on. Rothenberg "absolutely" wanted to re-sign him, he told reporters. "Bora can have any role he wants to have," he added. "He's a special talent and a special person."

It never happened. The federation decided at some point it wanted an American coach who could create a top-down national team structure with a clear, unifying philosophy. Both sides understood that this was clearly not Bora Milutinović. Perhaps he had done all he could. There is no counterfactual, but many of Milutinović's players doubted decades later that anybody else could have gotten them out of the group stage, however circuitously he got them there.

Milutinović's impact on his players was profound. "One of the most amazing moments of my life was after the World Cup, when Bora said to me, 'I'm proud of you,'" recalled Lalas. "That's how needy I was for his approval." Milutinović still calls Lalas every year on his birthday.

After he left the U.S., Milutinović was far from done working miracles. In 1998, he took Nigeria to the World Cup, although he only made it to the tournament when the death of the nation's dictator prevented Milutinović's replacement by another coach—in the power vacuum, there was nobody to sign off on his firing. He led Nigeria to the second round, becoming the first coach to do so with four different countries. In 2002, Milutinović guided China to its first World Cup qualification in forty-four years.

The Making of a National Team: Ricardo Pepi

Every time Ricardo Pepi goes home to Prosper, Texas, the place has changed.

In 1990, the city just north of the Dallas–Fort Worth metroplex counted 1,018 citizens; three decades later, there were a tad more than thirty thousand. Prosper grows and grows, bigger and richer, the leading edge of a suburban oil slick creeping from Dallas toward the Oklahoma border.

To get to Prosper, you set out from the north side of Dallas, from Plano and Frisco, where the large houses in the developments look so similar—brick facade, elaborate stonework, wrought iron fence—that you wonder how people manage to distinguish their own homes from those of their neighbors. A bumper sticker on the back of a large SUV has a message for other drivers: WELCOME TO AMERICA, NOW SPEAK ENGLISH. Next to that is a sticker of a smiley face. Navigate the jumble of overpasses and ramps and elevated highways, and then cut through the flat, empty scrublands due north. And there, suddenly, is Prosper, plopped right into the middle of the nothing, all of it brand-new. "When I haven't been home in a couple of months, and I go back in the summer, it's going to be completely different," Ricardo Pepi said. "I leave home at Christmas, and then I come back and I see new houses everywhere."

The Pepis' home looks exactly like all the ones next to it. New. Modern. Tidy. Manicured front yard. Not exactly small, but hardly ostentatious. On the inside, there is a lot of gray. A sign hangs over the back door: CON DIOS TODO ES POSIBLE. A living room wall is adorned with a mosaic of pictures, mostly from Ricardo's youth soccer career, a frame-by-frame timeline of a child so large the family still calls him Gordo even though he is tall and lean now. So much bigger than his peers was Ricardo that the parents of opponents used to demand to see his birth certificate—even if they had already faced him and seen it. When the exasperated Pepis complied, proving once again that Ricardo was, in fact, *younger* than the other kids, those opposing parents resorted to lobbing jibes at the preteen during the games. "*¿Cuándo se casará?*" "When is he getting married?" That kind of thing.

It's only been a few years since the Pepis moved to Prosper. They bought the place after Ricardo signed his first professional contract with FC Dallas's senior team, before he made the national team, before the record-setting $20 million transfer to FC Augsburg in Germany. He only lives here some of the year now, when he isn't in Europe or on the road. His family followed him to North Texas, only to get left behind again.

Daniel Pepi and his wife, Annette, were both born in Juárez, Mexico. She stayed there for all her childhood; Daniel crossed the border at seven and was raised in El Paso. Juárez and El Paso are twin towns cleaved by a heavily fortified boundary. Still, it feels like a single, rambling place to the locals. Daniel and Annette met on a soccer field. Daniel played in one of El Paso's men's leagues, a hub of social life there. Annette's family was as besotted by soccer as his was.

Daniel and Annette got married in 2002. She crossed the border to El Paso permanently. Ricardo was born in January 2003. Daniel was twenty-three years old when he became a father. Annette was sixteen. "I was young; she was younger," Daniel recalled. "We kind of started our life from nothing, trying to live day by day. Back in El Paso, life was not that easy. Starting a family, you have to work long days and sometimes it's really hard." The first few years were rocky. They found a house, only to move back in with his parents when they couldn't make rent. They bounced around. Then they scraped together enough money to buy a plot of land and a trailer in San Elizario, a speck of a town in the Chihuahuan Desert, tucked up against the Rio Grande and the Mexican border, consumed by the sprawl of El Paso but also very much of Juárez. San Eli, as the locals call it, was once a part of Mexico, until the Treaty of Guadalupe Hidalgo ended the Mexican-American War and made it a part of the U.S. Culturally, emotionally, it never stopped being Mexican. It's a town of skilled laborers, where people build their own homes with their own hands. Daniel, who had followed his father into the concrete-finishing trade at thirteen, now set about building his growing family a house on their lot. It took him six years. Annette bore two more children.

On the weekends, the Pepis went over the border to Juárez whenever they weren't at the soccer field. The food was cheaper. Her family was there. They would stay the night and brave the enormous lines at the checkpoint to return to El Paso on Sunday. Daniel still played in the local men's league—as a striker, and as everything else as well—and Ricardo hung around. The Pepis would get to the park as early as

8 a.m., when the games started, and stay there most of the day. Soccer was community. Cookouts. Drinks. Family. When he was four, Ricardo asked his dad if he could start playing soccer.

One weekend morning, Daniel and Ricardo had a game at the same time. Daniel decided that his game took priority; Ricardo would have to miss his. "We got into the car, and we started driving off to my game," Daniel remembered. "Halfway there, driving on the freeway, I think to myself, 'What the hell am I doing, man? It's not like I'm going to miss much. It's not like I'm having a career in this. And my kid's just barely starting. Maybe he does have a shot.' I turned the car around and we went to his game. Ever since that day, his games or my other kids' games were more important than anything else." Daniel Pepi the soccer player was retired; Daniel Pepi the soccer dad was activated.

Pepi made some kind of select team for a tournament in Las Cruces, New Mexico, an hour away. The coach put Pepi, a striker, in goal and gave him no further instruction. The Pepis and some other parents decided there and then to break off and form their own team, the Lions. Daniel became a coach. The team was on the road a lot, a kind of shoestring travel team facing moneyed opponents wherever it went. Keeping the preteen Pepi and his prodigious goal-scoring gift in competitive games became a financial priority for a family still only just getting by. "Sometimes we had to go to a tournament, go to Albuquerque, San Diego, Phoenix," Daniel said. "You used to do whatever you needed to do to get that money and take them. Sometimes we used to borrow some money. Sometimes I would ask for a loan at my job, or from my dad. Sometimes I had to pawn the title to the car. Whatever we had to do to just keep going."

Ricardo was conscious of the gulf in circumstances between the Lions and most of their opponents, the bevy of rich, largely white teams in the private, for-profit youth soccer scene. "It motivated me to do better than them because I know they had an easier way," he said.

"Being a Latino, you don't get as many opportunities as others get. It's either because of your circumstances or because people don't see the actual talent in you. Or people don't want to see that talent in you."

He may have been only a child, but Ricardo understood his family's sacrifices. "You start noticing these little things and start thinking, 'They're putting in a big effort for me to make it to these tournaments, so then I better go out there and actually make it happen,'" he remembered. "It was difficult because I just put a lot of pressure on myself. I wanted to help my family back in some way." He worked hard, and, knowing that he wasn't always the most skillful player on the field, he asked Daniel to do extra drills. Daniel was tough on him, pulling Ricardo from games when he dogged it. "When he thought I was being lazy, he would always get me off the field and he would take me home and say, 'If you don't want to play, then throw your uniform away, your boots away. You're not going to waste my time or my money.' It was really direct, but I feel like I'm here for that reason."

When Pepi was ten, in 2013, Daniel and his fellow dads handed control to a more experienced coach who took the team to FC Dallas's new affiliate in El Paso. FC Dallas was an established Major League Soccer team with a checkered competitive record but a sterling reputation for developing talent through its live-in, all-expenses-paid youth academy. A great deal of good fortune put Pepi on the radar of a professional team ten hours east. Had FC Dallas not recently decided to begin scouting El Paso, had Ricardo's new coach not sought an affiliation—over Daniel's objections, ironically—there's no telling whether anybody would have noticed him. He would hardly have been the first talented Mexican American to go entirely overlooked. He might have gotten lost in the tangle of minor leagues. Or he might have set out to try his luck as a free agent, a dime-a-dozen fringe prospect in the Mexican leagues, like hundreds of Mexican Americans have done.

The fact of FC Dallas's interest in Ricardo Pepi, now eleven, guaranteed nothing. After his coach recommended him for a tryout with the mother team's academy, Pepi broke his wrist and missed the tournament where he had hoped to get his chance. He was given another shot at a tournament in Guadalajara. Pepi, who had a preternatural sense for where the opportunities for goals would materialize, scored five times in the first game. He wondered whether the opposition was just weak or his own team very strong. By the end of the tournament, he had scored more than a dozen goals. "That's when I started to realize, 'I can do something here,'" he remembered. He announced to his parents that, one day, he would be buying them a nice house and allowing his dad to retire.

But Pepi blew a second tryout in El Paso. He got a third look in Frisco, where the team was based, and then heard nothing for a year. As a policy, the FC Dallas academy rarely allowed players younger than fifteen to move in from another market—it put too much pressure on them and there was plenty of talent in its own backyard. But just before he turned thirteen, Pepi received an invitation to come live and play at the academy full-time. He would have to leave home and stay with the family of another academy player. The Pepis had serious reservations, but they also didn't want to deny Ricardo the opportunity to make his improbable dream come true. It was a painful decision, sending their precocious son ten hours down the road by himself. They were a close family; they still are. Ricardo calls his parents before every game, or else he doesn't feel right out on the field. They talk and he promises to score a goal that day. His mother had not yet turned thirty when her oldest child left home.

"I just remember watching my siblings and my parents driving away, and I was like, 'Wow, this is a big sacrifice,'" Pepi said. "What made it harder was having my mom on the phone every night calling me like, 'Hey, I want you back. Come back,' and just crying on the phone."

Pepi thrived in Dallas. He scored so many goals in his own age group that the club quickly pushed him up in age. More goals. The next age group. Still more goals. "He just always had a knack for getting himself in good spots and having a short memory and taking chances and putting balls on frame," said academy director Chris Hayden. "He was an early developer. A lot of those kids get lost, too. The game is too easy for them." Some youth soccer stars level off quickly, or they never learn to cope when the game gets harder. But Pepi kept improving. Mexico invited him to play for its under-17 national team. A couple weeks later, so did the U.S., which brought him to the under-17 World Cup.

By that time, in late 2018, Ricardo Pepi had become, as a fifteen-year-old, the first signing for FC Dallas's new minor league affiliate team. He scored three goals in his first game as a professional in a 3–2 North Texas SC win. He scored again in his next two games. By the following summer, he was called up to the FC Dallas senior team. In 2021, he was an eighteen-year-old MLS All-Star and the youngest player in league history to record a hat trick. A few weeks after that All-Star game, the behind-the-scenes battle for his loyalty became public. Mexico and the USA both vied for his commitment to their national team programs—once a player has represented one country in a competitive senior national team game, they can no longer play for any other nation.

Not for the first time, Pepi was forced to contemplate his identity and make a judgment. He had grown up in a community that was assigned to the sovereign territory of one country but that felt more like another's. At home, they spoke Spanish—Daniel Pepi's English, in fact, was rudimentary until the rest of the family followed Ricardo to

Dallas after a few years. In Ricardo's school in El Paso, instruction was in English, but questions were often answered in Spanish. He spoke Spanish with some friends, English with others. "It's like the border is not there because growing up in El Paso, it feels like Mexico in some way," Ricardo said.

When the family watched soccer, which was often, they watched the Mexican league, their beloved Club América—it's still what they watch today. The Mexican national team games were a family event; U.S. games got no such billing. Ricardo Pepi was American; Ricardo Pepi was Mexican—still he had to choose.

In the end, it wasn't such a tough call. The United States badly needed a productive striker. Mexico, on the other hand, had several well-established forwards at that time. When Gregg Berhalter, rebuilding his national team ahead of the 2022 World Cup, made his pitch to Pepi, he promised to involve him in World Cup qualifiers with the senior team right away. Mexico had a different plan: to introduce Pepi slowly, passing through the under-20 team first. Pepi was still only eighteen, albeit with a full beard that lent him an aura as mature as his game. He would score thirteen goals in MLS that season and didn't think there was much more he could do on a youth national team to prove that he belonged on a full national team. "I felt like I deserved the opportunity," Pepi said. "The U.S. gave me the opportunity, so I made my decision. It was a difficult one, but it was also an easy one."

Early in his tenure, Berhalter sat down with his new national team and led it through an exercise to define its identity—both as a collection of soccer players and as proxies for the nation they represented. It's a cliché for a soccer coach to write up a team's values and objectives, usually to then tack them up on a locker room wall. But in this case, it was a fraught endeavor.

The player development system that feeds the U.S. men's national team not only selects who will represent the nation but also makes an implicit determination of who gets to call themselves American—in a soccer sense, anyway. The federation has made extensive efforts to improve scouting in the areas and demographics left out of the elite youth game, but this has proved a vexing problem. Which makes it all the more remarkable that the new senior national team has a sizable contingent of Black players. A dozen of them made the 2022 World Cup roster, overcoming bad odds, because the system has frozen out generations of minority talent that couldn't afford to play in front of the right people. Yet there remain startlingly few Hispanic American players on the national team. The U.S. brought four to the 2010 World Cup, three to the 2014 edition. That is, on twenty-three-man rosters.

Ever since Martín Vásquez became the first player to represent both nations—Mexico three times between 1990 and 1992 and the U.S. seven times in 1996 and 1997—several others have played for both countries between the youth and senior national teams. Fierce recruiting wars are fought over teenage talent, and some players careen between Mexican and U.S. youth national team camps and games, torn between their two identities.

As of 2024, the United States counts 37 million inhabitants who were born in Mexico or who have recent Mexican heritage, largely concentrated in Texas and California, Mexican territory until the middle of the nineteenth century. That's equivalent to almost a third of the population of Mexico. This demographic is the engine behind soccer's march into the American mainstream. Between 2012 and 2019, Latinos represented 52 percent of the growth in soccer fans in the United States, according to a study by Telemundo. No other national team scouts its diaspora in another country as aggressively as the Mexicans do north of the border. For a time, the Mexican federation employed two full-time scouts in the United States. The U.S., meanwhile, only recently got serious about scouting its Mexican American population seriously and systematically.

But when the U.S. goes after a player eligible to play for both nations, it faces a two-pronged problem. It fights the pull of the old country, for which the player's family may still hanker nostalgically. And it fights its own representation issue. "When you look at the makeup of the country, one would assume that a soccer-driven culture like the Latino people would be reflected at the national team level," said Mexican American former U.S. national teamer Herculez Gomez. "But it's not been the case. Players will go where they see a path, see an avenue. When you have individuals who you identify with, it's easier to feel inclined to join." The many Mexican Americans growing up in households steeped in Mexican soccer culture see one national team that looks entirely like them and another that has only a few players of the same heritage. Then again, the USMNT has fielded a lot more Hispanic American players than Mexico has, particularly at World Cups.

A split in the American fan base seems instructive in this paradox. For almost two decades, the American Outlaws have been the dominant national team supporters' group, a loud and colorful presence behind the goal at every USMNT game. Yet in 2019, Barra 76 emerged as a separate supporters' group that catered to Hispanic U.S. fans. At some five hundred members and six chapters by 2024, Barra 76 is far smaller than the American Outlaws, who counted more than twenty-four thousand members and two hundred chapters, but also consciously different. "We're showing a different side of the United States, a side we should be proud of," explained Elliott Montalvan, the New York City chapter leader of Barra 76. "We like to show that there are Hispanics here in the United States that do follow U.S. soccer and are very passionate about it."

"The Hispanic community in the States has gone without a voice," added Thomas Rosales, Barra's Phoenix chapter leader. "I never really saw myself represented in any of the supporters' groups. It doesn't resonate with me. It gets into representation. If kids see people like themselves having a good time, they will feel more geared towards supporting the country they were born and raised in rather than going with their heritage, which was the battle for me personally. It feels like you're choosing a part of yourself and turning your back on a part of your life."

Counterpoint: The American Outlaws have thousands of Hispanic members and proudly boast a diverse board and corps of chapter leaders. Days after the 2016 U.S. presidential election ushered Donald Trump and his virulently anti-Mexican messaging into the White House, American Outlaws members made a point of greeting Mexico fans warmly at a World Cup qualifier between the two nations in Columbus, Ohio. The larger fan group is so preoccupied with ensuring that it welcomes everybody that it even puts its chapter leaders through diversity, equity, and inclusion training. Still, some Hispanic fans felt like they didn't fit in.

This sense of alienation is understandable. U.S. Soccer sends mixed signals to Hispanic would-be fans. True, it displays its "One Nation. One Team" slogan in Spanish as well: "Una Nación. Un Equipo." And it made plenty of other efforts, like celebrating Hispanic Heritage Month every year with several social and artistic campaigns to mark the occasion.

Yet when it comes time to award venues for high-stakes home games against Hispanic opponents, the federation opts for overwhelmingly white cities where the risk of the opposing team's fans buying up the bulk of the tickets is low. In fact, the federation goes to enormous lengths to ensure solid home crowds. It uses census data and complicated ticket-selling schemes, granting early access to "insiders" and "members" of various tiers before putting the remainder of the seats on general sale—a key qualifier with Mexico in November 2021 in Cincinnati, for instance, was sold out before any tickets reached the open market. Competitively, this makes sense. And it's no different from what the USA's regional rivals have been doing for decades. Yet the upshot is that much of the Hispanic community that doesn't have privileged access to tickets through fan groups or federation memberships is excluded from the stadium with surgical precision, lest they root for the other team.

In a sense, U.S. Soccer has gerrymandered its own fan base.

Ricardo Pepi arrived on the international stage like an apparition. The boy from the edge of El Paso, coming to the aid of a desperate U.S. national team, was the physical manifestation of the fans' long-held fantasy of what might happen if the Latino talent pool was properly scanned.

Just two games and twenty-seven minutes into the USA's fourteen-match qualifying slog for the 2022 World Cup in Qatar, things had already started to look iffy. The Americans tied a weak El Salvador 0–0 in San Salvador. This was no disaster. The formula for qualifying is simple: Win your home games and pick up points here and there on the road. A tie was still a point. But you must win those home games. And the Americans failed to do that in the next match, lucky as they were to eke out a 1–1 tie against a surprisingly strong Canada.

That meant the Americans would need to win their next game in Honduras to keep their qualifying campaign on track. Still more points and another missed World Cup would become a very real possibility. It was early, sure, but a qualifying campaign slips into a tailspin quickly—just as it had for the missed 2018 World Cup. Now they were traveling to exactly the kind of environment in Central America where the USA had floundered in the past.

Twenty-seven minutes into that match, Honduras went ahead.

Things looked grim. Although the Catrachos appeared tired and overmatched, they were masters in the dark arts of gamesmanship—faking injuries, instructing ball boys to roll an extra ball into play to interrupt the game at crucial moments, working the refs with histrionics—a CONCACAF staple that invariably troubled the Americans. U.S. fans felt a panic take hold that swelled with each minute ticking off the clock. Here they were, back in the same old bind. For all the hoopla over a generation that was supposed to transcend these plodding skirmishes, the U.S. was back to struggling in the mud.

Shortly after halftime, Pepi knocked down a cross into Antonee Robinson's path. Robinson surged up the left flank to score the equalizing goal. And then, in the seventy-fifth minute, Pepi rose high and connected with a cross to head in the game-winning goal. The U.S. ran out to a 4–1 romp as some Honduran fans hurled trash onto the field. Pepi assisted on the third goal and the fourth came on a rebound from his shot. After the game, in the locker room, Berhalter awarded a visibly embarrassed Pepi not one but two game balls as his teammates chanted his name: "Pepi! Pepi! Pepi!" He had just become the second youngest American to appear in a World Cup qualifier, after Christian Pulisic. Thanks to the debutant, the Americans were back on track. And Pepi would score twice more in the next match, a 2–0 win over Jamaica.

By late 2021, fresh off those three national team goals, some of Europe's biggest clubs—Bayern Munich, Manchester United, AC Milan, Inter Milan, Ajax—were tripping over themselves to sign him. Days before his nineteenth birthday, Pepi picked a smaller club instead, Germany's Augsburg, whose €16 million outlay on him was six million more than it had ever spent on a player. It was a deliberate choice for Pepi. A stepping stone.

But he didn't score goals for Augsburg and he didn't score goals for the U.S. In fact, it would be almost a year and a half before he notched another goal for the national team. Ricardo Pepi lived in a new country, learning a new style of play with new teammates, eating new food, speaking a new language—new everything. He struggled for the first time in his soccer life. Strikers are supposed to score goals. It doesn't matter if they are teenagers saddled with the towering expectations of a record transfer fee, living outside of Texas for the first time, disoriented by their new surroundings. Two months before the 2022 World Cup, Augsburg sent Pepi out on loan to FC Groningen in the Dutch league. A reset, a chance to regain his shaken confidence. A demotion, too. But the goals returned. Still, it was too late for him to make the 2022 U.S. World Cup roster. Four players who identified as Hispanic American made it onto the twenty-six-man U.S. World Cup roster. Ricardo Pepi wasn't one of them.

The following spring, Pepi was back on the national team and scored four goals in three games. The last one came against Mexico.

PART IV

Striving

1995–2002

9 | The Boys of Bradenton

The day after the 1994 World Cup final, Alan Rothenberg walked out of the Rose Bowl flanked by Sunil Gulati and Hank Steinbrecher. Rothenberg put his arms around their shoulders. They had just put on the biggest World Cup ever. And, against pitiless odds, the home team hadn't embarrassed itself.

Now what?

That's what the trio of administrators pondered just hours after the end of the mega-event that dominated their lives for more than half a decade. "I want to win the World Cup in my lifetime," Rothenberg declared.

"That was the original thought," Gulati recalled. "How do we put ourselves in a position to win the World Cup? How do we get better?"

A pair of reports offered some guidance. In 1993, Steinbrecher hired Rinus Michels, the Dutch giant of soccer coaching, as a consultant. Michels was tasked with traveling the United States with his wife for three months and reporting back with his observations on the American game and how it might be improved. "Well, Hank, you have a problem," Michels told Steinbrecher. "You are a continent; you are not a country. The football you play in Los Angeles is very different from the football you have to play in Maine, because of your climatic conditions. The football you play in Chicago is very different from Miami." Steinbrecher was struck by the clarity of the report, which seems to have been lost to time. Michels pointed out that the Dutch federation took great pains to ensure that the Netherlands used the same coaching methodology from the senior national team all the way down through the local youth leagues, and that the U.S. ought to follow suit.

Four years later, the federation engaged a second coaching heavyweight to flesh out Michels's findings with a more detailed plan. The Portuguese Carlos Queiroz, who would coach on five different continents, produced a 114-page document with a clumsily photoshopped cover: a blurry picture of an astronaut standing on the moon, holding an American flag in one hand and a World Cup trophy in the other, kicking a soccer ball, beneath the all-caps banner WE CAN FLY. PROJECT 2010. The report quoted John F. Kennedy on the first page and laid out a road map for the U.S. to win the World Cup by 2010. Like Michels, Queiroz crisscrossed the country on a fact-finding mission, watching soccer, attending coaching conventions, and interviewing his counterparts. The result was an eleven-part plan that outlined a need for a national development structure from the age of six all the way up to the senior national team. It advocated for two national training centers to bring together the nation's most promising talent, eventually followed by sixteen regional centers and fifty-five state-level training centers.

Michels and Queiroz agreed: What the U.S. needed was a centralized soccer incubator. In 1997, U.S. Soccer was in the process of negotiating an apparel deal with Nike, which also tied in the federation's commercial rights. "After we had a deal, I said, 'Hey, by the way, I need something else,'" recalled Gulati. He asked Nike to pay for twenty beds for elite athletes at the IMG Academy in Bradenton, Florida, so that U.S. Soccer could keep its under-17 men's national team in residence full-time. In making its pitch, the federation stuck with the bold moniker on Queiroz's report. "The notion wasn't that we were going to win the World Cup in 2010," Gulati said. "The first audience for us was three people in Beaverton, Oregon. And Nike's motto isn't 'Just *try* to do it.'" Project 2010 would be folded into a larger $50 million Nike investment that also bankrolled a pipeline of young American talent into MLS.

Most of that under-17 group had been together since they were fifteen years old. They were picked from four regional select teams of high school freshmen and brought to San Diego for a tournament, which produced a team of twenty. They would come to national team camps for two weeks, either somewhere in the United States or abroad, and then go back home. It took a toll on their schoolwork. And it wasn't ideal for their soccer development either. "We're competing with the top players around the world when we're playing with the under-17 national team, playing Germany or France, we're on that same level," recalled Kyle Beckerman, a midfielder from Maryland. "But then when we're going home, we're going back to the Laurel Wildcats or Arundel High School. They're going back to Juventus and Paris Saint-Germain. Those kids were already in that professional environment."

Soccer players make the most gains in their early teenage years. The trick is to gather as many promising preteens as possible and to put them in an optimal training environment. From there, it's something of a lottery. The more of these precocious sprites you manage to collect, the better your chances that a few of them pan out. It's hard to project a sporting future for a boy not yet in puberty, which is why you have to develop them on an industrial scale. This arithmetic holds that winning a World Cup requires a willingness to throw hundreds of boys, if not thousands, into the crucible of competition and see which ones make it out. This tends to mean disrupting their education by sticking them in soccer academies where their priorities bear no relation to conjugation or chemistry. The process extracts a social cost in the miseducation of untold castoffs. Vast numbers of players must flame out for the few stars to emerge. And this requires a certain whatever-it-takes mindset that is a tough sell in the United States, where youth soccer is dominated by the white upper-middle class and fueled by the prospect of a discounted college education. Which is to say that in the new under-17 residency, school needed to be taken seriously.

John Ellinger, the under-17 men's national team head coach, learned at a national staff meeting in Chula Vista that he would be moving to Florida to live with his team full-time. As a former teacher, he was well suited to this job. But convincing the players, no matter how ambitious they might be, was sometimes tricky. "I remember when I told them during a trip to Italy that we were going into residence, some guys actually cried," Ellinger recalled. "'I've got to leave my home? Leave my friends?' Others were like, 'This is awesome, holy crap.'"

Whatever their reaction to the news, the players understood that they were embarking on a project with an uncertain outcome. "We were the guinea pigs because nobody knew if it would work or not," said defender Oguchi Onyewu, a member of the first Bradenton class. "We were asked at a very impressionable period in our adolescence to leave our surroundings to relocate together, leaving your friends, your family, everything you know. To really sacrifice all that for what you want to become, it was a concept that we needed time to wrap our head around."

To get to play on the national team full-time was "a no-brainer" to Beckerman, as it afforded a consistency in the environment and competition. The eleven-month camp was slated to start in January 1999 and run through the U-17 World Cup in November of that year, at a cost to the federation of more than $1.5 million. Players lived together in suites, took classes in the morning on an accelerated track intended to obtain their high school degrees early, and then practiced in the afternoons. "It was a professional mindset," winger DaMarcus Beasley recalled. "That experience molded me."

The federation was clear in its expectations. Onyewu remembers Gulati addressing the residents in 1998, all of them fifteen or sixteen years old, and telling them that the federation expected at least one of them to make the World Cup roster in 2002. "We're like, 'This guy is crazy,'" Onyewu said.

They were sixteen years old or thereabouts, yet expected to behave and perform like full-fledged professionals. The transition wasn't always seamless. Beasley, one of the top talents in the group, went home to Fort Wayne, Indiana, on several weekends because he was homesick. They found time for teenage tomfoolery, though. A few under-17 residents convinced a soccer player at the neighboring IMG Academy to drive a golf cart into a pond, promising that they would submit footage of the stunt to the wildly popular MTV show *Jackass*—which reminded viewers before and after every episode that it did not take submissions. Still, Ellinger had a potent, albeit unwitting, ally in his effort to maintain discipline. "I never had to worry about that first group getting in trouble because Anna Kournikova was still at Bradenton," Ellinger said of the tennis starlet. "They never went wandering when Anna was there."

The 1998 team had a clear standout. Forward Landon Donovan joined the group from inland California with an odd mix of arrogance and awkwardness. He didn't easily fit into the group socially at first, yet announced that he wanted to lead any tournament they entered in scoring. Soon enough, his new teammates understood that Donovan was ahead of them in his development. He had grown up playing with highly technical Hispanic players and a coach who emphasized ball work long before that was the norm. Still, the residency accelerated his development. "Until I went to Bradenton, I never practiced more than twice a week in my life," Donovan said. "I went from having to play outside by myself all day, or with my friends, to an organized setup where I could train five days a week, play on Saturday, and be in a real professional environment. I loved it. This was a dream—I was with the twenty best players in the country, playing soccer all day, every day. My career wouldn't have been what it was without residency."

By the time the U.S. embarked on the U-17 World Cup in New Zealand in November 1999, the team had not lost in twenty straight games and had won plenty of scrimmages against Division I college sides and even Major League Soccer teams. Along the way, they faced an eclectic array of opponents. "John Ellinger exposed us to *everything*," Donovan said. "He would take us to Central America, to Argentina, to Europe. We would play in some gnarly environments for a seventeen-year-old American that you wouldn't usually get. We were really battle-tested. Nothing scared us."

They made the semifinals at the U-17 World Cup—still the best the U.S. has ever done in that tournament—beating Mexico in the quarterfinals and losing to Australia on penalty kicks. Donovan was named the tournament's best player; Beasley its second best. "Still, when we get together, we go, 'We let that one slip. We should have won that whole tournament,'" Beckerman said.

The first under-17 cycle in residence had validated the project. The next year, the under-17 residency was expanded to forty players, creating cutthroat competition for spots on the traveling roster. From then on, players would live at Bradenton for several years and arrive as young as twelve.

Bradenton wasn't perfect. There were downsides to keeping the nation's best young players in a bubble. "The unfortunate thing is that guys came away from there thinking they had arrived already," said Thomas Rongen, the longtime under-20 national team head coach. "A lot of these guys were very talented and ended up failing in MLS because, all of a sudden, they had to sit and fight for a position. We created a lot of entitled guys as well."

Tab Ramos, who succeeded Rongen with the under-20 team, argued that the format was constricting. "The downside was that you just wouldn't see enough players," he said. A regular national team environment allows you to rotate players in and out, to try new ones, to bring in a camp composed entirely of second-string players, to keep a much larger talent pool. You can't do any of those things if you've brought a team into residence full-time. "Once you're committed to the players for at least six months, it's not like you can drop someone," Ramos said. "It helped the best players but it didn't help us to find *more* players." A month into a new cycle, you might find that a player was clearly lacking in something required to make it big, but you had uprooted him and made a commitment for at least a semester.

To players who weren't stereotypical alpha-male jocks, the environment could feel stifling. "I really didn't like it," recalled Robbie Rogers, who would become the first openly gay player in a major American men's sports league. "It was a time when I was struggling with my sexuality, and I was thrown into a kind of *Lord of the Flies* situation. Residency is just a bunch of young guys being young guys. I just didn't fit in there at all, and you have no space or time to escape."

Freddy Adu didn't entirely fit in either.

Adu was born in Ghana and learned to play soccer barefoot on fields littered with rocks and glass. An uncle in Maryland sent him new balls every so often, which bought Freddy access to pickup games with the older kids. When he was eight, his mother was one of fifty-five thousand people out of millions of applicants to win the American green card lottery—or was it the United States that had won the lottery?—and the right to immigrate with her two sons, who were both named Fredua but who went by Freddy and Fro. When they settled in

Rockville, Maryland, it didn't take long for someone to spot Freddy's gift. He ran roughshod over an under-14 tournament as a ten-year-old, whereupon Inter Milan offered his mother a six-figure contract for Adu to join its academy. His skill set seemed so unlikely for his age that people began speculating about his "real" birthdate, a matter that would haunt him for much of his career. To a prepubescent boy, the question was confusing. "I remember one time I went to my mom, like, 'Mom, is this true?'" Adu recalled. "My mom looked at me like she was getting ready to smack me." *Sports Illustrated* later hired somebody to check on Freddy's birth certificate in Ghana, who found no evidence that anybody was lying about his age.

Emilia Adu turned down Inter's offer on account of Freddy's age. The next year, he joined the U.S. under-17 academy in Bradenton instead. He hated it there at first, because all the other kids were at least three years older. On the field, however, he was right at home. In Adu's first scrimmage, the Americans faced an adult team from Finland that had competed in the UEFA Champions League the season prior, the world's foremost club competition. U.S. head coach John Ellinger watched in astonishment as a twelve-year-old Adu faked out four grown men and earned his team a penalty kick when the fifth defender took him down in the box. "At halftime I looked at him," Ellinger recalled. "And I said to him, 'Freddy, I can't wait until you're thirteen.' What a talent. He was an electric player to watch."

Major League Soccer couldn't wait either. Adu wowed observers at the under-17 World Cup in Finland in 2003, scoring on a dribble from the halfway line. Scouts from the biggest clubs in the world salivated. MLS, meanwhile, was desperate. In 2002, just six years after kicking off, it had contracted two teams and plans were drawn up to fold the league, just in case. MLS had stabilized somewhat by 2004 but was in no lesser need of an injection of excitement and exposure.

The introduction of a boy wonder, a genuine prodigy, represented its best chance to slow the gusher of money it was hemorrhaging.

MLS outmaneuvered a half dozen of Europe's leading talent factories by promising to slot Adu straight into its league. No need for him to bide his time, to work his way up, to clamber out of the cauldron and earn his shot with the grown-ups. He had already practiced with the senior U.S. national team when a deal was engineered to assign Adu to his hometown D.C. United, the league's early dynasty, even though the Dallas Burn had the first draft pick. At a guaranteed $500,000 annual salary, Adu would be the league's highest earner and make substantially more money than Landon Donovan, by then the national team's star.

At fourteen, Adu left Bradenton and became the youngest American professional athlete in more than a century, unloosing what would be labeled "Freddymania." Wherever D.C. United went, the crowds clamored for him. Before making his debut, he had already been interviewed on *60 Minutes*, appeared on MTV, and gone on David Letterman's late-night talk show. He was in a Sierra Mist commercial with Pelé, widely considered the greatest player ever, in which Adu won a scripted skills competition—the implication was none too subtle. The media couldn't get enough of the photogenic Freddy, because he was always good for a great quote or a fun TV segment. Nike chairman Phil Knight, who signed Adu to a four-year, $1 million contract as a thirteen-year-old, declared to *Sports Illustrated* that Adu could mean more to soccer than Michael Jordan had to basketball, or Tiger Woods to golf.

"At the beginning, I just thought it was the coolest thing in the world, to have a chance to go pro at such a young age and achieve my dream of becoming a professional soccer player and take care of my family," said Adu, who had gone from well-off in Ghana to fairly poor in the United States. "But you realize pretty quickly that there were a lot of expectations that come with that. My every little move on and off the field was scrutinized. I started feeling the pressure."

There was a reason why the European clubs in pursuit of Adu wanted him to play in their youth teams for a few years first: Fourteen-year-old soccer players have a lot more developing to do. D.C. United practiced in the mornings. In the afternoons, the team's younger players returned to the practice field to do extra work and sharpen their skills. Adu didn't have the chance to go out and practice in the afternoons because he was booked solid with commercial and media events every day. "When you're young, that's what you need to do to master your craft," Earnie Stewart said. "There were players that were less talented that eventually got more out of their careers than Freddy did."

The league flew Adu out to road games a day or two ahead of the rest of his team to make yet more appearances. He often had commitments after games as well, sometimes for several hours. After one road game, Adu was sent to Iowa for some commercial commitments while his team flew home. "I was young and naïve, and I didn't feel like I could say no to any of that stuff, being the face of the league and getting paid all that money," Adu said. "You felt obligated to do it. That's one thing I would do differently if I had a chance to do it over. I would say no to a *lot* of that stuff. I always put on a smile because I wanted to be a good ambassador for the league. It was just constant, constant, constant. I was like, 'Man, can I just go spend some time with my friends? Just hang out? I'm fourteen! I'm a kid!'"

Adu was a disappointment in MLS. And then he was a disappointment for eight different European teams and one in Brazil. His seventeenth and final appearance for the senior U.S. national team came when he was twenty-two years and twenty-three days old. By his late twenties, after meandering through fifteen teams in nine countries, Adu had washed out of the professional game altogether. Since playing his last professional game for the minor league Las Vegas Lights in 2018, Adu has worked as a private coach, offering skills training. Rather than spending his early thirties winding down a glorious career, he mentored a new generation of players mostly of the age he was when the sport anointed him as its savior. "I try to bring them the wisdom of everything that I've learned, both good and bad," Adu said. "It's brought my love of soccer back."

The Bradenton program ran for eighteen years, finally closing its doors in the spring of 2017 once Major League Soccer's youth academies had made it redundant. The national residency, designed as a stopgap solution, was rendered obsolete by the dozens of regional incubators—just as Queiroz prescribed. That process took longer than its instigators had imagined. In all, 450 players passed through Bradenton, 150 of whom went on to have professional careers. Thirty-three of them made the senior national team. That's a far higher success rate than the national centers of excellence of most federations. At the 2006 World Cup, the senior U.S. team featured four graduates of its under-17 program, more than any other nation in the tournament: Landon Donovan, DaMarcus Beasley, Oguchi Onyewu, and winger Bobby Convey.

Like Donovan, Onyewu, who went on to play in seven European countries and two World Cups, doesn't think his life would have turned out the same way in some alternate history. "Had Bradenton not happened, I would not have had the career I had," he says. "Bradenton put the best players in the country at that age group against each other every day. We'd wake up, we'd think football, we'd go to school, we'd finish school, we'd think football."

Project 2010 was a failure in the grand sense that the U.S. did not win the World Cup in 2010, even if its stated goal was never much more than a marketing tool. But it stocked the senior national team player pool with sound players for almost two decades, players who might have otherwise struggled to reach that level.

Before the program ended, it produced one more generation that would make an impact on the senior national team. In the fall semester of 2014, Tyler Adams arrived at the academy full-time as a high school sophomore. By then, Weston McKennie was in his final semester at Bradenton. And Christian Pulisic shuttled in and out of camp, on the verge of signing his first professional contract with Borussia Dortmund in Germany when he turned sixteen.

Even in Bradenton's heightened environment, Pulisic stood out for his competitiveness and passion for the game and by how upset he would get by losses. Adams, a year younger than the rest of the group, was impossibly mature, and emerged as a leader to whom it never seemed to occur that perhaps it wasn't his time yet. They were not all on the same trajectory, however. McKennie, a late bloomer who was far from the 6-foot-tall body he would grow into, lagged behind the group and would be cut and sent back to FC Dallas after that semester. "My memories are maybe not as beautiful as you think they are," McKennie said. "Tyler was always called in in place of me to go on trips. But we always had a great bond between all of us. We talk about it all the time."

Adams roomed with Pulisic or McKennie whenever he parachuted into camp. The next year, Adams and Pulisic had adjoining rooms, and McKennie came to hang out with them every night. "We were probably a bit naïve," Adams said. "We were living in almost like a fantasy world, waking up every morning and playing soccer every day. We didn't really know where it was going to take us at the time, but we all worked extremely hard to get to the senior national team. I think you can see when we play together now, there's an excitement about our game that you get to play with guys you grew up playing with, guys that you enjoy being around. The relationships and the friendships that I built there, I'm lucky to say that they do carry over onto the field now."

It was already evident, however, that Bradenton's utility was waning. The boys had fun, living like collegians and devoting themselves to soccer, but the environment was no longer necessarily better than that of the development academies they had at home. "I think as a player, it probably didn't make me any better," Adams says. "It challenged me because I was playing up in age, but in terms of the development path, it didn't make me take a leap forward."

Still, in the early 2020s, a new national team filled in around those three and their closeness spread through their peers by a kind of osmosis. Five former Bradenton residents made the American roster for the 2022 World Cup.

10 | Nightmare at the Château

One difficulty with international soccer is that performance at the World Cup can act as the sole arbiter of a coach's work. Almost half a decade of games and practices, planning, and pushing boils down to a few weeks, a bounce here, a blown call there, an injury, fortune, or misfortune. In 1994, everything had broken right for the United States—from Colombia's collapse to the soupy air in the Silverdome imparting just enough dip on Eric Wynalda's long free kick against Switzerland, to every other little stroke of fate. In 1998, it would all go the other way.

Yet in the summer of 1995, things looked rosier than ever.

After Bora Milutinović left as U.S. head coach, the job was floated to some of the same big names who turned it down in the previous cycle. Federation president Alan Rothenberg had his heart set on another star manager. While U.S. Soccer worked its way through its wish list, Steve Sampson was put in charge as the interim head coach. Sampson had started the last cycle on the World Cup organizing committee, where he served as vice president of competition. But as a coach, he didn't belong among the administrators, and the federation wanted an ally on Milutinović's staff. So Sampson was reassigned and became an assistant coach. When the World Cup ended, so did Sampson's employment with the federation. No college jobs were open and

Major League Soccer was at least a year from kicking off. So when Steinbrecher called Sampson, who had no professional head coaching experience, to ask if he would take over the team for the time being, the thirty-eight-year-old didn't hesitate. "Of course I said yes," he later recalled. "Who would say no to that opportunity?" With hindsight, Sampson acknowledges that he wasn't ready. "I should have coached at the professional level before being the national team coach. But what opportunities were there in the United States in 1995? There were none."

While the federation dithered on making a permanent appointment—hardly for the last time—Sampson began to post credible results. After a rain-shortened tie with Uruguay and losses to Belgium and Costa Rica, the Americans won the U.S. Cup with victories over Nigeria and Mexico—4–0 over the latter!—and a tie with Colombia. Two weeks later, the Americans were in Uruguay as a guest participant in the 1995 edition of the Copa América, South America's storied continental championship. Nobody expected much from the Americans in this fevered event, packed with international soccer heavyweights. Neither did U.S. Soccer. Which is why Hank Steinbrecher, its general secretary, didn't think much of making a promise to Steve Sampson, who wanted desperately to be made the full-time national team manager. "One day, Steve came to me and said, 'What do I need to do to keep this job?'" Steinbrecher recalled. "There were eight games left and I facetiously said, 'Seven wins.' Well, dammit if he didn't do that."

It was almost impossible to watch the Copa América on TV in the United States, but those fans who managed to were richly rewarded. That is, after the players and the federation resolved yet another labor standoff over match fees and bonuses. The players went on strike and refused to practice for three precious days on the ground in Uruguay. "They were incredibly unified," Sampson recalled. "The World Cup organizing committee and FIFA made a fortune. The players just felt they were disrespected, and in many respects, they were." Now here was Sampson, fighting to secure his own future, caught in the middle. He received a call three days before the USA's opening game against Chile and was informed that the federation would be dispatching the Olympic team as scabs. The night before the match, a compromise was finally reached and the regular national team practiced the next morning—just its second session on the ground in Paysandú.

The U.S. had never beaten a South American team on its own continent but, eager to prove a point after holding out for more bonus money, defeated Chile 2–1. Six days later, after a narrow loss to Bolivia, the Americans startled Argentina in an unequivocal 3–0 victory. The Argentines had rested several regulars on the assumption that the USA was no threat. Following the game, recently retired Argentine superstar Diego Maradona came to the American locker room to congratulate the players.

Mexico, the other guest team, loomed in the quarterfinal. El Tri, so nicknamed, was still smarting from the 4–0 loss a month earlier, but the U.S. prevailed again, on penalty kicks. The USA's travel from Paysandú to the semifinal in Maldonado was booked on a rickety-looking plane and several players balked at boarding it. Rather than taking a quick flight, the Americans rode a bus for five hours, which some players later said compounded their mounting fatigue. For the second summer in a row, Brazil knocked the USA out of a major tournament by a 1–0 score. Colombia finally exacted its revenge the '94 World Cup with a 4–1 walloping in the third-place game.

All the same, a fourth-place finish marked the finest American result at a prestigious international tournament since the 1930 World Cup. The federation's power brokers still harbored real misgivings about Sampson as a coach, but he had them in a bind. "Quite honestly, all of us knew that there were serious limitations, but at that point it would have been impossible to move him aside and bring in somebody else," Rothenberg said. "So, kind of against our better judgment, we stuck with Steve. And the results were unfortunate. He lost control of the players. He was very disruptive in the locker room."

There was still talk within the federation about replacing Sampson as late as October 1997, just eight months before the 1998 World Cup in France. His team looked unconvincing and grew increasingly vocal in its discontent, and Sampson's contract was not yet guaranteed through the big summer tournament. Rothenberg thought a coach should always be under pressure and never stopped talking to other managers. The joke went that the federation president carried a pink slip with him wherever he went, in case he decided to sack Sampson on the spot. The federation's leadership kicked around the idea of replacing him with Bruce Arena, an established college coach with just two years under his belt as a Major League Soccer manager. But Sampson clung on to the job with a historic 0–0 tie during a World Cup qualifier in Mexico City in November—the first time the Americans had avoided a loss on Mexican soil—that cleared the way to France. The U.S. ultimately qualified with a game to spare, but the performances on the field had been flat. Amid the celebrations, Rothenberg refused to declare outright that Sampson would be coaching at the World Cup.

"I was really hurt by that whole process," Sampson later remembered. "After we qualified for the World Cup, it took Rothenberg two months to make a decision on whether he was going to allow me to take the team to France. I should have taken a job in the MLS, because I had a lot of offers during that period of time. What it did, and maybe Alan didn't realize this when he was doing it, was I think it made me weaker in the eyes of the players. I think that hurt all of us."

All the while, Carlos Queiroz was at work on his report, which would beget Project 2010. As such, the federation had a much more established coach under contract, and Gulati met Queiroz in Japan to discuss the particulars of the job. Queiroz was being kept on standby in case Rothenberg decided to fire his head coach, and everybody knew it.

The Americans were drawn into a brutal Group F for the 1998 World Cup, pitting them against Germany, the European champions and early tournament favorites; a stacked Yugoslavia, which the U.S. would begin bombing under NATO auspices within a year; and Iran, another nation that was not historically fond of the USA. The only way this geopolitical hot pot could get any hotter, Rothenberg quipped, was "if FIFA designates an Iraqi referee."

A first-ever victory over Brazil in the semifinals of the CONCACAF Gold Cup in February 1998 preserved Sampson's job once more despite a loss to Mexico in the final. But a pair of defeats to the Netherlands and Belgium over the next ten days seemed to spook the beleaguered head coach. Sampson became unpredictable in the spring of 1998. First, he benched Alexi Lalas and Marcelo Balboa, the rocks of his defense and some of the team's emotional leaders. Sampson then switched tactics to an unconventional 3-6-1 formation in hopes of clogging the space around Germany's world-beating midfield. But it was his next decision that would haunt Sampson's tenure.

"We're playing in San Diego," Sampson recalled. "Roy Wegerle knocks on the door of my hotel room and says, 'Can I speak with you?' I say, 'Of course.' So he comes in and he tells me he's aware that John Harkes is sleeping with Eric Wynalda's wife. Here he was, the captain—an exceptional captain on the field—and, as it turned out, a very poor captain off the field, who felt entitled to do practically anything."

On April 14, Sampson announced on a conference call with reporters that he'd kicked Harkes off the team, blindsiding everyone. Sampson had only recently anointed Harkes as "captain for life." The explanation offered was that Harkes's indiscipline and initial refusal to play a new position in the reshuffled formation added up to some kind of critical mass that made his place in the team untenable. Harkes didn't want to play left back. He had taken part in a rowdy, drunken night out in Brussels two nights before a game, but so had several other players who had stayed out later. Years later, Sampson said he decided to keep the third reason to himself in an effort to protect both families involved, as Wynalda was not yet aware of the infidelity. Wynalda recalled, and several players echoed, that he and everyone else on the team had already heard. And that the players had pleaded with Sampson to reinstate Harkes regardless.

Harkes campaigned vociferously to return, but Sampson doubled down, telling *The Washington Post* that his former captain had skipped team flights, missed a team bus, gone out until 4 a.m., been habitually among the last to show up to team meetings, and questioned his position change. Harkes called the charges "outrageous" and "disgusting."

Sampson met with Harkes before the World Cup, hoping that his former captain would own up to the affair. "In two hours, not once did he apologize for his behavior," Sampson said. "He was not remorseful, maybe didn't want to admit it. If he had just apologized and owned up to it, I would have found a way to put him on that team." In retrospect, Sampson wished he had involved the team's leaders in his decision. "Did it impact the overall chemistry of the team?" Sampson asked. "Of course it did, and I feel badly about that."

On the eve of the World Cup, European police agencies arrested more than a hundred people in seven countries and charged them with planning a terrorist plot to attack both the England–Tunisia match and the Paris hotel where the USMNT was staying, and to fly an aircraft into a power plant. The plot was tied to the Armed Islamic

Group of Algeria, with the support of al-Qaeda leader Osama bin Laden. In the U.S. camp, meanwhile, Sampson ran afoul of his team's veterans once again. Martinique-born defender David Regis played in the German league and had an American wife. Sampson urged him to become a U.S. citizen in time for the World Cup. An officer turned Regis away when he showed up for his citizenship test because the session was full and told him to come back in a week. That would have meant missing the World Cup. But an ESPN crew tagged along with Regis on his big day and pointed its camera at the officer. A producer fibbed that they were live on the air, and that the officer was on national television, denying a would-be national teamer his place at the World Cup. They found some room for Regis to sit for the test after all. He was naturalized on May 20 and made his national team debut on May 23, just three weeks before the World Cup opener against Germany. That meant poor Jeff Agoos, the last player cut in 1994—who had helped Regis to prepare for his citizenship test, no less—was out of the lineup. The team's core did not appreciate Agoos's benching for the benefit of a newcomer. It didn't help that Regis was given Harkes's old number, six.

Sampson was forever changing things, cycling out players who had helped the team qualify and replacing them with untested ones. He brought in a psychologist just before the World Cup and made his players go see him. Everything felt unsettled. The back line had been remade in the year before the World Cup, and the lack of deference from some of the new players for the team's veterans only served to fracture the locker room further. "You think I cared what those guys were thinking?" recalled young Californian right back Frankie Hejduk, a hard-partying surfer. "I was trying to make a World Cup. I went into every training like it was my last. I respected those guys, but I didn't give a fuck what they were saying. They were a bunch of drama queens, to be honest. I would feel embarrassed if I was them."

Sampson would later argue that there was something else working against him: the launch of Major League Soccer in 1996. "Right in the middle of World Cup qualifying, it took players out of the best leagues in the world and brought them back to the United States," Sampson said. Players went from Italy's Serie A, the German Bundesliga, the English Premier League, and Spain's La Liga to a fledgling league that was competitively much weaker. "It was a massive detriment to the preparation of the U.S. national team for France," Sampson said. "Certain individuals just were not in form, were aging, were injured going into France '98."

If the team's veterans were making homecomings to MLS, the younger players were trying to achieve the opposite. "There were a lot of players who were trying to find a club in Europe, putting themselves and where they were going to play ahead of the team," said Claudio Reyna, a midfielder who captained Wolfsburg of the Bundesliga.

Just as Bob Gansler had in 1990, Steve Sampson decided that the USA would spend the World Cup in isolation. Only instead of Spartan barracks, he picked a luxurious but isolated château. Sampson toured France for the ideal location and settled on the lush grounds of Château de Pizay, where the England and France teams had stayed a few years earlier. "I felt that the players would appreciate the effort that the federation was putting forth," Sampson said. "And that we would have the opportunity to spend some really quality time together." Many of the players, it turned out, did not appreciate it.

Isolating was common at World Cups, something major soccer nations like Brazil or Italy might do. But their reason for doing so didn't apply to the United States. Those nations could only work quietly by cordoning themselves off from the throngs of fans who crowded them if they headquartered in or near a major city. The Americans simply didn't have that problem and just as in Italy eight years earlier, the players felt cooped up and robbed of a true World Cup experience. There was little to do at the Château de Pizay but feed the ducks and play cards—pots ran into the thousands of dollars as midfielder Preki Radosavljević strutted around toting a sock stuffed with his winnings. On a golf outing, *The New York Times* noted, Alexi Lalas shot a twenty-four on the first two holes, "presumably striking many of his shots as headers."

"It was a very strange World Cup," Marcelo Balboa recalled. "We were in a vineyard, two hours away from everybody. We were isolated with nothing to do but ride a bike into this little town that had two or three little buildings. It was a nightmare."

The controversial château and the surrounding vineyard didn't bother everybody. Goalkeeper Brad Friedel believed the setting became a proxy for other gripes. "I've heard so many stories about how the hotel was bad—we were in a beautiful place, out in the country outside of Lyon," Friedel said. "It was not a hardship."

Instead of mending a fractious mood, the isolation left the quarrelsome players with plenty of time to seethe, to split into stewing factions, to rail against their coaches. "That was the worst team I ever played with," recalled Thomas Dooley, who replaced Harkes as captain. "Absolutely the worst. I have never played with another team that was so unfocused or selfish. I could not wait to get out of there."

"I was probably arrogant and pompous and unreasonable and selfish in terms of the way that I thought of myself and what my expectations were," Lalas said. At several points in the following weeks, he and a few of the other disgruntled campers were on the brink of being kicked off the team and sent home. Balboa said that he was, at one point, cast out of the team by Sampson until the federation intervened.

Still, Sampson was outwardly bullish about the team's chances, making bold predictions about its World Cup future. "In ten to fifteen years, we'll win the title, there's no doubt about it," he told *The Washington Post*. "When we Americans decide to do something, we'll see it through." Rothenberg, meanwhile, ever the unsupportive boss, said that he did not think the U.S. would make the second round.

On the eve of the opener against Germany in Paris on June 15, Sampson's coaching staff showed the players a hype video, just as Milutinović had four years earlier. But unlike Bora's cut, this one featured not only the players but the head coach as well. He hadn't been the one to edit the video, but the players hated that Sampson was in it. The 1998 World Cup campaign had derailed before the American team played a single minute of soccer in France.

Two months earlier, the U.S. had played a friendly in and against Austria and dominated their strong opponents, winning 3–0. Everything clicked that day: the new formation, the new players introduced in favor of the old guard. But by the time the Americans kicked off their World Cup against Germany, whatever lightning they had bottled in Vienna had escaped, their fleeting chemistry floating away. Within nine minutes, Jürgen Klinsmann beat Regis to a header and nodded it back for Andy Möller to score. After an hour, Klinsmann capitalized on some shaky defending and made it 2–0. Germany had utterly dominated its opponents until the second goal, when "Die Mannschaft" decided it was bored of toying with the Americans and just rode out the game.

Sampson made five lineup changes for the game with Iran and switched the formation again. He had planned this before the tournament, but it caught his players by surprise. To them, it felt like he was abandoning his tactical scheme and lineup after just one game. The Americans were favored against Iran, which was playing under its third coach in seven months: Iranian American Jalal Talebi had been installed just three weeks before the tournament. The game was nearly called off entirely because of a minor diplomatic incident between the geopolitical rivals when the Iranian government instructed its World Cup delegation not to shake the hands of their American opponents before the game, which was a mandatory pregame ritual. FIFA threatened Iran with expulsion from the tournament if it didn't comply with the rules. In the end the sides agreed that Iran, whose players and staff were said not to share the regime's views on Americans, would not only shake hands but then pose for a group photo with the U.S. team, a World Cup first. A large crowd of anti-regime Iranians demonstrated before the game and booed their own players. Under a heavy security presence, the politically charged match finally kicked off.

The Americans made an assertive start and hit the woodwork twice before a completely unmarked Hamid Estili gave Iran the lead with a superbly placed header to beat Kasey Keller. The American locker room was dead silent at halftime. In the Iranian locker room, government officials collected the players' passports and threatened them and their families, Sampson says Talebi told him. (Talebi told ESPN this never happened.) In the eighty-third minute, Mehdi Mahdavikia doubled the Iranian lead on a breakaway. Just before Team Melli almost got a third, prevented well by Keller, the U.S. finally got on the board on a diving header by Brian McBride, who credited his prodigious heading power to the heavy metal he head-banged to. It would be the only goal the Americans scored at the World Cup. With a game to spare, they were eliminated. Sampson was criticized for his formation, but goalkeeper Brad Friedel thought the point was moot. "If you're not willing to win the header or not let your player beat you, or run back when you lose the ball, the formation is absolutely irrelevant," he reflected. "I think the players knew they could do better. The players at the time really wanted to blame everything on Steve. I would put eighty percent of the fault on the players for not adapting."

As far as the Americans were concerned, the game against Yugoslavia was academic. That wasn't true for the opposition, which needed a win to guarantee a place in the second round, and whose fans raised thousands of middle fingers in unison during the U.S. national anthem. Sampson shuffled his lineup once more. The Americans went behind in the fourth minute and played listlessly. The blood-soaked bandage McBride wore around his gashed head for much of the game was an apt metaphor. Out of all thirty-two teams in France, nobody posted a worse record than the Americans. "At the World Cup there are no points for nice try," ABC host Brent Musburger spoke solemnly after the game. "And for a country to have spent as much money as the United States on this soccer program, to score only one goal in three games is embarrassing."

The only thing left to do for the players was to take turns sticking the proverbial dagger into their lame-duck coach. "If this was the master plan, good god, it was pretty masterful," Lalas told *The Washington Post*. Sampson had wanted to send Lalas home at one point but was overruled by Rothenberg.

Decades later, Earnie Stewart winced when he thought back on that fateful French campaign. "We were not a team," he recalled. "One of the things the U.S. has always had is camaraderie and fight, and it just was not there. It was a mix of guys who seemed to have all kinds of different interests."

Behind the scenes, Sunil Gulati was already recruiting the next U.S. head coach. "We had Queiroz on ice," he said. "If Alan wasn't term-limited and had run again, we probably would have hired Queiroz." But Rothenberg *was* term-limited as federation president. And Gulati knew that his likely successor, Dr. Bob Contiguglia, favored Bruce Arena. So Gulati flew home in the middle of the World Cup to speak to Arena.

In Paris, Sampson and Rothenberg had breakfast a few days after the Americans were eliminated from the tournament. Sampson resigned. Rothenberg then proclaimed that Bora Milutinović and Carlos Alberto Parreira, who had been interviewed in 1991 and turned down the job in '95, were the leading candidates for Sampson's old job—and that a deal with Parreira might be only weeks away. Queiroz and the Norwegian Egil Olsen were in the running as well. Rothenberg said he'd probably appoint a foreigner. Also in the conversation, he said, was Arena, but he trailed the other candidates for his lack of international experience. Rothenberg announced all of this to the press, as was his wont, even though many in the federation felt it wouldn't be appropriate for a president to appoint a new coach less than two months before leaving office.

A quarter century after the doomed French campaign, the principals were still working out how to assign the blame. "It was the lowest point of my professional career," Steinbrecher recalled. "I look back on it with hives. I saw failure at almost every level, including my own."

"The regrets that I have are few, but '98 is one of them," Lalas said. "We wasted an opportunity. It was unnecessary, because we had gotten better individually and as a team, and yet we imploded."

The consensus, in the end, was that a World Cup was squandered. "That was probably the best national team that we had in the '90s," said Tab Ramos, one of the frustrated veterans. "We had everything. But we didn't really know how we played because of all the changes. And the chemistry of the group was not good."

After the third and final game in France, the USA's press officer found some of the team's official federation-issued game-day suits stuffed into dumpsters outside the hotel.

In 2006, Lalas became team president of the LA Galaxy. Six weeks later, he fired the team's head coach—Steve Sampson.

11 | Our Way

Bruce Arena is a big man with a personality that is larger still. The son of Italian immigrants grew up on Long Island, which would forever color his diction and his attitude. His sarcasm and bluntness reflected a lack of complication in everything he did. Caught on the wrong day, Arena seemed cocky and surly. Growing up, he had primarily been a lacrosse player but dabbled in soccer as a goalkeeper as well. He fashioned brief professional careers in each sport and made the national team in both. Arena appeared for the U.S. Soccer team just once, in the second half of a 1973 friendly in Israel—he missed out on a second cap because the junior high school where he taught needed him to cover study hall that day. He coached both sports at the University of Virginia, where he won five College Cups in six years in soccer and coached a raft of future national teamers.

Arena's philosophy was as simple as his speech, which belied his Ivy League education at Cornell. Soccer wasn't actually a very complicated sport, he believed, and coaching it successfully boiled down to little more than amassing talent and fostering clarity and chemistry. Get those three things right, and results were likely to follow. He also believed that he could have applied this formula to pretty much any other sport. He didn't get bogged down in ideology, like some of soccer's most celebrated managers. Whereas they took pride in complicating their work, Arena applied a pared-down approach and projected absolute confidence, one that felt so abundant that it could compensate for those who might lack it. In the tactical and technical aspects of the job, Arena was unremarkable. What separated him from his peers was his innate ability to coax dozens of grown men, most of them equipped with double helpings of ego and testosterone, into getting along. "He was an unbelievable psychologist," said Frankie Hejduk.

"He has what I refer to as the Arena Aura," said Hank Steinbrecher, U.S. Soccer's general secretary then. "When you're around Bruce, you just think you're going to win. Because when you go to his training sessions, there's nothing really special. It's just his mentality."

When Contiguglia was elected U.S. Soccer president, he decided that he wanted an American head coach, someone who understood the American player and the game stateside, and who could implement an overarching philosophy. Arena had won the first-ever MLS Cups in 1996 and 1997 and took D.C. United back to the final in 1998 while winning two international trophies. He prepared for the national team job with a gig as the U.S. Olympic men's soccer coach in 1996, albeit with modest results.

Arena would later admit that he had no idea what he was doing as national team head coach. But he injected the program with fresh energy and attitude all the same. "Bruce basically wiped out the memory of what happened in '98," goalkeeper Brad Friedel said. "When Bruce came in, there was no more excuse. If a player was out of the team and was unhappy and didn't train hard or was petulant in any way, it really stood out because he was the only one doing it, whereas in '98, it was basically half the team and it was just toxic on a daily basis. It was just an entirely different feel."

Arena seemed to grasp intuitively what his team was lacking and who could provide it, in both skill set and attitude. "He always found guys that he got the best out of," said Claudio Reyna. "He would see something in players that maybe others didn't, that would contribute to the team." And the head coach stimulated the players' competitive urges by forever pitting them against each other in everything, on the field and off, and keeping score.

Within the first six months of 1999, the rejuvenated Americans beat Germany and Argentina in friendlies. And then they played in the prestigious FIFA Confederations Cup. At that tournament, McBride got a quick education in Arena's communication style. After a forgettable first half, Arena laid into him at halftime. "Bruce is staring right at me," McBride remembered. "And he says, 'McBride, if you don't start fucking holding up the ball for us, you'll be off the field in five minutes. That's what you've got, five minutes to start fucking helping us win this game.' That happened quite a bit to different players." McBride would lead the Americans in scoring at that tournament. The U.S. beat Germany again and made a run to the semifinals, losing to Mexico in extra time but posting an impressive third-place finish. Arena's belief that his team could beat anybody was rubbing off. "There's this thing that Bruce does where not only do you trust him, but he gives you this desire to play together," McBride said.

Arena was both demanding and hands-off. He expected a lot of his players and staff but didn't bind them by rules—largely because he hated having to enforce them. Arena expected his players to be on time and to be ready to perform, but nothing more. For a player like John O'Brien, a young midfielder who emerged from the highly regimented Ajax academy in Amsterdam, that kind of freedom was a revelation. Friedel, playing for English mega-club Liverpool at the time, felt the same. "At Liverpool, it was like living in a fishbowl," he said.

"It was just football, football, football. If you were out at a club, or walking around, people used to call the team and say, 'Hey, shouldn't he be resting?' It was pressure."

The semifinal round of CONCACAF World Cup qualifying in 2000 was a slog. The Americans won only three of their six games and didn't advance until the last day. The final stage provided yet more CONCACAF shenanigans on the road. A local radio station parked a flatbed truck equipped with huge speakers in front of the U.S. team hotel, blasting music all night long. Showers in a locker room had no running water, forcing the Americans to douse themselves with bottled water before catching a plane home. Half a chicken flew at DaMarcus Beasley when he went to take a corner kick. The Americans suffered through a three-game losing streak. After the second of those losses, a 2–3 home defeat to Honduras, Arena delivered one of his signature quips. "Give our guys credit, they never quit," he said stoically. "They were running around like a bunch of idiots, but they didn't quit . . . idiots with heart."

Arena's men were the first U.S. national team to play a game after 9/11. And just before the Americans hosted Jamaica for their penultimate qualifier, the United States began bombing Afghanistan. Arena fretted over whether to tell the team. He did, giving a speech about patriotism and representing a country that was now at war. The U.S. didn't play well but took an early lead and got a late winner. A few other results fell favorably and, unexpectedly, the Americans punched their ticket for the 2002 World Cup in Japan and South Korea with a game to spare. Four months later, Arena's swaggering side lifted the Gold Cup for the first time in eleven years.

During the sixteen-game qualifying march to the World Cup, Arena cycled through thirty-one different players. But when he made his final roster for the main event, there were no fewer than eleven holdovers from the troubled 1998 campaign on the twenty-three-man roster. Although neither made the team, Arena had even brought back Tab Ramos and John Harkes for looks, in spite of their status as lightning rods in '98. Even though many players were the same, the new group somehow lacked any of the baggage that had tripped up the old one.

The work done down in Bradenton, meanwhile, began to bear fruit. In late 2000, an eighteen-year-old Landon Donovan became the first product of the under-17 residency to play for the senior national team after playing in the 2000 Olympics, where the U.S. placed an impressive fourth.

In his debut, Donovan scored and assisted in a 2–0 friendly victory over Mexico, of all teams. When the World Cup began, Donovan and DaMarcus Beasley, who had also broken into the senior national team, were both twenty years old. They were roommates bound by their youth and their hunger and fearlessness. By their own admission, decades later, neither one of them knew enough to be daunted by the occasion, and their confidence spread to the whole team. "We didn't have the pain of '98, we didn't live through that on the field," Donovan said. "We had no concept of failure. We didn't fear anybody."

The pieces fit together just so. The experience. The youth. The tactics. The confidence. The culture and the chemistry. The coach, overseeing it all. "I believe that no matter what sport Bruce would have coached in, he would have been successful," recalled Earnie Stewart. "It happened to be soccer."

For all he had already won at the club level, Bruce Arena was not inclined to inflate expectations of his national team. Whereas Steve Sampson promised a World Cup title within a generation, Arena did something like the opposite. "We're not going to win because we're not a good enough team," he announced. "I mean, how many countries have won it?" Seven, at that time. On the eve of the tournament,

Arena lowered the bar further still. "In the last World Cups, our record is 1-8-1," he said. "So they're not writing books about the U.S. in the World Cup yet." No, not yet.

The group-stage draw of Portugal, Poland, and cohost South Korea was manageable, even though the Portuguese were considered among the tournament favorites. At the American pretournament training camp in Cary, North Carolina, staffers began to get a sense that they had a special group on their hands. In the stifling heat, and on the back of a long club season for the European-based players, nobody complained about the endless conditioning. It brought them closer.

Arena also deviated from previous American coaches in another, more meaningful way. There would be no isolation for his players at the World Cup. This was a matter of necessity. The national team players were nervous in the wake of 9/11. Arena understood that if the players' families stayed elsewhere, his team would worry about them, rather than concentrate on soccer. So they stayed in the same hotel, one floor below the players. Partners, children, parents, grandparents, friends—all were welcome. While the security precautions could have kept the U.S. players as cooped up as they had been in 1990 and 1998, the presence of their loved ones instead turned them into a large, rowdy family—injecting an energy that nourished Arena and his players. The players got to be with their children when they weren't playing. There was a large family room where the kids hung out. Everyone mingled. Theirs was a happy camp. "It made a huge impact," said Reyna. "It gave all the players comfort. Things like that, it sounds like nothing. But many coaches—forget about it. Family in the same hotel? No chance." The Americans were criticized for their open camp. But several of Reyna's club teammates who played on other national teams told him after the World Cup how much the monthlong separation from their families had worn on them.

While he talked down his team's chances in the press, Arena professed confidence in the locker room. Immediately after the draw, he told his players they would beat Portugal, which seemed at the time like an absurd thing to say. But Arena had some inside information on Portugal's stacked offense. His assistant, Glenn Myernick, went to Europe to scout Portugal and had a chance encounter at an airport with Luis Figo, the team's superstar and the reigning world player of the year. For whatever reason, Figo confided in Myernick that he hadn't fully recovered from an ankle injury and was so worn out from the relentless onslaught of games that he would quite like to sleep for three days straight.

Arena repeated his belief that Portugal was beatable at the start of every team meeting, and it became a mantra. He found subtle ways of diminishing his players' awe for the Portuguese by taking little digs at their expensive clothes, their fancy cars. Before their tournament opener, Arena took his confidence public. "All things being equal, Portugal plays their best and we play our best, maybe Portugal is going to win," he told *The Washington Post*. "There's nothing wrong with saying, 'Maybe the other team is favored, and they're a little bit better than us on paper.' Until there's another method of deciding who wins the game, you go out and play."

Arena bet a group of reporters that none of them could name the correct starting eleven for that game. Sure enough, they couldn't. Because Arena fielded both Donovan and Beasley and plenty of surprises besides. Beasley, ever nonchalant, said no more than "That's cool" to the news that he would be making an unexpected start. "I was so naïve I didn't know what a World Cup was, what the games would be like," recalled Beasley. "I just wanted to play football. I didn't have time to think about what this meant, millions of people watching us play. I was just in the moment."

For thirty-six magical minutes, Portugal's golden generation disintegrated in the face of the fearless and super-fit Americans. In the fourth minute, Brian McBride's strong header from Earnie Stewart's corner fell right in front of John O'Brien, who slammed the ball into the Portuguese goal. And before the half-hour mark, a Landon Donovan cross took a freakish deflection and sailed into the net for the second goal. McBride's diving header made it three, stunning even the U.S. team itself. For the first time since 1930, the Americans scored three goals in a World Cup match.

Before halftime, Beto got Portugal on the board following some poor defensive work by the U.S. Jeff Agoos then scored an uncanny own goal in the seventy-first minute, but the U.S. hung on for its first World Cup victory on foreign soil in fifty-two years, storming the field as the final whistle sang. In a major upset, they had overrun a tournament heavyweight. The win represented a remarkable evolution. In the 1990s, the lumbering Americans mostly concerned themselves with playing the sport correctly. Even when they were competitive, the soccer they displayed was brawny but timid. Now, in a new century, they were confident yet still physical.

The U.S. had already been to South Korea and faced the home team before they met again in their next World Cup game. In December 2001, just eight days after they were drawn together into Group D, the Americans lost 1–0. Brian McBride remembers turning on the TV in his hotel room on that trip and noticing that most of the commercials repeated a few chants that sounded like they belonged in a soccer stadium. Half a year later, he realized that the entire nation had been in training for the World Cup, drilled through their TVs. In the picturesque stadium in Daegu, which opened up to a verdant mountainside, sixty thousand home fans in red performed those very chants from the TV in perfect unison. "It was the most amazing thing I've ever experienced on a soccer field," McBride said.

South Korea, like the U.S., had won its opener, beating Poland 2–0—its first-ever win at a World Cup, for which the nation's schools and offices let out early. That meant the winner of this second game would be through to the round of 16 with a game to spare. South Korea was good at all the things the U.S. was good at—running and cunning—and dialed up these skills even further. South Korea was the only team at the World Cup more fit than the Americans. "There was so much pressing, so much running," John O'Brien remembered.

Arena, for his part, couldn't keep all the opponents named Lee or Kim apart, hampering his tactical briefing. "To hell with this," he finally said. "They've got a bunch of really fast, fit guys that run all over the damned place."

This scouting report checked out. South Korea dominated the game and provoked a series of saves from the outstanding Brad Friedel—including on a penalty kick. In the twenty-fourth minute, Clint Mathis, described by ESPN announcers as "the swashbuckling redneck," found a seam up the middle on a deft scoop from O'Brien and scored. But the dam broke in the seventy-eighth minute. Ahn Jung-Hwan scored.

The equalizer sent the rabid Korean fans, who spent the entirety of the game drumming, dancing, and singing, into a frenzy, amping up the national mania a little further. By rights, the Taegeuk Warriors should have won the game after missing a huge, close-range chance in the final minute. But the Americans hung on again, this time for a single point. They were pleased. But battling the hosts with the outsize home field advantage, in the baking heat, had taken a toll.

Poland had nothing left to play for. After losses in its first two games, it was already eliminated from the tournament. The U.S., meanwhile, needed only a tie to advance. Failing that, it would need South Korea to beat Portugal in the other game, played simultaneously 115 miles away. The Portuguese had rebounded from their shock loss to the Americans by rolling over the poor Poles 4–0.

Judging by its first two games, you might believe that Poland didn't have any business at the World Cup. It had, after all, scored no goals and given away six. The Poles made six changes to their lineup and, with fresh legs and a point to prove, went ahead of the U.S. within three minutes. On the very next play, Landon Donovan wrongly had a goal disallowed for a perfectly legal shoulder-to-shoulder challenge. And that more or less decided the game, because Poland immediately scored again. And again. 3–0. The U.S. felt its hopes of the knockout rounds slip away.

But in the sixty-sixth minute in the other game, Portugal got a second red card and was reduced to nine men. Within short order, Park Ji Sung put the South Koreans ahead. Brian McBride had been taken out of the game for the Americans by then and was, like everyone else not on the field, paying more attention to the match in Incheon than the one in front of him. "On the bench, we're all eyes wide open, 'Did that just happen? Did they just score?'" he remembered. "As soon as we got confirmation, we were jumping up and down on the bench."

John O'Brien had the odd experience of being in one World Cup game while trying to keep track of another. So did the mostly Korean crowd at the U.S.–Poland contest, which cheered and groaned in moments that bore no relevance to the game they were attending. O'Brien tried to divine from their reactions what was going on.

The U.S. scored a late consolation goal, but it was irrelevant. South Korea upset Portugal after surviving a few late scares, and the Americans' own game no longer mattered. They were moving on. Their reaction was subdued. Suddenly, they weren't feeling so cocky.

A stroke of luck. Had the Americans won their group, they would have faced three-time world champions Italy in the round of 16. Instead, they got Mexico. And while their archrivals were hardly punching bags, they were at least familiar. What's more, the Americans had beaten them five times in their last six meetings. Animosity between the teams was already at fever pitch, and now the soaring stakes sharpened the contest even further. As did U.S. President George W. Bush's announcement to the team that he had made a friendly wager on the game with Mexican President Vicente Fox.

The Americans had delivered on expectations and were unburdened by pressure. The Mexicans, however, labored under the weight of a drought. The last time they reached the World Cup quarterfinals was in 1986, on home soil, a stage at which the nation felt it belonged. Surely, those gringos would not get in their way this time. "They were so arrogant at that time," Reyna said of their rivals. "We walked around the field before the game. They were on the other side of the field. At least half of them were looking at us, laughing, smiling at us. Completely trying to make fun of us. And we were just like, 'Fuck these guys.' There was something in the locker room that I felt there was no way we were going to lose this game. Everybody was so pissed off."

John O'Brien put his cleats into a Mexican ankle and could well have gotten an early red card that ruined his team's chances. Instead, a low cross from Reyna found Josh Wolff, who laid the ball back for Brian McBride to put the U.S. ahead in the eighth minute. "After ten, fifteen minutes, I knew we had them," said Reyna. "They were better. But we were better that day."

In the fifty-fifth minute, O'Brien courted controversy again as he punched away a corner kick in his own penalty area with his fist. Today, such an infraction would surely have been spotted by video replay and resulted in a penalty kick. Not then. "It was definitely a handball," O'Brien recalled. "It wasn't intentional." El Tri was more dangerous, attacking in waves as the Yanks bailed out desperately. But on a breakaway, Eddie Lewis found Landon Donovan with a deep cross to the far post, which the young attacker headed home to make it 2–0. The Americans were in shock, as was the nation that rallied behind them, watching in bars in the wee hours. The Mexicans, meanwhile, knew full well that they would be pilloried in their home country. Unable to kick the ball into the American net, Mexico resorted to kicking Americans instead. When the final whistle cried and the Americans had won their first knockout game in their World Cup history, their counterparts refused the traditional jersey exchange, or even to shake hands.

Team buses tend not to depart the stadium at the same time. The losing team usually leaves a lot sooner than the winning one. And yet, the American and Mexican buses pulled up alongside one another at an intersection outside the stadium. Memories differ on who started it—maybe it was Earnie Stewart, or perhaps Cobi Jones—but before long the celebrating Americans, a few beers deep, started pounding on the windows and screaming at their vanquished and moping nemeses. "They all come to their windows, every Mexican guy on their bus, and they're just flipping us off, we're getting F-bombs," remembered Frankie Hejduk. "You couldn't even believe the two opposite vibes. One team in its glory and just as happy as can be; the other team was in absolute misery. And it just happened to be our rivals. It was something you couldn't even dream of. It was a nightmare for them."

Two decades later, Mexican coach Javier Aguirre admitted as much. "I suffered the worst defeat of my career against the Americans in 2002," he said. "I've cried twice in football, and one of those times was out of sadness after losing to them."

If the USA felt like it had little to lose in the first knockout round, there was no downside at all to going up against Germany in the quarterfinal. Die Mannschaft was a blueblood national team, among the contenders every time it showed up to a World Cup. This was a free hit for the U.S.

The Germans might have hoped that the U.S. would be daunted by being on the same field with them. Any such notions were quickly dispelled. Bruce Arena urged his players to harness the brashness that had gotten them there. "Don't give them any respect," he told the players in the locker room before the game. "We should be in the semifinals. The worst nightmare for any country right now is to play the United States." Just minutes in, Landon Donovan broke through on goal alone and barreled toward Oliver Kahn, the world's top goalkeeper, before a dubious offside flag called him back. Kahn would be busy that day, faced with one American chance after another. The German team had had two more days of rest, yet they were wilting in the heat as the Yanks kept running at them. It all smacked of the 2002 U.S. World Cup team at its best: confident, composed, unimpressed. "All in all, that was probably the best team I've ever been a part of," Donovan recalled.

Yet midfielder Michael Ballack towered above the U.S. back line on a cheaply awarded free kick and snapped his header past Brad Friedel from close range. 1–0. The second half brought more American menace. No chance was bigger, or lingered longer in the memory, than Gregg Berhalter's lunge to volley a high ball headed on by Tony Sanneh at the near post from a corner. Kahn mostly smothered Berhalter's header, but the ball skipped toward the goal line, where Torsten Frings blocked it with his arm. Just as nobody spotted John

O'Brien's handball in the last game, denying the Mexicans their rightful penalty, nobody saw this one either. Karma.

Visible relief spilled from the German players when the game finally ended. The Americans were disappointed. They had outplayed a world power destined for the World Cup final. Several Germany stars agreed and told Arena as much. The U.S. had not yet arrived, the American head coach said, but "the gap has closed considerably."

On the team bus back to the hotel, somebody discovered that it was equipped with a karaoke machine. Dismay quickly dissipated as the team belted out songs the entire way. They played Frank Sinatra's "My Way" last. "We were singing at the top of our lungs," remembered Hejduk. "If there was ever a team that dominated Germany in that tournament, it was us. We deserved better. We did it our way, dude. We really did it our way."

The bus reached the hotel midway through the song. Nobody got off until they had sung the last stanza.

The Making of a National Team: Christian Pulisic

Christian Pulisic has two phones.

One is for his public life. It's where his social media accounts are housed, largely run by a team of specialists who help him post milquetoast holiday pictures or sponsor-forward snaps and videos of him in his gear, with his teammates, in action, holding the occasional trophy. He tries to stay off this phone. Because for every hundred positive comments, a single negative one has the power to ruin his day.

The other phone is personal. It's where his friends and family reach him. It has no social media apps. It's where he can wall himself off from the world and recede into his tight circle. If there are two versions of Christian Pulisic, this is the one that isn't curated. This is the one few people get to see. Christian Pulisic doesn't want to be public. He just wants to play soccer and hang out with his people. Take his boat out from the dock at his off-season home in Florida. Play guitar and basketball and endless online chess, and maybe a video game or fantasy football. Watch a rom-com, or *Monsters, Inc.* for the hundredth time. Recharge for the next game, for the next season.

American men's soccer spent half a century waiting for its first superstar, the first man who could both cross over into mainstream American fame and deliver the kind of career at Europe's leading clubs that made him credible abroad. In the absence of stars who emerged organically, the sport projected the label of First American Male Superstar—the U.S. women's national team mass-produced them, after all—onto all the young men who came along and showed even a glimpse of promise. Their names arrived in a flash, suddenly everywhere, in the mouths of everyone, and then, within only a few years, when the hype proved hollow, they weren't spoken of so much, slowly forgotten.

But then came Christian Pulisic.

A lithe forward from Hershey, Pennsylvania, who left the under-17 national team academy in Bradenton at fifteen to join German powerhouse Borussia Dortmund. He tore through Dortmund's youth teams and made his senior debut at just seventeen. Within months, he had become the youngest player ever to score multiple goals in the storied Bundesliga. Soon enough, he was also the youngest goal-scorer in U.S. national team history, after a rumor that he might instead represent Croatia, on account of his father's lineage, gave fans a fright. More or less from the moment he was put on the senior U.S. national team, he was its best player. Its fastest, its most technical, its most imaginative. A true attacker, a relentless runner. At twenty years old, Pulisic made a $73 million move to Chelsea in 2019, almost quadrupling the record for a transfer fee paid for an American. He was the first American to play regularly for a UEFA Champions League winner. You could imagine Christian Pulisic becoming just about anything.

Here, at last, was the guy with the talent, the pedigree, the eloquence, and the looks. Made in a lab for the purpose of appearing on magazine covers and late-night talk shows. The only trouble: Christian Pulisic is deeply introverted.

Pulisic harbors no interest whatsoever in being a star off the field, treating his swelling fame with a mixture of bemusement and hostility. "People have no idea who Christian is," said Tyler Adams, a close friend of more than a decade. "What is on the outside has nothing to do with Christian. He *always* has his guard up for what people might be hearing around him. When there's no cameras, this kid is the most down-to-earth, bubbly character that you'll meet, willing to talk about anything. He's so kind. A lot of people don't really know that. As someone that's so close to him, you want people to see what you see. But until you spend time with him, he's not going to give you that." Vanishingly few people get to spend time with Christian Pulisic, the real one—the loyal friend with the quick wit and the deep spirituality. To everybody else, he remains entirely walled off.

In the spring of 2024, Pulisic and Weston McKennie, leading players for storied Italian clubs AC Milan and Juventus, respectively, conducted a shared interview with ESPN. McKennie told a sweet story about the youth national team camp where they met when they were about thirteen. Weston was scared of elevators back then, so all week his new friend Christian would walk up and down all eleven flights of the hotel stairs with him out of solidarity. Pulisic looked visibly embarrassed as McKennie told the TV audience all of this. "I'm just not the kind of guy who would share stories like that," Pulisic said when the interviewer asked him for his own recollections, before adding, sarcastically: "I'm glad Weston has now put them all out there."

When he was five years old, Christian Pulisic taught himself to shimmy up a wall like Spider-Man and, to the horror of his parents, touch the ceiling before coming back down safely. By then, the son of two college soccer players already had a habit of endlessly kicking the ball back and forth, both right-footed and left-footed, with either of his parents. When Christian was seven, the family spent a year living in England while his mother—a teammate of Mia Hamm's in youth soccer—was on a teaching exchange, a year that immersed him in the game at all hours. Next, the family moved to Detroit, where his father, a former professional indoor soccer player, coached an indoor team. That gave Christian access to the team's Brazilian players, who taught him ball trickery. During the long Michigan winter, there was nowhere for Christian to play, so his dad set up an entire youth indoor league to provide him with competitive games year-round.

It's easy to assume that the Pulisics plotted out their son's path to stardom. But by all accounts, Christian's soccer obsessiveness was his own. He initiated the kickabouts with his parents. He insisted on playing and playing and playing. He just had the good fortune to be born into a family that could accommodate his fixation. He was athletic—at 5 foot 9, Pulisic can dunk a basketball—and competitive. The blend of all those traits earned him a weeklong training stint at the world-leading FC Barcelona academy when he was ten, which went so well the club invited him back twice. The next year, he trained at Chelsea, too—almost a decade before he would return as a pricey signing.

At eleven, Pulisic dominated under-14 games, dictating the pace of play even then. But he had a good deal of growing to do, lest his body get in the way of his ambitions. "He was tiny at that point," said Dave van den Bergh, a former U.S. youth national team coach. "It was always apparent, at every age group, that he was a very, very talented player. You just hoped he would grow into his body." When Pulisic finally did, he grew so quickly that it threw off his mechanics and he went through an awkward phase for the better part of a year.

Pulisic left for the under-17 academy in Bradenton at only fourteen. On December 13, 2013, Pulisic demolished the Brazilian under-17 team at the Nike International Friendlies, tallying a goal and an assist in a 4–1 U.S. win, earning the tournament's most valuable player award. That was the day—he has a tattoo of the date—when Pulisic realized he was good, and not just for an American. Others noticed as well. He had a training stint with PSV, in the Netherlands, and could have signed with its rivals Ajax as well.

German clubs, however, were more aggressive in tapping into the American market, whose players didn't cost anything if you signed them up young enough. Dortmund found out about Pulisic while scouting his under-17 teammate Haji Wright. Per FIFA's new rules, youth players weren't allowed to sign on other continents until they turned eighteen. Pulisic was only fifteen. A stroke of good fortune solved that problem, however. His grandfather Mate had immigrated to the U.S. from Croatia, which had joined the European Union just two years earlier. So his father, Mark, got a Croatian passport, and then Christian did as well. This accelerated his eligibility to play for Dortmund by two years. At fifteen, he was off to Europe to join the German academy while Mark accompanied him, taking a job as a youth coach at the club.

Christian, who spoke no German, was sent to a German public high school, where he often had no idea what class he was even in, and enrolled in an additional hour and a half of German lessons after school ended. His new teammates wouldn't pass him the ball and were rightly wary of him as a threat to their own spots. He couldn't play in his team's games until he turned sixteen half a year later. It was an isolating and frustrating time. He missed his mom, his older brother and sister, his friends. He missed playing competitive soccer games.

The senior U.S. national team needed Christian Pulisic right away.

Less than two months after Pulisic made his debut for Dortmund's first team, head coach Jürgen Klinsmann called him up for the U.S. in March 2016. At seventeen years and six months, that made Pulisic the youngest American ever to play in a World Cup qualifier. Later that spring, Klinsmann let Pulisic leave the national team camp for a few days to attend his high school prom back in Hershey, where the family had settled—after Klinsmann's wife explained to him what a prom was. In the absence of a workable commercial flight, Pulisic flew by private jet. The day after returning, he became the youngest player to ever score a goal for the men's national team.

Pulisic was the smallest player on the field. His reading of the game and quickness allowed him to get away from his defenders regardless. "Christian already could create separation between himself and the top-level players," said Tab Ramos, then an assistant coach on the national team. "And because he could do that, his physique didn't matter. You couldn't touch him."

For all his playing maturity, Pulisic remained a teenager away from the pitch. On his off days at Dortmund, he would drive three hours each way to Frankfurt because it had the nearest Chipotle restaurant. His apartment looked like an off-campus college kid's, with a pool table and a Ping-Pong table, TVs to watch his beloved New York Jets. The walls were decorated with blown-up photographs of Dortmund's famously raucous stadium. He had the swimming pool in the basement fixed up. When his father went home, Christian didn't leave the quiet part of town, a five-minute drive from the team's practice facility and far away from the nightlife. He didn't like to go out and get recognized. He'd sooner stay in and hang out with the smattering of other Americans playing at nearby clubs.

The attention that came with Pulisic's rapid ascent proved much harder to escape than the defenders hounding him. He hated the hours of phone interviews that Dortmund stacked up for him every now and then. He hated that it was getting harder to go places. He hated all the commercial work. His fatigue showed even to his teammates on the U.S. team. "You could just tell that he was fed up," Antonee Robinson said of one national team camp on the back of another long Dortmund campaign and post-season tour. "He just wanted to be home. He'd been footballed out. He kind of just seemed tired of it all."

Yet unlike all the other Next Big Things, Pulisic delivered. He played well for Dortmund, dribbling at defenders with abandon, and did the same for Chelsea in his first few seasons in London. He scored a goal against Real Madrid in the UEFA Champions League semifinal in April 2021, helping Chelsea to the European title. And when Chelsea's shopaholic new owners buried Pulisic on the depth chart with all their new acquisitions, he left for AC Milan and instantly became one of Serie A's top players. But Pulisic's growing status came at a steep price. He withdrew further into his private life. To the media, he was a bland quote, betraying no emotion of any kind. During press conferences he tended to look uncomfortable while his teammates sitting beside him on the dais seemed taken aback by the contrast with the person they knew privately. In the locker room, Pulisic came alive, growing into a leader and a team captain and ragging on his teammates with a quick wit. Occasionally, Pulisic broke from his placid character to talk publicly about his struggles with depression, hoping that he could help destigmatize mental health issues.

Yet no matter how plain Christian Pulisic made himself, how carefully he guarded his private life, that pesky outside world just kept asking him questions. Then again, maybe there just wasn't that much to share. So focused was Pulisic on his soccer career that he didn't have a serious girlfriend until he was twenty-six.

"It will always seem kind of crazy to me that people want to talk to me," he wrote in a photo-heavy coffee table book he published on the eve of the 2022 World Cup. "This whole transition from being a quiet guy minding my own business to having to be a footballer talking in the media about everything and anything still doesn't come easy for me."

When, in the fall of 2024, Christian Pulisic was asked about his personal life during a casual chat with a few reporters by a practice field in Austin, Texas, his affect changed instantly. The intrusion into this armor of privacy interrupted the flow of humdrum soccer questions. He lowered his eyes, and his mouth formed something like a grimace. He might have even been blushing a tad.

Was he, Pulisic was asked, more comfortable in the spotlight away from the field these days? Early in his second season with AC Milan, Pulisic had established himself as the leading goal-scorer on one of Europe's most storied clubs. He was appearing in more TV commercials. And he had even let his girlfriend, professional golfer Alexa Melton, post pictures of them together on Instagram, although there were none on his own account—a once-unimaginable peek behind the veil.

Had living a public life become easier on him at last?

Pulisic groaned audibly. "I still struggle with that stuff," he finally mustered. "But I think it's important for me to step out of my comfort zone a little bit. I'm doing the best I can."

PART V

Stagnation and Ambition
2003–2014

12 | Not Much of a World Cup

By the time the U.S. tumbled gracelessly out of the 2006 World Cup in the group stage, winless again, a concerning pattern had begun to show. In 1990, 1998, and 2006, the Americans had fallen at the World Cup's first hurdle, expelled from the tournament after three group-stage games. In 1994 and 2002, they made the knockout stages. A boom-and-bust cycle. Or, bust-boom-bust. A promising World Cup campaign, suggesting that the program was at last on the right path, invariably followed by a disappointing one and an inquest fueled by self-doubt.

No one thing went wrong in 2006. A difficult draw made things hard for Bruce Arena's team from the outset, although it didn't dissuade a record-smashing twenty thousand American fans from following the team to Germany. It took five minutes for that campaign to fall apart, when the Czech Republic's skyscraping striker Jan Koller nodded in the first of the three goals the U.S. conceded without offering retort in a flat performance. In the next game, the Americans gained their only point of the tournament against the eventual world champions, Italy. A gritty tie ended 1–1, although both goals were scored by the Azzurri—one in each net—and three players were expelled with red cards before the second half had really even begun.

Clint Dempsey scored the only American-made goal of the campaign against Ghana, but an unlucky 2–1 loss ended the tournament prematurely.

Sometimes the timing of a World Cup favors you. Sometimes it catches you out. The older national team players had already peaked when 2006 came around. The new generation wasn't quite ready yet. "Two years later, with that same team, I think you would have had different results in all those games," said Frankie Hejduk, who was injured in 2006 but traveled anyway, as a kind of curator of team chemistry. "But that's the World Cup."

Timing and misfortune weren't the only factors. "Something about it didn't feel as fresh," John O'Brien said. "In '02, a lot of people were excited to be there and do something, and '06 had a different flavor to it." The team wasn't as close-knit this time around. And not as disciplined. In his second cycle, the liberties Arena afforded his players became a liability rather than an asset. "It's a really fine line to give players enough freedom where they can express themselves," said Brian McBride. "Sometimes, it goes a little too far, when people start going out and partying and doing things and think it's OK." The 2002 team policed itself; the 2006 team didn't. Arena didn't interfere.

Nobody saw Arena's 2002 World Cup team as much of a threat before it snuck to the brink of the semifinals. By April 2006, however, FIFA's rankings listed the United States men's national team as the fourth best in the world, ahead of several serious World Cup contenders. This was patently absurd, a product of FIFA's famously flawed ranking system, but expectations and the team's profile were nevertheless inflated. At the same time, complacency set in. "There was a strong investment in the first four years in building a team, in being a solid group," said Gregg Berhalter. "As things progressed, I think we just forgot about that."

The team's breakout stars from 2002 admitted in retrospect that they weren't properly prepared four years later. "I thought I was way better than I was and I forgot about what made me successful," Landon Donovan said. "I just assumed that I could step onto the field and everything was going to be fine. It was a huge learning lesson, very eye-opening to know that you can't just flip a switch and that, if you don't do all the little things right, you're, at best, an average player. That tournament was so valuable for the rest of my career, because you have to feel that pain to realize you never want it again."

"Mentally, I thought we'd do the same thing we did, have the same kind of run we did in '02," echoed DaMarcus Beasley. "We got punched in the mouth real quick in the first game. That killed us, killed our spirit. We were talented. It wasn't a bad group. I just think, mentally, my mind wasn't where it should have been during that World Cup."

John O'Brien's roommate, young backup goalkeeper Tim Howard, snuck two beers into his bag after the Americans were eliminated by Ghana. On the team bus, he revealed his loot and handed a beer to O'Brien. As Howard cracked his open, he said: "That wasn't much of a World Cup, now was it?"

13 The Fruits of Imperialism

If Thomas Rongen strikes you as a movie character, that's only because he is. He speaks with gusto, almost as loudly as his colorful outfits, which emphasize his creased, ever-tanned face beneath his ash-gray hair. After all these years, his accent is still faintly Dutch, even if everything else about him is unmistakably American.

In 1979, Rinus Michels made a call back home to Amsterdam. The famous Dutch coach of the Los Angeles Aztecs in the North American Soccer League was in need of a "water carrier" as the Dutch call it, a midfielder who can cover a lot of ground, do a lot of running. And he had to be young and cheap. Somebody pointed him to Thomas Rongen, a twenty-two-year-old amateur. Rongen became an NASL journeyman who spent a summer living with Johan Cruyff and his family in Washington, DC, when they were both on the Diplomats. Cruyff was the world's best player of the 1970s—a man blessed with such preternatural confidence that he once gave a team bus driver, who had gotten lost, directions through a Florida town where Cruyff had never been before. Somehow, Rongen was one of a precious few people afforded proximity to Cruyff, one of the sport's true eccentrics, who enjoyed attending his players' surgeries when he became a manager. Rongen parlayed his brush with two of the game's great minds into a coaching career that included stints as manager of four different Major League Soccer teams and a decade in charge of the under-20 U.S. national team. In 2011, he led the national team of American Samoa to its first competitive win ever, a feat turned into a movie featuring Michael Fassbender as Rongen.

In 2008, Rongen's under-20 U.S. national team scrimmaged a Norwegian youth team from the Stabæk Fotball club in Guadalajara, Mexico. During the game, Rongen and his counterpart got to talking, and that's when he learned that one Stabæk player had a U.S. passport. Rongen wandered over to the corner flag, and when the player in question, Mikkel Diskerud, arrived to take a corner kick, Rongen confirmed his nationality with him. Indeed, Diskerud's mother was from Arizona. Just like that, Diskerud was on the American radar. He would go on to play thirty-eight games for the USMNT, making the 2014 World Cup team.

Rongen got a call from a former youth national team player of his, Bryan Arguez, who played for Hertha Berlin. They caught up for a while and then, Rongen recalls, Arguez said, "By the way, Coach, there's four guys playing here with American passports." They were Terrence Boyd, John Brooks, Jerome Kiesewetter, and Alfredo Morales, none of whom were familiar to U.S. Soccer. All of them would soon join the American program and eventually appear for the senior national team. Rongen was onto something. He asked U.S. Soccer for a budget to start compiling a list of dual-national players who were raised and developed elsewhere but who might be convinced to join the American program. His superiors were skeptical, questioning whether there were enough such players out there to make this effort worthwhile. And they weren't sure that dual-national players would be entirely loyal and committed to the U.S. cause. Besides, recruiting players who by rights belonged to another federation was not done then. Rongen was given the go-ahead all the same but told to be subtle about his work and avoid the appearance of overtly poaching players.

When Big Soccer, a popular online soccer forum at the time, got wind of Rongen's project, its users began contributing research, fleshing out his list. The amateur sleuths were particularly adept at finding players who had left the U.S. at a very young age, before the federation was aware of them, to try their luck in Europe. They put Rongen onto Tony Taylor, a striker active in Portugal who played a dozen games for U.S. under-20 and under-23 teams before switching his allegiance to Panama.

Within a year, Rongen had some four hundred names on his list of dual-national players eligible for the USA, a huge number of them born-and-raised Germans fathered by American servicemen. The U.S. armed forces have populated more than forty bases in Germany since World War II, siring a stunningly large pool of soccer talent, the apparent beneficiaries of some potent mix of American nature and German nurture. "The mere fact that we are imperialistic and are throughout the world in the name of democracy has also allowed us to tap into soccer resources that we really didn't have any idea about," Rongen said.

Some of those players were estranged from their fathers. Jermaine Jones, who had already played three games for Germany, later admitted that he switched allegiances to the U.S. in the hope that his serviceman father, who had been out of the picture since Jermaine was a young child, might notice him and come back into his life. He did, and Jones played sixty-nine times for the U.S. Some German American players had never met their fathers at all. Some spoke almost no English. And most weren't in contention for the more prestigious German national team. Playing for the U.S., as many did, opened both an alternative path to the World Cup and a means of connecting with their roots.

Rongen hardly invented the notion of a player switching national teams. Alfredo Di Stéfano, arguably soccer's first international superstar in the 1950s, represented three different countries before eligibility rules were tightened up. Dual nationals played for the U.S. from the very beginning of the program. A smattering of players who had already represented another nation featured as early as 1926. Joe Gaetjens played for Haiti before *and* after going to the 1950 World Cup with the U.S. and scoring the goal that felled England. But for all those decades, the federation's effort to find foreigners with American ties was haphazard. In the late 1960s, U.S. Soccer decided to go on a concerted recruitment drive. This campaign bagged Coventry City striker Gerry Baker, who had been born in New York to English parents. No European First Division player had represented the USMNT before him, not that Baker helped the cause much (seven games and two goals, both against Bermuda). The endeavor soon fizzled.

Earnie Stewart, the Dutch-born son of an American airman, wrote U.S. Soccer a letter in 1990 just to let the federation know he existed. A promising forward in the Dutch league, Stewart had been called up to the under-21 Dutch national team in late 1989 but hadn't made the game-day roster. If he had gotten on the field, he would have been ineligible to play for the U.S., which he went on to represent 101 times and at three World Cups.

The U.S. lucked into Thomas Dooley a few years later. At the time, Dooley was a thirty-one-year-old veteran of the German league. By then, he had missed out on three separate opportunities to make the German national team because of injuries. His prospects with the world champions had grown dim. At one of Dooley's games for FC Kaiserslautern, his agent had a chance meeting with a woman who worked for U.S. Soccer and asked about the player with the English-sounding name who spoke no English. Dooley, his agent informed her, had an American father, a serviceman who abandoned the family when Thomas was only one year old. The father left behind some sports trophies and tennis rackets that Thomas and his older brother played with growing up in their father's absence—"Playing with some memories." As teenagers, Thomas and his brother talked about going to the United States to track down their father. They never did. So the idea of the United States writ large stood in as a kind of substitute father figure. Thomas listened to American music and watched American movies, drove a Corvette and watched the Super Bowl long before that was a common thing to do in Europe. He was unaware of the other kind of football in the United States, however. "I didn't know they even had a national team," Dooley said. "I didn't know that soccer existed in the United States."

And then, out of nowhere, came an offer to play for the U.S. national team. "It was like winning the lottery," Dooley said. "I dreamed about America. It was just so outstanding. It was the most important place for me to visit, but I never had the chance. And then overnight, you cannot just visit but you don't even have to pay, and you can play for and serve that country. It was an unbelievable feeling." Dooley made his debut in 1992 and captained the U.S. at the 1998 World Cup. He took every call-up to a game on U.S. soil as an opportunity to explore another part of the country.

These recruits mostly fell into U.S. Soccer's lap. Rongen realized that the world's breakneck globalization was changing the nature of international soccer. Pretty soon, it would be common for a young player to have two passports and a claim to perhaps a few more. As the notion of nationality became squishier, opportunities emerged for enterprising national team programs. Rongen's list anticipated the all-out recruiting wars that were a few years away. By the time he set to work in earnest, the American program had already found itself on the wrong end of the decisions by two high-profile players, Giuseppe Rossi and Neven Subotic.

Rossi grew up in New Jersey but had risen through Italy's youth national teams while working his way into the Manchester United first team. U.S. senior national team head coach Bruce Arena, however, refused to recruit him. "We're not chasing around eighteen-year-old players that can't get games for their club team and tell me they want to play for Italy," he said then. Rossi stuck with the Azzurri and grew into a world-class striker, scoring a wonder goal against the U.S. at the 2009 FIFA Confederations Cup, although injuries ruined his career.

Subotic was a Serbian refugee of the Bosnian War who wound up in Salt Lake City and then at the academy in Bradenton, Florida. He had been unhappy on the U.S. under-20s—still under the care of Rongen, as it happened—disgruntled by his playing time. Bob Bradley, then the senior national team head coach, arranged for Subotic to practice with the U.S. in Switzerland. Subotic had just established himself as a starter with Mainz, a team in Germany's second tier managed by a young, little-known manager named Jürgen Klopp. On the eve of the training camp, the U.S. federation received a call from Subotic's agent, who announced that his player was injured—which Bradley knew to be a lie—and wouldn't be taking up the American invitation after all. When, in 2008, Klopp brought Subotic along with him to Borussia Dortmund, a Bundesliga powerhouse, Bradley traveled to Dortmund to try to speak with the defender. To no avail: Subotic chose to represent Serbia.

The failed pursuits of Rossi and Subotic convinced the U.S. program that it needed to redouble recruitment efforts. Bradley met with German Americans Jermaine Jones and Timmy Chandler and tied them down in 2009 and 2011, respectively. The pair would combine to make almost a hundred U.S. appearances. This was the way of the world now. Recruitment had become a part of the national team head coach's job. "It doesn't matter where they're from," Bradley said. "It just matters that when they come through that door, they are in all the way."

Recruiting national team players raised questions about patriotism and loyalty and careerism. Gregg Berhalter, like Bradley, believed that a dual national ought to buy into the team's culture first and foremost, but that there was no sense in submitting recruits to some kind of purity test. "What you're building is a team that represents the United States, of guys that will fight for each other, will do anything for each other," Berhalter said. "And you need to make sure that the people you're bringing in are open to *that*. That's the important thing. That they're not just looking for attention or to raise their career."

A sense of pride in the country dual nationals represented helped, of course, but if that feeling was lacking, Berhalter believed it could be developed. "Ideally, you have a guy that is connected to what you're representing," Berhalter said. "But you can help build that."

14 | The Bradley Competency

By 2006, Bruce Arena had been U.S. Soccer's head coach for almost eight years. He had lifted the program to a higher plane, but new U.S. Soccer president Sunil Gulati, who had risen to the pinnacle after decades of unpaid work for the U.S. national teams. A head coach staying in charge for two World Cup cycles was unusual; three was exceedingly rare. Staleness tends to set in. Arena wanted a new contract before the World Cup, but he was offered no more than an option on one. Now, to his fury, Arena wouldn't be kept on for a third term.

Gulati targeted several big-time coaches. He traveled to Argentina to meet with José Pékerman, who had just resigned as the Argentine head coach following a quarterfinal elimination at the hands of Germany at the 2006 World Cup. Pékerman was lukewarm on the prospect of taking on the American job. His countryman Marcelo Bielsa, however, was not. Bielsa had been Pékerman's predecessor with the Argentine federation and hadn't worked in several years. He was known as one of the sport's foremost thinkers, yet "El Loco" was also one of its leading characters. True to his reputation, Bielsa convinced the Four Seasons hotel in Buenos Aires, where he and Gulati were scheduled to meet, to let him into Gulati's assigned room before the

U.S. Soccer president checked in. When Gulati opened the door, he was startled to find that Bielsa had already set up his projector and the rest of his extensive materials. Over the course of a five-hour presentation, Bielsa dazzled. But his price tag was prohibitive. And he didn't speak any English. Unlike most other federations, U.S. Soccer expects its men's head coach to proselytize, to seek out publicity and spread the good word about its sport to a distractible nation.

Besides, Gulati had a clear favorite: Jürgen Klinsmann, the man who bested Pékerman on penalties in that quarterfinal in Berlin. Klinsmann had remade Germany from a dour, plodding results machine to a fleet-footed young team, exceeding expectations at the World Cup on home soil by placing third. It was exactly the sort of résumé Gulati wanted: a big name as both a player and coach, with the know-how to upgrade the program and, as a bonus, an understanding of American soccer's quirks. Klinsmann had moved to Southern California after retiring as a player in 1998. (Gulati, as the deputy commissioner of Major League Soccer, had previously tried, unsuccessfully, to convince Klinsmann to sign with the LA Galaxy by promising him that he would only have to play in the home games.) Now Klinsmann would be the kind of appointment that would send a signal to the soccer world, the sort of move that excited even the federation's jaded broadcaster, ESPN. It was easy to see Klinsmann's appeal. He was charming, sunny, and energetic. Privately, he was funny and blunt. Gulati and Klinsmann met, and the federation president walked away enamored with the breezy German. "You walk into a thirty-minute meeting with Jürgen, and he's never said it, but you come out of the room believing you can win the World Cup," Gulati recalled. "He's so exuberant. It's not false bravado. That's his personality."

Klinsmann, in turn, was keen. Gulati floated the idea to Bob Bradley, a seasoned and successful MLS coach, that he might become Klinsmann's assistant. Bradley would function in a similar role as

Joachim "Jogi" Löw had under Klinsmann with the German national team, as a strong number two, handling tactics and practices while his boss worried about other stuff. "That was our thinking," Gulati recalled. "Be the assistant to Jürgen and in a way you'll end up coaching the team. Let Jürgen do the big picture, the motivation, the press, all of that stuff. And have somebody else to do the X's and O's."

The matter was moot, however, until Klinsmann agreed to take the job. And hiring him was hardly straightforward. Klinsmann innately distrusted soccer federations, the sport's establishment, and authority of any kind. He demanded wide latitude to do as he saw fit, to hire and fire anyone within the federation whether they reported to him or not. He wished to upend the federation's hierarchy and report to Gulati alone, bypassing several layers of experienced and well-paid executives to speak directly to the volunteer president. Nobody had ever been given that kind of power and Gulati wasn't inclined to offer it now. Neither was the federation's CEO and secretary general, Dan Flynn, who predicted that Klinsmann would be unmanageable. The two sides agreed on the money fairly quickly, even though the number was substantial, but negotiations dragged on for weeks and then months when nobody budged on the issue of power. "I still today have the opinion that the head coach has to report just to the president of a federation," Klinsmann explained years later. "Because he has the most responsibility on his shoulders. Why would he then report to anyone other than the president that he has the agreement with?"

When talks with Klinsmann fizzled out, Gulati interviewed Bradley for the full head coaching job. The New Jerseyan was appointed as interim manager in December 2006. The federation gave Bradley a temporary appointment because it wanted to buy him time to win over some of the team's skeptical leading players. He did. In Bradley's first four games, the Americans beat Mexico, Denmark, and Ecuador, and tied Guatemala. By May 2007, Bradley had earned the job permanently. In the following months, Gulati sounded out Bielsa about a role as the federation's technical director—he proved too expensive again. After a decade and a half in charge of some of Europe's juggernauts, Italian star coach Fabio Capello signaled that he wanted a job out of the limelight, arousing the interest of U.S. Soccer. Gulati approached him about a dual role as technical director *and* coach of the under-23 Olympic team. A week after speaking to the American federation, Capello took the pressure-cooker England job instead.

Whereas Arena was the wisecracking uncle, the guy you pictured manning the barbecue while holding court at the family reunion, Bradley looked and carried himself more like an army general than a soccer coach. He was cleanly shaved, without fail, and kept what was left of his hair closely cropped. He seemed to own no clothes that might be mistaken for fashion. Bradley was hardly without humor and harbored a deep love of sports and Bruce Springsteen. But a veneer of seriousness and intensity masked these passions. He was a plainspoken Princeton man who, when he saw fit, flashed an intelligence that intimidated even the cleverest people. "Bob is three times smarter than all of us," one federation staffer said. "The worst thing you can do in a conversation is let Bob talk first because he's already thought through every angle, pro and con."

Bradley, who had officially served as Arena's assistant in three jobs and informally for much longer, appreciated his mentor's talent for cultivating a warm culture and marveled at his ability to turn sarcasm into a team-building tool, although Bradley was pretty sure nobody else could pull it off. But Bradley had his own methods and his own ideas. He would be more direct with players than Arena, who avoided conflict. "Bob was very matter-of-fact, he was black-and-white," striker Herculez Gomez said. "There is no gray in Bob Bradley's world. There's no bullshit. With Bob, it was very structured, in the best way. He could be very hard, very difficult on some players. But as a player, all you want is to know your role."

In Carlos Bocanegra, Bradley appointed a captain as consistent and undramatic as the coach was himself. And then Bradley set about raising the demands on his players. "Bob was hard in the way that he challenged you and pushed you," said Stu Holden. "But he was also good about putting his arm around you and having a conversation and getting to know you as an individual. That built trust."

While Arena had virtually no team rules because he didn't want to enforce them, Bradley brought more discipline and implemented structure while remaining careful not to diminish the players' joy in coming to camp. "Trying to be clear and to establish what we're all about and have standards, that part of it was important," Bradley remembered. "But, also, you needed a group that got along. You needed to appreciate coming to camp, seeing guys that were your friends, so I never wanted to take any of that away. I just wanted to make sure that, together, we were clear on what it meant to come into the national team."

Early in Bradley's national team tenure, Sacha Kljestan played for Chivas USA in Los Angeles, in whose stadium Bradley had an office. Anytime Kljestan walked by, Bradley would be holed up watching game film of some player on his radar. "He was just always watching some game from Europe on this little computer, probably some illegal stream that he had to find in order to watch Oguchi Onyewu playing for Standard Liège," Kljestan recalled. DaMarcus Beasley had the same memory of Bradley from when they were both with the Chicago Fire—Bradley forever analyzing tape at a little desk in the corner of the locker room.

Bradley introduced a new rigor to the national team, a meticulousness that had no precedent. "Bob just started to examine everything," goalkeeper Brad Guzan said. "A player sliding over half a yard to the left or right."

"Bob's superpower was his attention to detail," added defender

Oguchi Onyewu. "Really sharpening edges and making you aware of elements of your game that you needed to focus on."

The players were left with no doubt about Bradley's benchmarks. "He expected us to be as detail-oriented and as devoted to our craft as he was," said midfielder Mo Edu. Every minute of practice was coordinated and fit into some larger idea. Bradley roamed the field giving constant one-word instructions to his players, peering in one direction and somehow catching what was going on everywhere else as well. "He was just on you always," winger Robbie Rogers said. "If there was a bad touch, he would be on you. Some players probably thought that was excessive, but he was a perfectionist in a way that I thought really improved the group as a whole and really helped me."

Sometimes a loss acts as a catalyst. In the summer of 2009, the American men played in the FIFA Confederations Cup in South Africa, a high-profile dry run for the World Cup there the following year. They blew a first-half lead in a 3–1 loss to Italy, the defending world champions. And then they were hammered 3–0 by Brazil.

Yet Bob Bradley saw something he liked, something promising. "We lose 3–0, but there was a real sense that, in a tough moment, everybody stuck together," the head coach recalled. Improbably, he saw green shoots in a second heavy defeat in a row, a team putting it all together. The Americans had a mathematical chance of advancing to the semifinals of the eight-team tournament with a big win over Egypt and a friendly result in the other game. A 3–0 U.S. win accomplished just that, sending Bradley's team to a semifinal against the European champions, Spain. The Spanish were undefeated in thirty-five games and destined both to win the 2010 World Cup and to repeat at Euro 2012. But to the world's shock, the U.S. won 2–0. "Spain kicked our ass. Let's be honest, they kicked our ass. They were so good," remembered Bocanegra. But the U.S. had blended its athleticism with a dogged defense set up in rigid lines. Then they simply took what few scoring chances the Spaniards allowed them. "It was really that gritty American mentality: We're going to fight until the end; we might not be as good as you, but we're going to be really hard to beat, grind you down, work harder than you. We had a few good moments, finished our chances. That's how this sport goes sometimes."

In a rematch with Brazil in the final, the Americans took a two-goal lead before losing 3–2. Still, there was a feeling that Bradley's men had unlocked a formula, tapping into something essential.

The experience brought a tight-knit team even closer. They were the rare group that got along well but could also handle the tough truths. "All of our personalities were really in sync with one another," Onyewu said. "There were no bad apples. There was no contention amongst us. Everybody really just wanted the team to perform."

Bocanegra first saw that chemistry spark during a bar crawl in Chicago following the victory at the 2007 Gold Cup—"There was no social media then, which probably helped everybody still have careers later in life." When the team's European-based players reported for national team duty, they often flew into Miami. Jet-lagged and exhausted from the club games they usually traveled directly from, they would have dinner and a beer, and then a contest to see who could stay awake the longest. That sort of thing drew the team close. Even though Bradley tended not to rotate his lineup much, resentment over playing time never reached the kind of critical mass that can tank a team. Following the lead of the happy-go-lucky backup goalkeeper Brad Guzan—Tim Howard's perennial understudy in goal, no matter how well he played in the Premier League—the players set their own interests aside. "The group of guys on that team was really selfless," Bocanegra said. "You had some guys who got headlines and guys who didn't, but it didn't matter, everybody was pulling in the same direction."

15 | Virality

When the Americans returned to South Africa for the 2010 World Cup, they secluded themselves in a lush resort north of Johannesburg. They enjoyed each other's company there. The Americans joked and laughed and sang. They roughhoused and dumped water on unsuspecting teammates for the sin of reading a book. They swam and played golf and Ping-Pong. The team's contingent of Black players had long conversations about the meaning of a first World Cup in Africa. Third-string goalkeeper Marcus Hahnemann went hunting in a wild game reserve and shipped the carcasses of his victims home to Seattle. Clint Dempsey, a country boy at heart, got some poles and a license and spent his afternoons fishing for huge catfish and carp while his teammates goofed off.

Stu Holden and defender Jay DeMerit rechristened their room as Studio 214, where DeMerit—who went undrafted by MLS but nonetheless worked his way up from England's ninth tier to the Premier League—gave teammates haircuts. They wrote chants for every teammate. They even had one for their coach, who carried a portable DVD player with him everywhere he went and was liable to pull a player aside at any time, in any place, to show him some footage of a game situation where he really ought to have been positioned a few yards over.

It became a running joke, but not because he was wrong. Bob always had a point.

We all know they play a 4-3-3
because Bob's seen it on the DVD.
He's Bob Bradley, he's Bob Bradley,
the leader of Uncle Sam's Army.

On the way to practice, the whole team would sing the songs on the bus. Then they had an intense session, going in hard on one another. The occasional scuffle broke out, but nobody took anything personally. It's easier to get over that sort of thing when you like all your teammates.

The Americans were hampered at the 2010 World Cup, however. They lost Charlie Davies, the zooming striker, to a car accident that nearly ended his career—and his life. Stu Holden and Oguchi Onyewu, important players both, made it back in time from major injuries but had barely played all season.

Then again, the U.S. had stronger support than ever before. Justin Brunken and Korey Donahoo, hardcore USMNT fans from Nebraska, had grown frustrated by the lack of consistency in fan support around the national team. So they founded a new fan group, the American Outlaws. In their first excursion, the Outlaws took a bus of about sixty fans from Nebraska to USA–Brazil in Chicago in September 2007. Soon, they started putting on night-before get-togethers, pregame tailgates, and colorful marches into the stadium, where they sang and drummed and chanted behind one of the goals for the duration every single match. By the 2010 World Cup, there would be hundreds of Outlaws members in South Africa, leading the chants of the mass of countrymen who bought up fifty thousand tickets—making American fans better represented than any other nation but the host country.

Dauntingly, the Americans faced England first. The island nation talked itself into believing that their Three Lions were among the favorites to win the World Cup, as it did every four years despite the awkward fact that it had actually won the thing only once, back in 1966. David Beckham was injured, but much of the supposed "golden generation" remained. And in Wayne Rooney, the English had one of the world's most dangerous forwards. Sure enough, Steven Gerrard put England ahead in just the fourth minute. But a long, dipping shot from Clint Dempsey slithered under goalkeeper Rob Green and evened up the score before halftime. The sides played to a stalemate in the second half as England ramped up the pressure. Tellingly, U.S. goalie Tim Howard was named man of the match, even though he'd been hurt within half an hour when an opponent crashed into his ribs.

USA WINS 1-1, the *New York Post* announced on its front page the next day. GREATEST TIE AGAINST THE BRITISH SINCE BUNKER HILL.

In the very first minute of their next game, Clint Dempsey planted an elbow into the jaw of Slovenia's Zlatan Ljubijankić, somehow escaping punishment, but the Slovenians punched back with two goals before halftime. "As much as everybody was excited about the point against England, at halftime of the game against Slovenia, we were done," recalled Michael Bradley, the head coach's son and the team's midfield anchor. "We were out. We were staring down the barrel of playing a third group game that would mean nothing and we were headed home early. We had a hard halftime. We were saying to each other, 'We are not fucking going down like this. This is not how this ends.'" Bob Bradley's men pulled together and Landon Donovan scored just minutes into the second act, blasting a shot at Samir Handanović's face from close range, giving the Slovenian goalkeeper no choice but to duck out of its way. Late on, Bradley equalized with a lunging toe-poke. And Maurice Edu appeared to have bagged the match-winner, only for the goal to be inexplicably disallowed.

A blend of frustration and relief coursed through the American team after the game. Landon Donovan entered the locker room a few minutes later than his teammates had after conducting a postgame TV interview. By then, the rest of the Americans had already worked through their feelings, vented and hollered, said what needed saying, assuring one another that they wouldn't make a slow start in their third and final group-stage game. Donovan, of course, didn't know what had happened in his absence and came into the locker room hot, misreading the mood. He hurled one of his cleats at the ground and yelled, "That's not good enough!" It startled his teammates. "I just cared so much," Donovan remembered. "I was pissed off that we had let forty-five minutes go in a World Cup. Because I had let three times ninety minutes slip by in '06. I knew the pain of feeling that and I didn't want to go through that again."

The team dealt with the awkward moment the way it addressed many of its issues: through song. Holden and DeMerit quickly composed a ditty to mark the incident.

Landon threw his shoe,
But it's OK, we drew 2–2.

"Everybody was jumping up and down, cheering and laughing," Holden said. "Landon was singing along with it. That was a perfect example of the team we had created."

The U.S. needed a win against Algeria. Its survival depended on it. Algeria ceded much of the initiative to the Americans in their winner-take-all group-stage finale, even though the Fennec Foxes had a plausible path into the round of 16 as well. Soccer can be a sport of frustration. Sometimes the team that dominates ball possession and hogs the scoring chances loses anyway. Algeria had not yet scored in the World Cup but had given up only one goal, losing 1–0 to Slovenia and tying England 0–0. Now the Americans crashed into that same determined back line, wave after wave of attacks washing up against the tightly packed banks of Algerian defenders. The U.S. kept coming close. A disallowed goal. A ball off the post. An open net missed. Ninety minutes ticked by slowly and then quickly and then they were gone altogether. The U.S. still hadn't scored and would be eliminated in the group stage for a second World Cup running—as would Algeria, incidentally—unless it managed a goal in the final minutes of injury time.

That's when, in the ninety-first minute, Tim Howard launched a quick counterattack with a long throw up the right flank. Donovan ran at the Algerian box and laid the ball off to Jozy Altidore, who squared it to Dempsey. Dempsey's effort was smothered by goalkeeper Raïs M'Bolhi, but the ball trickled free for Donovan, who swept it into the empty net. In the space of a few seconds, of a throw and a few kicks, the American campaign in South Africa went from catastrophe to success. At the final whistle, the Yanks piled onto a delirious human heap, celebrating their 1–0 escape from ignominy.

Donovan's winning goal—cheered on by ESPN announcer Ian Darke and his memorable "Go, go, USA!" call—sent overflowing soccer bars and packed viewing parties into delirium all over the United States. The viral supercut of the nation collectively losing its mind over soccer—soccer!—didn't reach the team for several days, isolated as it was at the resort. Back then, locker rooms at World Cups were still treated as sanctuaries. Not even FIFA itself dared enter. But after the Algeria game, there was pandemonium around the Americans. President Bill Clinton, on hand for the game, shared beers with the players and chatted with Tim Howard about books. NFL star Reggie Bush got into the locker room, too, somehow. And at the center was Donovan, who'd been through a lot that summer. He was separated from his first wife, actress Bianca Kajlich, but blew her a kiss on live TV. Meanwhile, he learned during the tournament that a woman in England, where he briefly played for Everton leading up to the World Cup, claimed that she was pregnant with his child—a claim that would become public a few weeks later, before Donovan denied paternity. Donovan later admitted that he suffered bouts of depression during his career. But through all the personal turmoil, he was in a good place in South Africa. "I had done so much work on myself in therapy to be able to compartmentalize," he said. "I had so much awareness, meditating to make sure I was staying present."

Among other things, Donovan worked out how to coexist with Clint Dempsey, with whom he shared the team's limelight. They both had egos befitting their status, yet the former was a soft-spoken, conflict-averse California boy, while the latter was a Texan tempest of rage and ambition. They tolerated one another, but little more, usually giving only lukewarm celebrations when the other scored. "These were two alphas," recalled midfielder Mo Edu. "I think that rivalry brought out the best in both of them. They had this desire to always do something in a match, to be the headliner. It drove the team."

"Clint and I, during our careers, we were competitive," recalled Donovan. "The good thing is that it made U.S. Soccer better because we wanted to win but we also wanted to be the man."

Donovan and Dempsey would combine to score four of the USA's five goals in South Africa. The fourth and final one came on Donovan's sixty-second-minute penalty against Ghana in the round of 16, canceling out Kevin-Prince Boateng's fifth-minute goal—the third time in four games the U.S. went behind first. But Asamoah Gyan ran through the American defense and rifled a volley out of Howard's reach in extra time of a sloppy game, knocking out an American team that felt it ought to have made the quarterfinals. Bill Clinton was back in the locker room after the match, offering some soothing words about "getting your ass kicked" and how often it had happened to him in his political career.

The elimination was a disappointment, an opportunity squandered. Not least because a record 19.4 million Americans watched the U.S. vs. Ghana game, turned on to it by Landon Donovan's dramatic winner over Algeria. "To this day, we have the feeling that there was more there for us," said Michael Bradley. Get past Ghana, and the U.S. would have faced Uruguay in the quarterfinal. A tough task, but not an impossible one. It would have represented a breakthrough.

This was the fickle nature of the World Cup. "The reality of the three World Cups I played in is that they all came down to one play," Donovan said.

Something fundamental had shifted. Without anyone in an official capacity ever saying it in so many words, expectations crept from surviving the group stage at the World Cup to some ethereal next level. The American fans wanted more. Deeper runs at the World Cup. Prettier soccer. A tangible sign that their team belonged on the world stage.

To a vocal segment of the fan base, Bob Bradley became an anachronism. He coached in a tracksuit, rather than a jacket and tie like many of his contemporaries. He didn't say interesting things, speaking in long, run-on sentences that were purposely devoid of meaning. He didn't do anything interesting tactically. The same players, more or less, doing pretty much the same things. Over and over. They did it well, usually beating inferior teams and competing with superior ones. It was all very competent if a little unexciting. That was Bob Bradley: relentlessly competent. There was a great deal of merit in that. But Bradley had no interest in taking credit, in doing the kind of self-promotion that had become common among soccer managers. A new age had dawned that expected coaches to style themselves as personalities, playing distinct roles in the game's theater—the charmer, the villain, the intellectual, the anti-intellectual. "He didn't need to be loved by people on the outside," said Stu Holden, the midfielder who became a TV analyst after retiring. "I don't think he cared. You look at a lot of modern coaches, the Pep Guardiolas and the Jürgen Klopps, a lot of them know how to play the media and use it to their advantage and create a narrative about themselves and their teams. People on the outside did not get to know Bob the way his players did on the inside."

"I put the team first," Bradley explained. "I always felt that, as national team coach, what we put out on the field was the most important." Nobody got to see the long hours he put in, preparing to make the most of every minute his players were in camp, to understand them and their tendencies, studying opponents. "It was never about me. It was always about the group."

In this vacuum, fans formed their own opinion. And a sizable number of them held something else against him: his son, Michael. By the 2010 World Cup, Michael, a spitting image of his father, had worked himself up to being a steady contributor for a solid Bundesliga team in Borussia Mönchengladbach. He was one of the U.S. program's best players in his position. When he finally faded from the national team picture 151 appearances later (good for third all-time), he did so as one of the national team's finest central midfielders ever. Yet the whiff of nepotism clung to him, even though he was first brought into the national team by Bob Bradley's predecessor, Bruce Arena. Still, it seemed that no matter how well Michael played, how much he gave to the team, there was no escaping his last name. "Certain players and former teammates had opinions about opportunities that were given at certain stages in Michael's career that perhaps others wouldn't have gotten," Holden said. "But Michael is a damn good soccer player. He's one of the best midfielders we've had. Perhaps he was given different opportunities, but Michael earned a lot of what he got. I don't think you can question his place in that lineup."

The Bradleys were both scrupulous in avoiding perceptions of favoritism or alliance, working as professionally as they could. "The most important thing was always the team," said Michael. "Everything my dad did and everything that I did was always to make sure that the relationship that we had never took front seat." But it was hard not to see one as an extension of the other. They were wired the same way, and they were uncommonly close. Michael on several occasions called Bob his best friend; the instant he retired, he joined his father's coaching staff on a club in Norway. On occasion, their mutual intensity came to a head and they got into loud disagreements in the locker room over tactics or some such details of the game. Teammates sometimes felt on edge, like Bob was in the locker room even when he wasn't, in the guise of Michael. "You knew he was one of your teammates, one of your boys. That he was going to give an honest effort, work his ass off, that he cared as much as anybody," Holden said. "But you would always find yourself thinking twice before you spoke in a certain way about the coaching staff or things within the team in front of him."

Taken together, the flimsy grievances against Bob Bradley conspired with a baseless belief that the American program had gone as far as it could under an American coach. What the team really needed, the fans believed, was a foreigner, somebody steeped in the game from birth, to bring in that je ne sais quoi that was, well, undefinable. Perhaps the inability to verbalize what, exactly, such a coach would introduce that was presently lacking should have been a red flag. Certainly, a big-name foreign coach wouldn't be able to bring foreign players along with him. The talent pool would be the same—which is to say, not nearly deep enough to suggest that the U.S. was underperforming. In fact, one of Bob Bradley's unexpressed skills was hiding the many holes in his team. This foreigner-favoring doctrine rested on a belief that such an outsider could make the players better, when actual coaching is not in the remit of the national team manager—there simply isn't time in the few days and weeks that he gets to work with his team, every other month. The pretext for importing a new national team coach, then, was thin. The pool of viable candidates—those who combined a brand name with even a rudimentary understanding of the complex structure of the American game—was even thinner.

In the background, yet looming over this conversation, lingered Jürgen Klinsmann, who had taken only one job in the four intervening years but was fired by Bayern Munich before his first season was over. In a lot of ways, Klinsmann was the polar opposite to Bob Bradley. A world champion player, the cunning striker who dominated Europe's legacy leagues in the 1980s and '90s, blending panache and a killer instinct. He transformed the look and feel of the German national team at the 2006 World Cup, becoming the cheery face of the home team and earning a national Order of Merit. He had that next-level scent about him. That European aura that the American soccer community adored.

Sunil Gulati talked to Klinsmann again. Klinsmann impressed with his presentation, his vision and ambition, his promise of more attractive, attacking soccer. They agreed on money again. And talks broke down over control again. Gulati called Bob Bradley to offer him a new contract. Bradley accepted and got on a plane that very night to a press conference announcing his re-signing. Gulati urged Bradley to freshen up his program. Make some changes. Players told the federation president that things were starting to feel stale, as they naturally would after four years. Hire some new assistant coaches, perhaps. Find some new ways of doing things. None of that happened.

In the final of the 2011 CONCACAF Gold Cup, the Americans met their Mexican archrivals at the Rose Bowl in Pasadena. Before a rapt crowd roaring for the visitors, El Tri undid an early 2–0 U.S. lead with four unanswered goals. A few days later, Gulati met Klinsmann in Germany during the Women's World Cup. This time, after five years of flirtation, Klinsmann agreed to abide by U.S. Soccer's existing power structure. "We basically said to Jürgen, 'If we're ever going to work together, it's going to have to be easy,'" recalled Gulati. "'Because I'm not going through this nightmare stuff again.'" They met in New York and worked out the details of the deal. Gulati told Klinsmann to sign or else the federation would be moving on from him once and for all. Klinsmann signed.

Gulati waited to fire Bob Bradley until a few weeks after the Gold Cup final, following his son Michael's wedding. The conversation took just five minutes. It was about results, Gulati and Dan Flynn explained. Bradley wanted to argue about it. "His view was that the Mexico game was a phenomenal game," Gulati said. "OK. Fine. But we got embarrassed in the end."

"I knew that they had met with Jürgen," Bradley remembered. "I didn't like the way it was handled, I made that very clear with Sunil. I said, 'Listen, if you want to get rid of me, get rid of me. I'm fine with that. Just make sure you get someone good. Because I don't think you appreciate how good the work has been.'"

16 | The Great Leap Forward

It was easy to see the appeal of Jürgen Klinsmann, an irresistible package of worldliness, pedigree, innovation, and exuberance. Klinsmann smiled constantly and chuckled easily. He carried himself like a man whose confidence it was no longer possible to shake.

In his introductory press conference, Klinsmann promised to remake the U.S. men's national team and, without saying it in so many words, American soccer as a whole. By playing more assertively, reflecting an American can-do attitude. By playing prettier soccer. By tapping into the deep but virtually untouched Hispanic American talent pool. The whole event, attended by a phalanx of foreign press crowding into a Midtown Manhattan Nike store, felt like a pep rally. You might well have walked away from the thing believing that Klinsmann would probably find the formula for world peace somewhere along the way. This was the power of his magnetism, the pull of his personality. As U.S. Soccer president Sunil Gulati said of his three men's national team head coaches more than a decade later: "Bruce will get players to run through a wall. Bob will figure out how to tunnel under the thing. And Jürgen will have the players believing they can jump over the wall."

Klinsmann was born and largely raised in the German town of Göppingen, just outside of Stuttgart, the son of a baker who rose as early as midnight to start his sixteen-hour workday. As a teenager, Jürgen apprenticed to his father in the bakery, working from 3 a.m. until it was time to go play soccer. Jürgen earned his baker's diploma as a backup to his soccer career, but from the time he scored sixteen goals in a single game when he was nine—and 106 goals in a stretch of eighteen games—it seemed unlikely that his life would take him anywhere other than the big time.

Even as a child, Klinsmann was uncommonly driven in his pursuits. When he was ten, sensing that he had outgrown his boyhood team, he engineered a move to a bigger club by tracking down his prospective coach and knocking on his door unannounced. Once he turned professional, Klinsmann's brother, a decathlete, noticed that Jürgen lost speed in the second half of games and could stand to improve his running technique. So Jürgen took it upon himself to shirk soccer convention and engage a track coach to make him faster, behind the backs of his disapproving soccer coaches.

Klinsmann took his first trip to the United States in 1984. He was nineteen and had just saved Stuttgarter Kickers from relegation to the third tier of German soccer with a breakout nineteen-goal campaign. As a reward, the club's chairman paid for the entire team to go to Florida on vacation. Klinsmann was deeply impressed by the country's sense of limitlessness. "I was overwhelmed with the beauty of Miami and Fort Lauderdale," Klinsmann said. "I couldn't believe it. I thought, this is not true, I'm on a different planet here." Meeting the great West Germany striker Gerd Müller in Florida also left a mark on Klinsmann. Der Bomber had been Klinsmann's childhood hero. Now a few years retired from the Fort Lauderdale Strikers, he'd stuck around to run a steakhouse. The image of Müller, a heavy drinker making a living by regaling German tourists with stories of his glory days, frightened Klinsmann. "I saw him and said to myself, 'Hopefully I don't need to tell old stories once I'm not playing anymore.'" He resolved to always press ahead to the next challenge, never stopping to dwell on his accomplishments.

Throughout his winding career at major clubs in Germany, Italy, Monaco, and England, Klinsmann lived frugally and invested much of his earnings in rental property. Long after arriving as one of the preeminent strikers of his generation, he still drove a battered thirty-year-old Volkswagen Beetle in defiance of his growing fortune. He went long stretches without employing an agent. He picked the teams he signed with less by their status than for their promise of adventure, weighing where he would like to live and what he hoped to experience. Along the way, Klinsmann learned hard lessons about the value of promises in professional soccer. When he left Inter Milan to sign for AS Monaco rather than Paris Saint-Germain, he did so on a vow from up-and-coming Monaco manager Arsène Wenger that Klinsmann would form a front line with the Liberian superstar George Weah. Wenger immediately sold Weah to PSG and admitted to Klinsmann that had he been up front about his plans. He knew the German would not have signed—which was true.

Klinsmann never completed the German high school diploma that would have entitled him to continue his education, and this shortcoming ate at him. So he embarked on an alternative education. Lacking the patience to read books or watch TV—he would never acquire the stamina to watch entire soccer games, not even when he became a coach—he picked his vacation destinations by what they could teach him, going to places like South Africa and Namibia in the early 1990s.

As he accrued status within the German national team—aided by the team's World Cup trophy in 1990 and runs to the Euro finals in 1992 and 1996—Klinsmann grew increasingly meddlesome in the team's affairs. He demanded a say in matters far beyond the scope of his team captaincy, like where the national team would be based for a major tournament.

Klinsmann retired after the 1998 World Cup, before his thirty-fourth birthday. He settled with his American wife and children in Huntington Beach, California. There, he spent much of his time working out and playing in a local men's league—under the name Jay Göppingen, to keep the press away. Klinsmann took Spanish and computer lessons, learned to fly a helicopter, noodled on his laptop at Starbucks. "I went back to school," Klinsmann said. He audited college classes and took courses on human resources at Adidas headquarters. He restyled himself as a kind of Silicon Valley type, employing buzzwords taken straight from tech's disruption culture. "I fell in love with California because people let you be the way you are and at the same time, they want you to do well and push you," Klinsmann said. "You don't have to justify yourself for whatever you want to do, they just wish you well."

After six years out of the limelight, Klinsmann appeared on German television and gave such a sharp analysis of the German team's myriad failures at Euro 2004 that he was promptly put in charge of the team despite having no previous coaching experience. He became instantly controversial, dumping a raft of regulars and upsetting his new employers by hiring non-Germans to his staff. He set out on an aggressive agenda of modernizing not only the team's playing style, but everything else it did as well. Klinsmann hired a sports psychologist years before they were commonplace. He wanted his players to read more, take computer courses, and open email accounts to connect the team. On the field, results were mixed, contributing to the mounting pressure on his position. There was only sporadic evidence that Klinsmann's plan was working, and it didn't sit well with the German press or public that he continued to reside primarily in California.

But in 2006, on home turf, Germany overperformed at the World Cup, reaching extra time of the semifinal before losing to eventual champions Italy, and all was forgiven. In the wake of the tournament,

Klinsmann declined to renew his contract, saying he just wanted to return to his family and "a normal life." He left the team in the hands of his longtime assistant, Jogi Löw, who built on Klinsmann's foundation, finished third at the 2010 World Cup, and won the whole thing in 2014 in Brazil.

Now Klinsmann would be applying the same blueprint to the United States men's national team.

The U.S. federation hired a famous German to coach its men's national team. He would be given a large salary and a sprawling mandate to change things as he saw fit, to push the team up to the next rung of international soccer's food chain. He was worldly and spoke lots of languages, and he had recently medaled with Germany at the World Cup. He lived in the United States and possessed deep insights into American soccer and its issues. His years-long study of American sports coalesced into well-formed thoughts on the psychology and sociology that would shape his project. He had lobbied for the job for some time.

His name was Dettmar Cramer. The year was 1974.

Cramer had coached Japan and Egypt and was an assistant when West Germany lost the 1966 World Cup final to England. U.S. Soccer poached him from Hertha Berlin with a then-massive $220,000 four-year contract offer. But after just six months and a mere two games in charge—both losses—superstar defender Franz Beckenbauer convinced Cramer to return to Germany to take over Bayern Munich. The two had been close ever since Cramer managed to overturn Beckenbauer's ban from the national team for impregnating a woman out of wedlock. Cramer twice won the European Cup, the continent's biggest club prize, in his first season and a half in charge of Bayern.

In 2011, Jürgen Klinsmann became the sixth U.S. men's head coach with German heritage. Klinsmann signed a contract worth a whopping $2.5 million annually—Bob Bradley made $915,000 in his final year, which was double his 2006 starting salary—owing to his market value and the federation's improved financial picture.

Klinsmann's breeziness was a welcome change of pace from Bob Bradley. "My first impression of Jürgen was that he was an awesome dude to be around," recalled midfielder Benny Feilhaber. "He seemed like a very upbeat, optimistic person. He was so happy and smiling and bubbly all the time and that just went through the players. I liked him right away."

Klinsmann was a fount of ideas, innovations, and alterations. "He wanted to change shit up," midfielder Mo Edu said. "There were a lot of things being introduced, changing up the way we ate at camp, having a dietician, testing for food sensitivities, traveling with our own gym setup." One such test discovered a gluten sensitivity in Edu, which helped him tailor a diet to better feed his performance.

There seemingly wasn't anything Klinsmann wouldn't consider if it might help to push the program forward. "What we tried to do was stimulate the players, to make sure they were introduced to different ways of doing things," Klinsmann said. In the process of reinventing things, his outsize fame was a tool he wielded effectively. "Jürgen was a huge, huge name to have with us wherever we went," said Tab Ramos, head coach of the under-20 men's national team and a member of Klinsmann's senior team coaching staff. "He made U.S Soccer welcome everywhere and opened doors for a lot of players."

What Klinsmann wanted above all was for those players to move to the best clubs they possibly could. He reached out to a few German, English, and Swiss clubs in an unsuccessful attempt to get Herculez Gomez to the next level. He did this for other players, too, steering several to the Premier League, firm in his belief that it would better serve the national team. His public proclamations to that effect drew the never-ending ire of the MLS commissioner. "Don Garber was saying I was detrimental to the MLS because I told all the players to go to Europe," Klinsmann said. "But I would do that still today. And funnily enough, all the U.S. players are in Europe now."

During his own career, Klinsmann styled himself as a mellow bon vivant, but he was utterly ruthless on the field. "As a striker, he had a real killer instinct, and I think he wished that was something that more Americans had," said winger Robbie Rogers. Klinsmann found it curious that the players weren't as goal-hungry as he had been, so he went looking for a new kind of player. He even gave a minor league player and a collegian a chance—the latter, Jordan Morris, became a mainstay.

Bobby Wood was among the new recruits. The Hawaiian striker went to Germany at fourteen for a training stint with 1860 Munich that never really ended. "It was horrible," Wood recalled. "It was a culture shock, a tough experience being alone at such a young age, so far away from my family." The club knew how to take care of German kids in their dorms but had no idea how to look after a youth player who didn't speak the language and was twelve time zones from home. The German boys, with whom Wood already had a hard time fitting in, went home for the weekend, leaving him by himself. But he stuck it out. Unlike most of those boys, he made it to the Bundesliga.

Klinsmann liked guys like Wood, who had gone to Europe early and scrapped their way through the murderous competition in the youth academies, emerging at the other end. They had survived a kind of soccer Darwinism. The head coach did all he could to support the players fighting their way to the top, as he once had. "It was probably the best thing that happened to me, personally," Wood said of Klinsmann's hire. "He had whole setups for people overseas. If you needed somebody to talk to, treatment, he wanted to help every person possible. He opened a lot of doors for me."

A long-standing gripe among those on the fringe of the national team, or just beyond it, was that Bob Bradley seldom gave new players a chance. Whether they were getting minutes for their club team or not, Bradley favored his European-based regulars over MLS standouts. While Klinsmann preferred his players to be active in Europe, he didn't rule anyone out on account of the prestige of their club. "He didn't look down on guys playing in MLS, whereas I felt that was more the case with Bob," said Kyle Beckerman, a member of Bradenton's original class who spent his career in MLS and became a USA regular under Klinsmann after being ignored for years. "In the Bob regime, there were guys not playing with their club team but playing with the national team, which I thought was bizarre." To the 2014 World Cup, Klinsmann would bring ten MLS players; Bradley had taken only four in 2010.

In the early years of Klinsmann's tenure, the U.S. posted a series of remarkable results. The Yanks beat Italy on Italian soil, a first. They won in Mexico for the first time in more than two dozen attempts. They beat Germany. They reclaimed the Gold Cup in 2013. The early rounds of qualifying for the 2014 World Cup were a slog, but the U.S. ultimately qualified for Brazil comfortably.

"He pushed the envelope," Gulati said of Klinsmann. "I think other people would say he pushed the envelope in ways that weren't proven. But we had a good run for a while."

Klinsmann came as advertised, all charm and chaos. He delivered buzz and shock in equal measure. Yet the job of a national team head coach isn't really to make waves. It's to cultivate a sense of calm and predictability. So limited are the hours and interactions with your players that the most successful national teams are those that get their players ready for games simply and efficiently.

In his first camp as manager, Klinsmann stripped the traditional last names from players' jerseys and gave the starters generic numbers one through eleven, rather than their longtime digits—never mind all the fans who had bought a DONOVAN 10 or ALTIDORE 17 jersey. The new head coach wanted to signal to his players that what mattered was the team, not them. By the next camp, however, he changed his mind. Inconsistency would be a hallmark of Klinsmann's tenure.

Early on, many of the changes accrued to the players' benefit. "Off the field, he really upped everything," Kyle Beckerman said. "The difference in nutrition, hotels, the way we traveled, was something I immediately noticed."

But before long, it became hard for the players to make any sense of it. "One camp you went in," said Stu Holden, "and there was a dietician and it was this whole thing and you were going to be on this plan with these blood works and using this machine and these trainers. And then you came in two camps later and none of that was even in play anymore—the trainers had been fired and there was another set of sports performance guys."

There were breathing sessions for a spell and empty-stomach runs at dawn for a while, to draw down body fat. One camp, yoga was in; the next, it was out. "There was a lot of change," said goalkeeper Brad Guzan. "You're with a national team such a short amount of time that you want that stability, that understanding of what it's going to be like for the next X amount of days."

All that programming didn't resonate with everyone. "He almost treated us like we were kids," defender Omar Gonzalez said. "There were all these classes, making sure you were eating properly. Come on, we're there to just play for our national team. But the coaching part was always sort of lacking. There was always a field trip. The schedule was full. Guys were tired."

Klinsmann was uncompromising in his methods. If he didn't get what he wanted from the federation's administrators, he didn't hesitate to go over their heads and plead his case to Gulati, putting the president in an awkward position. Klinsmann insisted, for example, that the team travel with a portable gym so the players would always have the same equipment available to them. It was a nice idea in theory, but in reality it meant hauling treadmills all over the world, even though only a few players ever used them. The head coach wanted the team administrator on call 24/7, which simply wasn't necessary. To Klinsmann, however, it was a matter of principle that his wishes be carried out. He was unyielding on this, and everything else. Once he had decided on a course of action, and these decisions came constantly, Klinsmann would not be waylaid by decorum or half measures.

For a time, Klinsmann benched Michael Bradley, the emotional heart of the team, at the very peak of his prime. He would do the same to star striker Jozy Altidore. Klinsmann made Clint Dempsey captain even though the Texan was clearly uninterested in the role. "He knew that I didn't want to be the guy who was doing all the media and stuff like that," Dempsey recalled. "I just wanted to score goals. He made me captain even though I'm not the guy who wanted to be captain. There were other leaders on the team."

"I was a huge fan of his," Klinsmann said of Dempsey. "He was one of the best players ever in the U.S. But he had also the brain for being a captain and looking after other players and the chemistry of the team and speaking up when things are bothering him. My wish was to give him even more responsibility."

This was hardly the only area where Klinsmann seemed to be overdoing things, overcooking his management of a veteran team with an established culture. For all his rigidity, Bob Bradley treated his players like adults. So long as they wore team-issued gear on the field, he let them dress as they pleased off it. They could eat and drink what they wanted. Klinsmann, on the other hand, wanted to control everything. His players had to wear matching team tracksuits all the time.

It was the European way, but it was one of the small things that would come to grate on the players. Those who were active in Europe saw their time with the national team as a little reprieve from their strict clubs, which usually treated their players like unruly teenagers in a reform school, going so far as to lock them in hotels the night before home games. National team camps were once joyous occasions, a chance to hang out with their countrymen for a while. Now, snacks had to be lean and high in protein. Soda was verboten. Klinsmann tried to wean Tim Howard off his beloved peanut butter and jelly sandwiches with all-natural alternatives, which the muscle-bound goalkeeper couldn't bring himself to eat.

A gap grew between the things Klinsmann said and the things he did. In those days, only a handful of national teamers played in Europe's Champions League, the best competition in club soccer and the level Klinsmann told them to aspire to. Midfielder Sacha Kljestan played Champions League soccer for three straight years with Anderlecht in Belgium but spent most of that time wondering why Klinsmann was ignoring him. "And then he calls me back into the national team when I'm playing for the New York Red Bulls," he said.

In 2014, the national team held its annual January camp for out-of-season players in Brazil, to get acclimated for the World Cup there that summer—even though most of the campers were long shots to make the roster. Benny Feilhaber was on the roster. He had already made thirty-eight national team appearances under Bradley and, at twenty-six years old, was entering his prime when Klinsmann was hired. He was exactly the sort of creative player Klinsmann had promised to empower to deliver the pretty soccer he envisioned. Yet in two and a half years, Klinsmann had played Feilhaber just twice.

Halfway through the camp, Klinsmann wrote six names on a whiteboard during a team meal in a dining room in São Paulo and then calmly announced that those players had been cut, catching everyone by surprise. This kind of public execution is not done in soccer, or any team sport for that matter. "It was the weirdest thing ever," said Feilhaber, who read his name on the board that day. "Jürgen did some shit that is so strange to me."

"It was very abrupt and very cutthroat," echoed midfielder Dax McCarty, who was in the room. Feilhaber confronted Klinsmann and made a case that, yes, it had not been his best camp to that point, but that Klinsmann had given him far fewer opportunities than his performances at the club level merited. Five minutes after their meeting, the team manager called to tell Feilhaber that Klinsmann wanted to see him again. "He uncut me," Feilhaber recalled.

"Benny put Jürgen in such a mind-pretzel he ended up keeping Benny in camp," McCarty remembered.

But after that camp, Klinsmann never called Feilhaber up again, even though he was an MVP finalist in MLS the following year. "I played forty-four games on the national team and none of those were at my peak," he lamented.

Behind the scenes, meanwhile, things weren't much clearer. In his negotiations with Gulati over the course of five years, Klinsmann pushed for the power to hire and fire just about anybody in the federation. He never got it. All the same, he attempted to fire almost everyone who had preceded him at the federation, trying to dislodge staffers who tended to stay on as coaches came and went, providing continuity. Klinsmann failed in these efforts, but longtime federation employees who believed deeply in their mission to grow the game would find out after the fact that they were nearly pushed out, which made for a demoralizing work environment. The staffers whom Klinsmann recruited himself, meanwhile, didn't always strike the players as well prepared for their jobs. When Sacha Kljestan reported to his first camp under Klinsmann, assistant coach Thomas Dooley asked Kljestan what role he played for his club. "I was in shock," Kljestan remembered. "I've gone from Bob Bradley, who was the most prepared, watched everything, knew everything about every player that was playing in Europe. And then it was, 'Are you guys even watching the games?' That was absurd to me."

Ultimately, almost every person Klinsmann hired would also be dismissed by Klinsmann, who believed to his core that the way to extract the most from his people was to keep them on edge, to give them a sense that their jobs were perpetually on the line and closely intertwined with their most recent performance. "In a certain way, it should not be a relaxed environment," Klinsmann said. "If you want that, then you play for an amateur team and have a beer afterward. If you want to go to a semifinal in a World Cup, you need a certain tension within a team. It drives the energy, the ambition, and I think that's necessary."

Every now and again, he shoved someone over the precipice. Carlos Bocanegra had been team captain since late 2006 and had earned priceless experience playing in two World Cups and in four of Europe's biggest leagues. Years later, several of his teammates called him the best captain they had had in all their careers, someone who provided stability even as the waters around the team roiled. But out of the blue, Klinsmann had a different idea. In March 2013, on the eve of the USA's first game against Honduras in the final round of qualifying for the 2014 World Cup, he decided to bench his popular captain.

Because he didn't trust anybody to keep his lineup secret, Klinsmann had a habit of only telling his players who would start hours before the game, keeping them in suspense far longer than they were accustomed to. That's how they learned, not long before the game against Honduras, that their leader wouldn't be with them in San Pedro Sula. The team was stunned. Bocanegra himself found out only hours earlier that he would be replaced by a center back pairing that had never played together. "He pulled me aside before the full team meeting. I was blindsided," said Bocanegra. He never represented his country again.

The U.S. lost that game to Honduras, 2–1, and before its next match, *Sporting News* published a long story that cited several players complaining anonymously about their coach. They blasted Klinsmann for constantly making changes, both on the field and off it, without any apparent objective or logic. They also criticized his lack of tactical preparation for the games. Klinsmann's assistant, Martín Vásquez, who had also worked with Klinsmann in his short and unhappy spell at Bayern Munich, came under fire for his own tactical shortcomings.

After the article published, as it happened, the team went on a long winning run and earned a berth for Brazil without incident. All the while, the federation went on a PR campaign to burnish Vásquez's credentials, only for Klinsmann to fire him just three months before the World Cup.

Klinsmann's constant changes extended to team rules that he kept dreaming up but never enforced. Cell phones were banned, for instance, but since nobody bothered to crack down on them, players commonly made calls standing in front of the no-phones signs Klinsmann had hung. Or Klinsmann would make a show of breaking up the language cliques that grew in his locker room—courtesy of the many German Americans he came to rely on—and insist that everybody speak English. And then he'd walk into the locker room, head straight for the German Americans sitting together once more, and unabashedly address them in German before finally switching to English and speaking to the rest of the team.

Practice was often chaotic, with coaches disagreeing on what players were supposed to be doing and stopping mid-session to confer. Some players felt that the team practiced too often, yet also at too low an intensity. Clint Dempsey remembered two-a-day practices right after returning from the grueling European club season exhausted, aghast at being asked to do yet more conditioning. Whereas practice sessions under Bradley had been tightly orchestrated and crisp, with players competing hard, Klinsmann's were lax. "The training sessions weren't as feisty and fierce as before," said DaMarcus Beasley.

Many players didn't feel ready for the games. Klinsmann changed lineups and formations willy-nilly. Often, players worked out the tactics themselves in the tunnel on the way out to the field. They started to see through their manager. "My guess is he probably wanted to do the things that he said," Feilhaber said. "But I never thought he was a very good coach. He's a nice guy off the field and, at best, you can say he's probably a good motivator. But he's not an X's and O's guy; he's not tactically sound. He wouldn't give us any information before the game. It was more like, 'Go out there and compete. Win your one-on-one battles.' There's plenty of games where you can go back and we looked all over the place. It just didn't look like there was any cohesion or any understanding. It was just a bunch of players on the field. Guys didn't exactly know what to expect from everybody else. And that's so different from Bob. We knew exactly what Bob wanted from each position."

"We did not do a lot of tactical work," echoed Sacha Kljestan. "Like, nearly zero. It flabbergasted me. It seemed like we spent a lot of time doing other things that just didn't matter. He would have a guy come and speak to the team about breath work and how important that was. And he brought in a guy that ripped a phone book in half. It was just stuff where it was like, we could be watching video and talking tactics."

Klinsmann could be hard to read, his reasoning tough to follow. But he was capable of showing his players immense warmth. When midfielder Stu Holden was recovering from yet another injury, Klinsmann flew over to England to watch Holden play in a reserve game for

Bolton Wanderers, facing teenagers in front of a few rain-soaked spectators. "I was fucking godawful in the first half, and I was only going to play forty-five minutes in this game," recalled Holden. "So I'm in the locker room after halftime and everybody else has gone back out and I just put my head in my hands and I started to cry. In comes Jürgen, and it's just me and him sitting in this locker room, the first time I've met him and he's just talking to me as a human." The coach assured Holden that he would make it back to the national team, that the federation would help him rebuild fitness, that he was still a part of the program.

"I wanted to show him that the coach is here for you," Klinsmann recalled. "'You've been through so much shit. Don't worry. You take it one day at a time.' That's the only thing that mattered."

"Whatever happened with Jürgen later," Holden said, "that always stuck with me as a guy that genuinely cared. And he was true to his word."

Holden recalled Klinsmann being central to the locker room's merriment when things were going well and chemistry was good. He would sing along with the songs, cherishing the camaraderie. But Klinsmann had a switch. He could cut a player loose and never look back. Holden did make it back to the national team, but knee injuries forced him into an early retirement. Klinsmann offered him opportunities and resources until the end. But when Holden became a broadcaster, that all changed. "The first time I ever said anything negative towards him, I ended up on that shit list," said Holden. "From then on, Jürgen and I never had much of a personal relationship, unfortunately."

17 | Launch

By the time the 2014 World Cup drew near, Klinsmann had already ditched his longtime assistant and the team's captain. Now he set his sights on even bigger game.

Landon Donovan was on a different trajectory from the moment he left California to join Bradenton's inaugural 1999 class of Project 2010. At fifteen years old, Donovan didn't shrink from trash-talking players from the MLS champion D.C. United in a scrimmage, drawing the ire of his opponents. But his skill underwrote his confidence. Once, on the same youth national team, the coaching staff showed Donovan and his teammates a video of Ronaldo, his generation's best striker, a compilation of the Brazilian's dazzling array of scoring moves. Donovan asked to borrow the video. The next day, he pulled off Ronaldo's signature move in a game, faking out the goalkeeper with a hip swivel and rolling the ball into the empty goal. "I had never been exposed," recalled Donovan. "Soccer wasn't on TV the way it is now. I didn't really know anything about soccer around the world. It had never actually occurred to me that you could dribble by the goalkeeper and pass the ball into the net. It was this huge, eye-opening moment for me." Decades later, under-17 head coach John Ellinger still hadn't worked out when Donovan found the time to practice the move, figuring he must have done it in his hotel room.

Donovan signed with Bayer Leverkusen of the Bundesliga in 1999. He was seventeen and enjoyed playing soccer every day and living on his own. First-team minutes proved elusive, however, and he grew disillusioned. He was also homesick. Donovan once flew home from Germany to California just so he could spend sixteen hours with friends and family before flying back. Leverkusen allowed him to spend four seasons on loan with the San Jose Earthquakes from 2001 through 2004. Donovan thrived, broke out at the 2002 World Cup, and helped Major League Soccer find its footing. He returned to Leverkusen for a brief spell in 2005 before reportedly passing on a move to the Premier League and spending most of the remainder of his career with the LA Galaxy. Europe, however, kept tugging at him. He went on loan to Bayern Munich in early 2009 for an unsuccessful stint under Jürgen Klinsmann. Donovan twice joined Everton for brief and happier periods. But he always came back to California. Playing in Europe, where the elite competition was, didn't make him as happy as being at home.

For all he accomplished in MLS—six championships and so many records that the league named its MVP award after him—Donovan's is also a story of the paths not taken. He was a cerebral, introspective sort, who didn't hesitate to tell a roomful of reporters about the failures of his first marriage. He just wasn't a careerist, the way soccer players are expected to be: uninterested in climbing the ladder, hopping to ever more prestigious clubs. "I've tried to make decisions in my life based on what I think will bring me joy, on what's good for myself and the people around me," Donovan said. "I do what feels right in the moment, at the time, and that can change. It's who I am."

It made for something of a scattered career, which he ended somewhere between three and five times, depending on how you count the retirements. “I think about and second-guess a lot of things, every day,” Donovan said a few years after retiring for the final time.

“I was building the plane as I was flying it,” Donovan added later. “I didn’t have mentors. I didn’t have people who had been through it, who could say, ‘Hey, man. You’re not good enough yet. You need to just keep training.’ I didn’t have anyone who could appropriately tell me that. I really wish I had had that.”

The trouble for Donovan wasn’t merely that there was no blueprint for him to follow as America’s first standout men’s player. He also carried the burden of all that extra attention and expectation. At first, he enjoyed the status. But it took a cumulative toll. At the start of his career, Donovan would be excited to play all through the MLS season. In his late twenties, the season would start to drag and tire him out by September, rather than in November when the games ended. “The next year, it would be August,” Donovan said. “And the next year, it would be July. We were not only players, we were also ambassadors all the time. We were trying to sell the game to America. Taking all of that on for so many years just started to wear me out. It’s been a long struggle to push the game forward.”

At thirty, Donovan briefly interrupted his career to take a break in Cambodia—“Just being somewhere where I wasn’t counted on, relied upon, responsible for anything,” Donovan later explained. “People didn’t know me.”

Landon Donovan understood that he wasn’t a lock to make his fourth World Cup roster in 2014, even after his seminal goal in 2010. His sabbatical began after scoring the winning goal for the Galaxy in the 2012 MLS Cup final on December 1. By late March 2013, however, he returned to practice with the Galaxy, and five days later he was back playing competitive games. But while he was away from the game, Donovan missed three World Cup qualifiers. In June 2013, Klinsmann chose not to select him for the next three qualifiers. He brought Donovan back for the 2013 Gold Cup, which the U.S. won with a B team powered by Donovan, whose five goals earned him honors as the tournament's best player and top goal-scorer. When he rejoined the national A team in September, however, Donovan had been gone more than a year—he'd missed the September and October camps in 2012 because of injuries.

An idea metastasized, in Klinsmann's mind anyway, that Donovan, still only thirty-one, was disposable. Klinsmann invited thirty players for his World Cup training camp at Stanford, Donovan included, to fight it out for the twenty-three roster spots for Brazil. "I don't have doubt," Donovan said then. "I'm very confident in my abilities and I think I'm deserving to be a part of the squad. But I have to prove that and I have to earn it." It felt inconceivable that the Americans should leave him at home. Team leader Michael Bradley, who seldom made meaningful proclamations, said that if the Americans hoped to make it past the group stage, "We need Landon."

Donovan later denied that his relationship with Klinsmann was strained, although others felt that it was tense. "I could sense that the relationship between Jürgen and Landon was an uneasy one in moments, was not so straightforward," said Bradley. And ever since Donovan's sabbatical, the coach had been saying that he would have to earn his way back onto the team. Donovan and Klinsmann had history. When Klinsmann managed Bayern Munich, he expended significant political capital at the club to sign Donovan on loan from the Galaxy. But Donovan barely played, and his difficulties only served to put a bigger dent in the embattled coach's reputation at the cutthroat club.

Klinsmann and Donovan seemed like kindred spirits, exuding the same Californian calm. Yet the middle-aged Klinsmann still possessed a ruthlessness that Donovan simply didn't have in him. Now, as a coach, Klinsmann preached ambition and couldn't abide Donovan's public struggles with motivation—which masked, as he later revealed, private bouts of depression. Klinsmann ought to have understood the pressure of stardom as well as anyone, admitting during his career that the unabating expectations weighed on him. But though Donovan's predicament was relatable to him, Klinsmann cut him no slack.

On May 22, 2014, the U.S. had a hard but otherwise unremarkable day of practice. Late in the day, something felt off, and it showed in the body language of the players Klinsmann took aside. That's when federation staffers realized that the head coach was making cuts for his final roster. Klinsmann hadn't told a soul that this would be the day. The cuts weren't slated for another week. Not even the other coaches knew what Klinsmann was up to. But midfielder Brad Davis could tell from the excommunicated players' faces. "I didn't think I would get a spot," he remembered. "As practice is going on, I'm going 'Please don't come up to me. Please don't come up to me.'" Klinsmann never did.

Mo Edu wasn't so lucky. He was doing a gym session with half the team while the rest were on the field. "I'm watching from afar thinking, 'Oh, shit,'" Edu said. On his way back to the locker room, he walked briskly, keeping his head down. He made it to within a few yards of the locker room, almost home safe, when Klinsmann called after him for a chat. That's when he knew.

Then, as staffers looked on in horror, Klinsmann nabbed the seventh and final player he let go that day: Landon Donovan.

"I wasn't the best player in the country at that time, that's for sure," Donovan said later. "But I felt like I was good enough to help." He scored eight goals in ten national team games in 2013 alone—the highest rate of his career.

"The hard part was that, at the time, it felt malicious," Donovan added. "That was hard for me to swallow. If I could have looked myself in the mirror and said, 'You know what? I'm really not one of the best twenty-three options to go help this team win,' then I could live with that. But I didn't feel that way. And I'm not sure anybody else who was around did either. It just didn't feel right. It was also frustrating because I knew that Jürgen would have nothing to do with U.S. Soccer within a few years. I knew he didn't really care about soccer in America."

Klinsmann felt that, upon his return, Donovan never reached the level he played at before taking a sabbatical, even though his statistics were strong. "I saw the other players clearly ahead of him," he said. "I knew it was going to be a huge, huge issue. He's Landon. I knew that if you leave Landon out, oh my God, the entire country will scream at me. But there my responsibility was to be fair to the other ones who were fighting for that spot throughout the entire season, and in that time in Stanford, were better than him."

Donovan returned to the locker room and packed his things. "I'm going home," he told a few now-ex-teammates before clearing out quickly. By the time the rest of the twenty-three survivors returned from the practice field, their less fortunate peers were already gone. Klinsmann announced that those present had made the team. The elation of making it to Brazil quickly wore off when the shock that Landon Donovan was not in the room set in. Meanwhile, the federation's communications team scrambled to get out ahead of this cataclysm, preparing the press release they couldn't have imagined writing. Even federation president Sunil Gulati only learned of the roster cut heard round the world after the fact, to his consternation—his family had been close to Donovan.

The Donovan decision distracted from other surprises. Klinsmann cut several veteran locker room leaders in favor of German Americans whose perceived preferential treatment was a sore point within the team. Goalkeeper Tim Howard realized that several of his recruited teammates, whose English ranged from fluent to stilted, didn't know the words to the national anthem. He printed out the lyrics, told them to memorize them, and then staged a practice session before their first game. Among them was the eighteen-year-old winger Julian Green, active for Bayern's reserve team and all of thirty-one ineffectual minutes into his U.S. career. Somehow, Klinsmann put more stock in the totally unproven Green than in his program's all-time leader in both goals and assists.

Years later, both the players who did and didn't make that 2014 World Cup team voiced a wide range of opinions on what had and hadn't gone wrong during the Klinsmann era. But on one matter there was total consensus: Landon Donovan should have gone to Brazil.

"I thought leaving Landon home was a terrible decision," said Sacha Kljestan. "Landon was probably still the second- or third-best player on that team."

"There's a couple names where you scratch your head and go, '*This* guy over Landon?'" Omar Gonzalez said. "Some guys went along for the ride and didn't even see the field. We could have used Landon."

Bruce Arena probably summed it up most concisely after the roster announcement was made: "If there are twenty-three players better than Landon, then we have a chance to win the World Cup."

When Brad Davis got back to the hotel room he had shared with Donovan, he found a handwritten note from his exiled roommate. In it, Donovan lauded Davis for his work and his dedication. He deserved to go to his first World Cup, Donovan wrote, and should make the most of the experience of a lifetime. "For him to have the grace in that moment to take the time to write me a letter," Davis remembered, "it was extremely meaningful to me."

A few months after the World Cup, U.S. Soccer arranged a rare send-off game for Donovan in Connecticut, a friendly against Ecuador. He and Klinsmann had a difficult conversation in the hotel restaurant about what had happened. "It was clearly uncomfortable for both of us," Donovan recalled.

Julian Green played fifteen minutes for the United States in Brazil and never became a national team regular.

Twelve days before the United States played its opening game against Ghana at the 2014 World Cup, an interview appeared in *The New York Times Magazine* in which Klinsmann proclaimed that the Americans could not possibly be expected to compete in Brazil. "We cannot win this World Cup, because we are not at that level yet," Klinsmann was quoted from an interview he had given half a year earlier. "For us, we have to play the game of our lives seven times to win the tournament. Realistically, it is not possible."

The backlash was immediate. Klinsmann's clear-eyed statement sounded defeatist and unforgivably un-American. Around that time, a major international poll published by *The New York Times* asked people in nineteen World Cup–bound countries whether they believed their national team would win. Only four countries had a plurality convinced of their chances: two-time world champion Argentina, five-time world champion Brazil, defending world champion Spain . . . and, yes, of course, the United States. Before the 2002 World Cup, Bruce Arena expressed the same pessimism as Klinsmann had a dozen years later; coming from Klinsmann, however, the man installed precisely to elevate the program to a new plane, this kind of defeatism rankled.

Nevertheless, Klinsmann signed a contract extension in December 2013 for four and a half years, contingent on getting to the second round in Brazil, that pushed his salary north of $3 million per year and gave him the added title and power of sporting director. Klinsmann had pushed for a new contract as a show of support from the federation. U.S. Soccer, for its part, fretted that if the U.S. showed well in Brazil, it might lose Klinsmann to a higher-profile job. "He'd become a part of the brand of the national team," explained Gulati. "He was the face of the team." Less than a week before Klinsmann's new deal was announced, the Americans drew a brutal group for the World Cup—a group of death, in soccer parlance. It contained Portugal, powered by Cristiano Ronaldo in his full pomp; a German team that would go on to win the whole tournament; and Ghana, which had eliminated the U.S. from the 2006 and 2010 World Cups.

Brazil presented a panoply of challenges. Heat. Humidity. Malarial outposts in the Amazon rainforest. But the Americans had an advantage over everyone but the home team. The American Outlaws fan group had by then grown into the thousands and traveled to the World Cup en masse, fueling American ticket sales of almost two hundred thousand, more than three times as many as even Argentina, a neighboring nation that reached the final. AO's growth baffled even its leaders. "We didn't have a five-year plan," Justin Brunken said. "We had like a one-week plan. We never thought we would get to where we are. All we wanted to do initially was try to bring all the fans together and let good things happen."

The U.S. suffered three injuries in the first half of their opening game against Ghana alone. Clint Dempsey, who put the Americans ahead in just the twenty-ninth second of the game with a delightful dribble, broke his nose but played on. Jozy Altidore's pulled hamstring took him out of the game in the twenty-first minute and, as it turned out, the rest of the tournament. Ghana equalized with less than ten minutes to play when André Ayew whipped the ball past Howard. But John Brooks, a halftime substitute for Matt Besler—another hamstring victim—had had a dream earlier in the day. During a nap, he imagined that he would score the game-winner that day in the eightieth minute. It turned out to be the eighty-sixth, when the defender slammed home a towering header, his first goal for the national team. The U.S. won 2–1, but the collateral damage was considerable. It had no alternative to Altidore. "What killed us in Brazil was that Jozy got hurt in the first game," said Michael Bradley. For the rest of the tournament, the U.S. would be forced to move several key players out of position to fill the Altidore-shaped hole in the lineup.

Still, the Americans surprised a more talented Portugal in the oppressive heat and humidity of Manaus, a city deep in the Amazon rainforest. Jermaine Jones scored a stunning equalizer with a swerving long shot to cancel out Portugal's early goal off a defensive miscue. Clint Dempsey bundled in a goal off his stomach for his second score in as many games. But late in injury time, the Americans lost the ball and Silvestre Varela got his head onto the end of a deep cross from the otherwise anonymous Ronaldo, scoring a 2–2 equalizer. The Americans outplayed the stacked Portuguese team and would have qualified for the knockout rounds with a game to spare had they hung on for the win. It wound up being academic. Even though the U.S. staggered to a mirthless 1–0 loss to Germany in sodden Recife, with Klinsmann losing to his old assistant Jogi Löw, Portugal's defeat of Ghana meant the U.S. moved on anyway.

Still, the spilled points against Portugal and the capitulation to Germany meant that the U.S. faced Belgium, an ascending global power, in the round of 16, rather than plucky Algeria. In a wide-open game, the Americans gave up endless scoring chances to the soaring Belgians. But soccer is a funny game. Tim Howard set a World Cup record for saves in a single match with fifteen, frustrating the disbelieving Belgians. And with time ticking down, American striker Chris Wondolowski even had a chance to stick a tricky bouncing ball into the sliver of daylight between the crossbar and Thibaut Courtois's sprawling 6-foot-7 frame. Wondolowski missed—a moment that would haunt him even though the difficulty of the shot didn't warrant the crush of criticism he received. Klinsmann, for his part, frequently reminded Wondolowski that the linesman had his flag up for offside, and that the would-be goal would not have counted anyway.

Belgium finally vanquished Howard in extra time, when Kevin De Bruyne and Romelu Lukaku each scored unsavable goals. Julian Green became the tournament's youngest scorer with a dink to put the U.S. back in it, his first touch in his first appearance in Brazil. Jermaine Jones stabbed a loose ball just wide of the goal. And Courtois denied Dempsey one-on-one. A lopsided game produced a narrow scoreline, but the Belgians had compiled an unheard-of thirty-eight shots, twenty-six of which were on target. "The team was really right at the limit," Klinsmann reflected.

During Klinsmann's first World Cup cycle coaching the U.S. team, the Americans beat some first-rate teams, survived the World Cup's group of death, and came within a touch or two of the quarterfinals. Yet they were stranded in exactly the same place as four years earlier: in extra time of the round of 16, losing 2–1. The soccer hardly looked any better. And the USMNT only survived the group stage on goal difference, a tiebreaker.

The Making of a National Team: Antonee Robinson

On its face, there is no good reason for Antonee Robinson to be a pessimist. There is something joyous in the appearance of Jedi—that's what everybody who knows him has called him since he was a preschooler, Jedi. The defender charges up and down the left flank, indefatigable, celebrating goals with backflips that make his carefully kempt curls wobble. He is tall and lean, smiling easily beneath a set of sharp cheekbones. He is the auteur of dazzling card tricks that turn into viral videos, capable of solving a Rubik's Cube in under a minute, a proficient self-taught pianist.

And yet, the pessimism. "When we book vacations, I'm always expecting the hotel's going to be crap or the flight's going to cancel, or

I'm going to miss the flight," Robinson said. He speaks in a thick Scouse accent, acquired during a childhood in Liverpool. It offers a fine addition to the beautifully American bouillabaisse of brogues in the U.S. national team locker room. "Until I actually get to my hotel and I'm sunbathing by the pool, I don't believe the holiday's going to go ahead."

As a teenager, he didn't believe that he would be joining Everton Football Club's first team for a preseason training camp until he boarded the plane. When he was called up for the U.S. national team, the whole enterprise felt unreal until he met his new teammates. He was named to the roster for the 2022 World Cup as a nailed-on starter at left back but was convinced he'd be injured in his last club game with Fulham or that something else would get in the way. After he made it to Qatar, he fretted that the last week of practice would trip him up somehow. Not until he'd completed his first World Cup match against Wales did he finally accept that he was indeed at the World Cup.

But Jedi also had plenty of reason to be suspicious of good things happening to him, considering that his career existed in defiance of all the bad luck and long odds he had overcome.

Antonee Robinson's Jamaican grandmother settled in White Plains, New York, tethering the family to the United States. Her son Marlon, Antonee's father, joined her there as a child. Marlon played soccer for Duke University before moving to England, where Antonee and his two siblings were born. When Antonee was four or five—nobody made a note of his exact age because who could have known it would ever become relevant?—his father, who was also his youth soccer coach, asked him and his teammates to pick nicknames for themselves. That's when Antonee became Jedi, for his love of Star Wars and his Jedi costume and his lightsaber toy. The self-styled Jedi was a gifted soccer player, possessed of a withering competitiveness. Losing to his brother in *FIFA* on the PlayStation sparked frightful eruptions of anger. "I'd bite the cable and break it, smash the computer, take the CD out, throw it at him," Antonee recalled. "I'd get so angry. It was a bad problem." It was the kind of competitiveness that was socially problematic yet an indispensable ingredient in the making of a great athlete, the central character trait that every national teamer shares.

Everton first scouted Antonee when he was seven and offered him a place in its academy. It did so again when he was nine. But his dad thought Jedi was still too young to leave the team Marlon had built around his son. At eleven, Blackburn Rovers made a move for him, but Everton pointed out it had been waiting on Jedi for all those years, so Antonee joined his hometown team.

Around that same time, Marlon got American passports for his children in anticipation of an IT job in the United States. When Jedi joined the Everton academy, the family called off the transatlantic move. This is the irony of Antonee's U.S. national team career: If he had moved from Liverpool to the United States when he was eleven years old, it would have been less likely that he would go on to represent the USA at the World Cup. Downgrading from one of the world's leading academies at Everton to a ramshackle youth development system stateside would have diminished his chances considerably.

Jedi set out to become the youngest player to ever suit up for Everton's senior team, a club known for giving teenagers a chance. But when he got to the academy, he had a hard time just getting on the field. While teammates were invited to England's youth national teams, Jedi mostly rode the bench, just good enough not to get cut, but not so good that he might play meaningful minutes. "I was kind of a filler player," he remembered. "Some age groups, they'll be giving out contracts to guys because they need a team for that age group to allow these bigger prospects to play. I was kind of there to make up the numbers."

He worried that he wouldn't even get the standard two-year

developmental contract, called a scholarship, given to teenagers as a bridge from youth soccer to the pros. He was the second-string left back, after all, after he was moved back a line from his original position as a winger, and one of the smaller players on the team. Yet to his immense surprise, he was offered a contract over the starting left back. "'How does that make any sense?'" Robinson remembers thinking. "Eventually, they offered him one at the end of the season, but I was just like, 'Why have they even bothered giving me a scholarship when I don't play? They don't have any intention of playing me.'"

Robinson grew and played more. That's also when the injuries started. The left knee. Then the right knee. There is never a good time for injuries, but Robinson's always seemed to happen at the most critical junctures of his fragile career. He stared down a daunting recovery deadline with his first contract running out. Everton would surely let him go this time.

But he was back on the field two months early, played well, and was named the club's under-18 player of the year. Everton gave him a one-year contract as a senior professional. The two left backs ahead of Robinson on the first team depth chart got injured. At last, some good luck. Then, of course, he got hurt as well. Everton, a Premier League team, renewed his contract for two years but sent him out on loan to Bolton Wanderers in the second-tier Championship league. Robinson would, in fact, never play for Everton's first team in an official game.

In the latter stages of that season with Bolton, in the spring of 2018, Jedi got his first call for the senior U.S. national team. It would not be his first time in a U.S. jersey. He had been called into the American under-18 team for a single camp a few years earlier. And while Everton wouldn't release him to play in the U-20 World Cup for the Yanks, he always appreciated that the U.S. program saw something in him back when he was a long-shot prospect, if he was any kind of prospect at all. He wasn't a marginal youth player any longer. Robinson moved to Wigan Athletic that summer and after another season and a half in the Championship, in late 2019, he got a bit of news he could scarcely process. AC Milan, one of Europe's most regal clubs, wanted to sign him.

"I was told they were interested in me in November and I didn't believe it," Robinson remembered. "Got to January and I didn't believe it. And then it was like a couple days seeing all the news stories come out, but I was like, I can see they're interested but it's not going to happen." Milan sporting director and all-time great defender Paolo Maldini called him the day before Jedi was supposed to fly out to Italy for the standard medical testing. He still didn't believe it. Something would surely come up. Probably his knees, which had long scars running down them, betraying all they had been through. At Milan's practice facility, after he made his flight and the plane took off on time and nothing else got in the way, Jedi finally started to believe. "I had to put a Milan training kit on, and I was like, 'Fuckin' 'ell, this looks good on me. This could happen.'"

The Milan doctors discovered ectopic heartbeats. Some of Robinson's heartbeats weren't strong enough, forcing his heart to overwork and swell. He needed a procedure. Milan backed out of the deal. "It didn't happen," Robinson said. "And that sets me right back to not expecting anything to fucking come through." He cried his eyes out.

Robinson's heart surgery was scheduled for March 2020. The outbreak of the COVID-19 pandemic delayed it. He was told to cut caffeine out of his diet in the meantime. When his surgery was finally rescheduled a few months later, the pre-op exam showed that the ectopic heartbeats were gone. He no longer needed the heart ablation. When he was told the surgery wouldn't be happening, Robinson figured the procedure had failed, because of course he did. The cardiologist returned and explained to him that the surgery hadn't been necessary in the first place, and that this was the best possible outcome.

Jedi moved to Fulham of the Premier League instead of Milan and did so well that he was rumored to be on the radar of Manchester City and then Liverpool and every other mega-club in need of a left back in the following years. He became the starter for the United States in 2021 and had a strong World Cup in 2022. He played faultlessly in Qatar, hurtling up and down the left flank indefatigably and contributing to the attack by overloading the wing. Mostly, he became a fan favorite as a sort of Renaissance man whose unexpected gifts away from the field light up social media. Like the card trick Robinson learned when he was fifteen. "I'm gonna tell you a story about what happened to me the other night," he begins in a viral video. He's in Fulham's meal room, talking to an audience of teammates who have gotten to cut the deck of cards he is holding several times. "I met these girls, they were two redheads." Jedi pulls the first two cards from the top of the deck: two red queens. "I'm speaking to them for one, two, three minutes," he says as he cuts the deck three times. "Their friends came over; it was two brunettes." The two black queens flip onto the table. "I say, 'Hi, I'm Jedi, nice to meet ya.'" Joker. "What are youse doin' tonight?" "Ah, we're going to a par'y at 673 King Street." A six, a seven, a three, and a king. It goes on like that until he's worked his way through the whole deck, each new twist in the tale coinciding with a corresponding card. When he finishes, his teammates go wild.

Robinson readily admits that it's all a ruse. He stacks the deck, lets his audience cut the cards several times, but always unwittingly doing so in a way that doesn't disturb the order of the cards. It's mostly a memory trick. Just as he learned that once you understand its patterns and movements, solving a Rubik's Cube is a skill that can be learned. Same goes for the piano. They are things you can manipulate, shifting the odds in your favor. Unlike the whims of fortune.

PART VI

Rebuilding

2015–2021

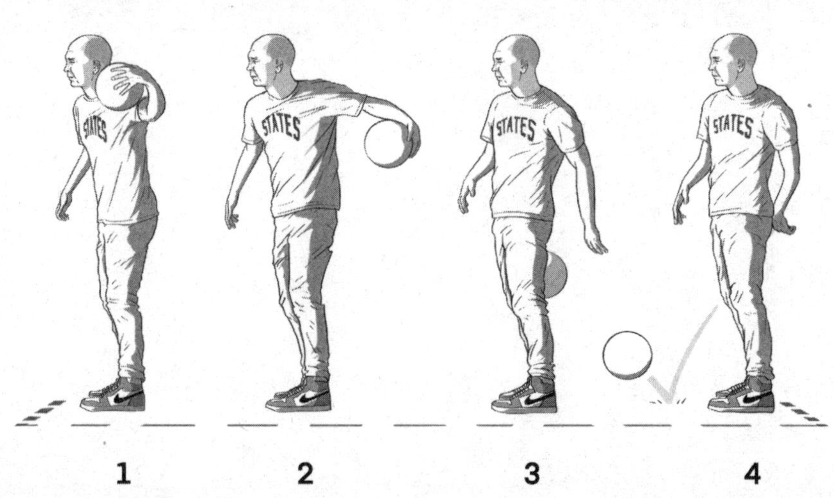

18 | The Crash

Less than six months after the 2014 World Cup, Michael Bradley lost faith in Jürgen Klinsmann. In Clint Dempsey's telling, Bradley approached him during the 2015 January camp about his feelings on the manager.

After Bradley had ended his European career in January 2014, leaving AS Roma to sign a $39 million, six-year deal with Toronto FC in Major League Soccer, Klinsmann criticized the move. Dempsey had had his own such run-in with Klinsmann. The fire and fury that propelled Dempsey from Nacogdoches, Texas, to Tottenham Hotspur, a Premier League juggernaut, had always impressed Klinsmann. But then Dempsey returned stateside for his own enormous contract in MLS in the summer of 2013—$24 million for three and a half seasons with the Seattle Sounders—five months before Bradley did. Klinsmann called out his star forward publicly for shelving his ambition, something that still didn't sit well with Dempsey many years later. "Look, if I'd had more money and not had to take care of people, I probably would have stayed in Europe," Dempsey said. "But my first house was a trailer on my grandma's pasture, bro. One of my greatest accomplishments is being able to tell my mom and dad they could retire and I'd take care of 'em."

Dempsey's career stood as one long defiance to the odds. His parents, who had five children between them, couldn't afford to nurture Clint's soccer talent. A tragedy intervened when Clint's older sister died of an aneurysm at sixteen. The money no longer going to her budding tennis career freed up resources to take Clint on the six-hour round-trip drives to a high-level soccer team in Dallas. His father worked construction and sold some of his guns to keep Clint on the field. They took on debt anyway. As a teenager, Dempsey wasn't in the picture for a residency in Bradenton. Dempsey was quiet off the field and ferocious on it. He would do anything to get ahead, caring not one bit if he ruffled feathers with his insolence. The first time he played on the under-20 national team in a scrimmage against the LA Galaxy, Dempsey nutmegged the great Alexi Lalas on his very first possession. By the time he was thirty, he had ridden his existential hunger all the way to Tottenham, by way of Furman University, the New England Revolution, and Fulham FC.

Once Clint Dempsey got to the summit, he never let the attitude that served him so well diminish. He once punched through a glass windowpane upon learning that he would not be starting in a game. But as the stakes of his career mounted, he turned inward. His hard edge, his slangish and direct manner of speaking, could come off wrong. So he avoided media and commercial engagements. Whereas he had once rapped under the moniker of Deuce on a hip-hop track for a Nike campaign as an MLS rookie, he now dialed his public persona way down. He took little interest in matters that didn't pertain to his own play, his family, or his hobbies. "As you get older, you start making more money, more pressure comes along with the role that you have," Dempsey explained. "I became more reclusive, didn't want to bring too much drama. I wanted to be able to play the game that I loved and make enough money to take care of my family."

By 2015, Dempsey was team captain but Bradley its emotional

leader, owing to Dempsey's apathy toward the job that Klinsmann had foisted on him against Dempsey's wishes. Bradley diagnosed deepening problems on the national team. And together, they had the clout to push for change. Dempsey wasn't interested in scheming, just as he hadn't been when Michael's father, Bob, was the head coach. "I told Michael straight up, 'Bro, when they came to me talkin' about your daddy, do you think I talked? Naw. I didn't talk. So why am I gonna talk now? My job isn't to pick the coaches. My job is to go out there and play,'" recalled Dempsey. "I didn't do his dad like that. I wasn't going to do Jürgen like that. I told him, 'I just want to score goals and go fishin'.' I'm simple. I'm not gonna try to get people fired and change coaches. They want to fire him? Cool. That's on y'all."

The chasm between Klinsmann's description of his team's style and what it actually produced grew ever wider. To hear him talk, the Americans were a swashbuckling side that struck fear in the elite teams. But out on the field, the Americans looked a confused, muddled mess with no apparent plan.

The mood in the team was fractious and growing more divided. At the World Cup in 2010, the national team counted its unity as one of its biggest assets. But the current incarnation splintered into factions as the culture slowly grew toxic. For years, joining up with the national team had been a joyous occasion. "You're linking back up with your guys you haven't seen in two months, catch up," Sacha Kljestan said. "It was always the honor, and then it was just fun. It was always so exciting with Bob, even though Bob was strict, just to be around the guys." Now many players and staffers dreaded national team camp. "It became more of a drag."

A friendly game in Chile bookended that 2015 January camp. It encapsulated all that was amiss under Klinsmann. For starters, nobody seemed entirely sure what Klinsmann hoped to accomplish by traveling all the way to Rancagua to play a Chilean B team in a small, old stadium. Meanwhile, the U.S. lined up in an odd 3-5-2 formation it hadn't practiced, with several players posted well out of position. The Americans lost 3–2. What, exactly, was Klinsmann doing? "He lost the culture of the team and the trust of the players by making too many moves that people were second-guessing," Stu Holden said.

Things didn't get any better at the Gold Cup that summer. The Americans made hard work of the group stage, which they typically breezed through, and only looked coherent in their quarterfinal win over a meek Cuba. Then the U.S. lost its first-ever competitive game to Jamaica on home soil in the semifinals. Publicly, Klinsmann blamed the referees; privately, he suspected match-fixing, according to a story in *The Ringer*. Neither excuse scanned.

The first few bouts of qualifying for the 2018 World Cup didn't restore confidence. The U.S. won only one of its three games. Sunil Gulati and Dan Flynn had apparently seen enough. In April 2016, they approached Bruce Arena about returning to the national team job. The Galaxy, for whom Arena had won three MLS Cups in a four-year stretch, signed off on releasing its manager and a salary was worked out as well. But Flynn canceled a meeting to finalize agreements and then went quiet. Unbeknownst to anybody else at U.S. Soccer, he awaited a heart transplant. When Flynn got the call instructing him to report for surgery immediately or lose his place in line, he understandably forgot about his work.

Here was Gulati's predicament: Changing head coaches mid-cycle would take up an enormous amount of time and energy between the actual logistics of it all and having to explain himself to the press and various stakeholders. Meanwhile, he already had Copa América Centenario on his plate. The South American confederation, CONMEBOL, agreed to stage an extra edition of its signature regional championship in the United States to mark the tournament's centenary. It promised a windfall for the chronically insolvent CONMEBOL and another mega-event to help propel the sport stateside—while, as a bonus, buttressing the case for awarding the U.S. the 2026 World Cup. But in May 2015, most of the CONMEBOL leadership was caught up in sweeping indictments by the FBI and IRS for taking an alleged $110 million in bribes related to the media and marketing rights for that very Copa América Centenario. Nobody directly involved with U.S. Soccer was implicated, but Gulati was at work trying to save the tournament—which would wind up netting U.S. Soccer some $75 million in profit, per ESPN, bankrolling federation projects for several years. Without Flynn, his CEO and general secretary, Gulati simply didn't have the bandwidth to take anything else on.

And so Klinsmann survived.

It was, ironically, a solid performance and a kind quarterfinal draw against Ecuador in the Copa América Centenario that bought Klinsmann more time—even though Lionel Messi's Argentina rolled over the USA 4–0 in the semis. The Americans made the final round of World Cup qualifying without further drama. Then the wheels came off.

The path to the 2018 World Cup began with a November 2016 home game against Mexico in Columbus, Ohio, whose dated MLS stadium acted as an impregnable bastion whenever the Yanks hosted their archrivals. The U.S. beat Mexico there in World Cup qualifiers in 2001, 2005, 2009, and 2013, all by the same 2–0 score—or *dos a cero,* as the U.S. fans taunted their counterparts. The loyalty to Columbus was a superstition cloaked in a statistical fluke.

To mend the rifts in his team, Klinsmann proclaimed a "unity week" ahead of the game during which only English was to be spoken. During the entire week, only two people were fined the hundred dollars for violating the language rule: assistant coach Andi Herzog and Jürgen Klinsmann, for speaking German to each other during a team lunch.

Klinsmann abandoned the 4-4-2 formation that had worked fairly well at the Copa América Centenario and rolled out the unfamiliar

3-5-2 formation that had bombed in Chile almost two years earlier. This incomprehensible decision was summarily exploited by Mexico. El Tri overran the Americans with one scoring chance after another and went ahead in the twentieth minute—the first time in history the Mexicans had so much as scored in Columbus. It could have been worse; Mexico hit the post twice. When an opponent was injured and the game briefly interrupted, Michael Bradley and Jermaine Jones hollered at Klinsmann to abandon his failing tactical scheme and return to the team's old formation. He did.

The Americans recovered and wrested control of the game. Bobby Wood equalized. But defender Rafa Márquez, the Americans' feisty old foil, scored a late winner for El Tri and sparked another reckoning on the American side. It was the first time the U.S. had lost a World Cup qualifier at home since 2001. Klinsmann blamed his players in the press, pointing the finger at the very central midfielders, Bradley and Jones, who had talked him into the adjustment that brought them back into the game. They weren't battling hard enough, Klinsmann argued, never mind that his formation left them outnumbered.

In its next qualifier, the U.S. couldn't even keep the game close in San José, Costa Rica. Los Ticos romped over the disjointed and seemingly uninterested Americans in a 4–0 humiliation. Klinsmann figured that politics played a part in both of the losses. Donald Trump had just been elected president of the United States. "That gave these two games a completely different psychological edge," Klinsmann said.

At any rate, on November 21, 2016, six days after this catastrophic start to the ten-game final stage that would send three of six CONCACAF teams directly to the World Cup in Russia—and a fourth to an intercontinental playoff—Jürgen Klinsmann was finally fired and replaced by Bruce Arena. "The game in Costa Rica really broke our back," Gulati said. "By that time, we were hearing more about the dissension in the locker room and Bruce was a safe pair of hands." The

Klinsmann experiment had petered out. Rather than claiming a place among the sport's elite nations, the U.S. threatened to miss out on its first World Cup in a generation.

In retrospect, two things can be true. Klinsmann was the most qualified man for the job; Klinsmann was the wrong man for the job. He had the résumé, the name, and the ideas to suggest that he would inject the program with new energy. He also lacked the organizational skills, the tactical foundation, and the attention span to carry out those ideas. As it turned out, the program needed a general contractor, not an architect.

But tempting as it is to proclaim one manager's tenure an unqualified success and the other's an abject failure, it's rarely that clear-cut. Arena, Bradley, and Klinsmann each had one successful World Cup and a second cycle that disappointed, whether they got to finish it or not. In the end, they were all, in something approximating equal measure, the beneficiaries and victims of a few bounces. "If you look at the records of those three guys, they're almost identical in terms of win percentages," Gulati said. Bradley's was 53.7 percent, Klinsmann's 56.1 percent, and Arena's 54.7 percent.

In some ways, Klinsmann made the job of his successors easier—by improving the team's working conditions, for example. In others, he made it harder—systematically dismantling the team's culture and leaving it with an aging and quarrelsome core. "I think he pushed us hard and he took the image of the game to a higher level—partly because of his own force of personality," Gulati said later. "But progress is not linear."

Klinsmann, ever the optimist, maintained that had he not been fired, he would not only have qualified for the 2018 World Cup but made an unprecedented semifinal run as well. "I knew that team inside out," he said. "I knew exactly how to get them to reach their highest level of potential. I would have taken them to the final four in Russia."

After more than five years under Jürgen Klinsmann, the return of Bruce Arena offered a kind of radical clarity. "You wouldn't see Bruce late at night with his little lamp on in a hotel room, writing X's and O's down in a notebook," said midfielder Dax McCarty. "He came in and simplified everything. He wanted to play to players' strengths. He built guys' confidence back up in the way only Bruce can do. Bruce had this Bruce charm where he could explain something to everyone without explaining it, by telling a joke, and everybody would accept it as gospel."

Whereas Klinsmann wanted a hand in everything—whether he understood it or not, down to how the team's press shop was run—Arena was comfortable delegating. He was sixty-five and liked to say he was playing with house money at this stage of his coaching career. He was back in charge of the national team to prove a point, to redeem the failure of his 2006 World Cup campaign.

A 6–0 thumping of Honduras put the U.S. back on track to qualify. But things were hardly straightforward after that. In Arena's first seven games, the Americans won three, tied three, and lost once. The team's issues had not been resolved. Other than teenage Christian Pulisic, who would lead the entire final phase of CONCACAF qualifying in scoring with five goals, no young American had really made much of a mark. The aging team lacked structure and factions persisted. The locker room mood remained unpleasant and disgruntled players caused problems.

Still, after the U.S. hammered Panama 4–0 in a commanding performance, everything appeared to be under control. Four days later, a tie against Trinidad and Tobago would suffice to send the U.S. to an eighth straight World Cup. And even absent a tie, Honduras would need to beat first-place Mexico, and Panama would have to vanquish second-place Costa Rica to deny the Americans a berth in Russia. ESPN's predictive metric gave the Americans a 93 percent chance of qualifying for Russia. In Trinidad of all places, where the Americans finally made it back to a World Cup for the first time in four decades since they reached Italy in 1989. The outcome against the long-since-eliminated Soca Warriors was so predictable that only 1,500 tickets sold for the game. A storm flooded the perimeter of the field. Keen to spare their cleats, the American players got piggyback rides to the field to practice the day before the game. Images of the scene zipped around on social media, which Arena later blamed for embarrassing and motivating the Trinidadian hosts.

Arena kept his lineup exactly the same as against Panama, even though some players were worn out. "We'd had such a dominant performance that he didn't want to make any changes," McCarty said. "I think that turned out to be a very big mistake, because we were very leggy and it looked like guys couldn't get around the field."

"The field was crap," recalled midfielder Benny Feilhaber. "And we didn't have a great mentality." The first half took a shocking turn when American defender Omar Gonzalez scored a fluky own goal. And then Trinidad got a second from a thunderbolt of a long shot, stunning goalkeeper Tim Howard.

Clint Dempsey, a sub under Arena, came on at halftime. The coaching staff had few other ideas for how to turn the tide. It was just one of those days. Pulisic quickly scored. In the seventy-seventh minute, Dempsey hit the post with a shot. Then the American advance stalled. The second goal never came. Meanwhile, Honduras improbably came from behind to beat Mexico. Panama did the same against Costa Rica.

It was all over. From a scenario in which it was almost impossible not to succeed, the U.S. somehow extracted failure. "The confluence of events that occurred that night to not qualify was just crazy,"

McCarty said. "You can't make it up. It was a really tough moment in all of our careers. A lot of tears were shed."

Looking back, captain Michael Bradley pointed out that the video assistant review referee system may have bailed the Americans out, had it been introduced half a decade earlier. "In a VAR world, we probably would have qualified," he said. The Panamanian goal that wound up conspiring to eliminate the United States didn't actually cross the goal line, after all.

All the same, the finger-pointing began. Sunil Gulati's position as president of U.S. Soccer became untenable, and he eventually announced that he would not run for a fourth term. He tried, as ever, to take an objective view of the national team's collapse in qualifying. "We don't evaluate the whole program on Dempsey's shot going six inches wide," he said later. "If we qualify, it's not as if we've done everything right. And if we don't qualify, we haven't done everything wrong. But for a game that you win nine out of ten times and two other games going the wrong way, we qualify."

But Gulati had been in the sport long enough to understand how these things worked. "Jürgen has said if he'd stayed on, we would have qualified; Bruce has said if he'd come on earlier, we would have qualified," Gulati reflected. "So I guess that only leaves me to blame."

On the charter flight from Port of Spain to Miami, Tom King, U.S. Soccer's managing director of administration, reminded Arena that the U.S. still had a friendly game with Portugal on the schedule and that he ought to start preparing. "Are you crazy?" Arena responded. "I'm not gonna be coaching." Two days later, Arena resigned.

It was time to rebuild.

19 | The Brotherhood

There was a lot to do, and Gregg Berhalter wasn't certain he wanted to be the one doing it.

The new men's national team head coach would need to exorcise the demons of the failed 2018 World Cup qualifying campaign. Revive the program's credibility. Rebuild with an inexperienced generation. Convince disillusioned fans to believe. Resuscitate the team's culture. Update its playing style. Nurture all the emerging young talent. Recruit dual nationals in an increasingly competitive landscape. And do it all under the auspices of a federation quickly cycling through leadership and controversies.

"There was some hesitancy," recalled Berhalter on becoming the men's national team head coach. "There was some part of me that was cautious about it."

Following fifteen years as a professional player in Europe, spent in the Netherlands, Germany, and England, Berhalter finished out his career in three final seasons with the LA Galaxy—the last of them in a dual role as one of Bruce Arena's assistant coaches. The Galaxy's ownership also had a stake in a second-tier Swedish team, where Berhalter became the first American-born coach to take charge of a European professional team in 2011. But his eighteen months with Hammarby in

Stockholm were unremarkable, and he was fired for his failure to get the team promoted to a higher division. In his next job, however, Berhalter made the playoffs four out of five years—and the MLS Cup championship game once—with a Columbus Crew team whose owners were more interested in moving the franchise to Austin, Texas, than investing in its success. He built a system and a culture in Ohio, spotting talent and then getting the most out of his players. Between this body of coaching work and his experience playing in two World Cups for the U.S. in 2002 and 2006, Berhalter was clearly qualified for the national team job when Arena resigned. But it was a tough gig in the best of times, perhaps more so than ever now. The kind of job that could wreck your résumé.

What's more, the federation was in no rush to put its faith in Gregg Berhalter. After Sunil Gulati decided not to run for another term as president, a coaching appointment would have to wait until a new president was elected. Once Carlos Cordeiro was installed in that role, the federation overhauled its structure. Coaches would no longer be hired and fired by the president and the federation's general secretary but by a general manager, who first had to be identified and hired. By the time Earnie Stewart was appointed to this position and ready to begin thinking about which coach to hire, it was already June 2018, eight months after the loss to Trinidad.

While the Klinsmann era had been a failure inasmuch as the U.S. had regressed on the whole, his appointment nevertheless raised expectations for his successor. Fans hoped for another big name. Tata Martino was available. He had recently coached FC Barcelona and reprised his work with Lionel Messi in charge of the Argentinian national team. Further buttressing his first-rate résumé was the work he did with Atlanta United, turning an expansion team into Major League Soccer champions in the span of two years. Martino, however, didn't speak much English. As such, Stewart didn't consider the Argentine in the final round of candidates. "I believe in culture," Stewart later explained. "I believe in communication. I believe in being able to connect with players." So the new head coach had to speak English—because a substantial slice of the job still consisted of selling the sport. And, ideally, he would be an American. No country, Stewart pointed out, had ever won a World Cup with a foreign coach in charge. "It's not the absolute data point, but it says something, I think." Martino took charge of Mexico.

"There was a brand of soccer that we wanted to play," Stewart said. "I needed somebody who could help me with that piece." Berhalter had a track record of delivering all the things Stewart wanted in a coach. So did the other finalist for the job, Oscar Pareja, the Colombian FC Dallas coach who had come to the U.S. as a player two decades earlier. Berhalter spent more than a year as the presumptive new national team coach. When he was finally appointed in December 2018, there would be no honeymoon period. A subset of U.S. fans didn't like that Gregg's brother Jay was the federation's chief commercial officer.

Berhalter felt a personal compunction to take the offer in late 2018. "Having represented the United States in World Cups and for twelve years, it was really close to me," Berhalter explained a few years after his appointment. "I put up with a lot of shitty conversations about what American soccer is—I'd had enough."

During the long delay, useful work was done. Interim manager Dave Sarachan, Arena's longtime assistant pressed into service as his temporary successor, ripped the national team down to the studs, phased out the veterans who fell short of making it to Russia, and mined a rich seam of young talent. Hardly anybody was paying attention. An unheard-of twenty-three players made their national team debuts in the year Sarachan was in charge, and they were, almost without exception, young, promising, and untested. Tyler Adams and

Weston McKennie—who scored against Portugal in a 1–1 tie—were introduced to senior international soccer under Sarachan, as were Antonee Robinson, Tim Weah, and scores of others. While the federation sorted itself out and the fans grieved for the World Cup, a new generation settled in—absent any expectations or scrutiny and a year sooner than it otherwise might have.

But U.S. Soccer was watching, and its leadership harbored high expectations for the young team—the federation's new president, Cindy Parlow Cone, declared that she wanted the USMNT to consistently rank among the world's eight best national teams.

Gregg Berhalter loved his time playing on the youth national teams, because he found a crowd of fellow obsessives. "It wasn't like we were into girls," he said. "We were into soccer." Frankie Hejduk roomed with Berhalter in youth national team camps from the time they were teenage prospects. Even as a young player, Berhalter was diagramming tactical scenarios. "After the game, he'd be drawing triangles," Hejduk recalled. "He had a whole notebook. 'We should have done this here, that there.' Like, 'Why didn't you do this? Why didn't you do that?' All I did was listen." Hejduk knew Berhalter would be a coach. "He micromanages everything. He's so detailed. He's an über-obsessive."

In 1994, after his junior year at the University of North Carolina, twenty-year-old Berhalter went on a training stint with German powerhouse Schalke 04. He met the under-21 U.S. national team in the Netherlands for a camp, arriving at the airport in Amsterdam some twenty minutes before the rest of the team did. Just then, Rinus Michels, one of the fathers of modern soccer, consulted for U.S. Soccer, and he welcomed the team at the airport. Berhalter took the opportunity to pick the famous coach's brain until the rest of the delegation showed up. Bob Gansler, the American coach on that trip, was aghast.

"His face turned white," Berhalter remembered. "He says, 'Gregg, do you know who you're talking to?'" Berhalter knew perfectly well and wasn't going to let the opportunity slip away. Michels tagged along with the team as they played several Dutch clubs. He was so impressed by Berhalter that he put in a call to PEC Zwolle of the Dutch Second Division, which offered the young American central defender a contract. Michels even wrote a letter of recommendation to help Berhalter secure a work permit.

Berhalter winding up in the Dutch leagues was not only a coup for a player never considered a serious prospect but also fortuitous in that it was the ideal place for him to develop. The Dutch soccer scene reflects the nation's innovative, collectivist ethos. Players are free to question their coaches and exercise this option liberally, expecting the man in charge to explain his decisions. "When you're in Holland, after every training session you have a debate with the players about it," Berhalter recalled. "After every game, you talk with people about it. People love to talk about soccer, and you really learn a lot. I went to Holland just out of university and totally unprepared for professional soccer. I thought I was the X's and O's guy. *Everyone* is an X's and O's guy there. That was the fun part of it, the debates. Everything I thought about soccer I had to forget about. At times my confidence was so low and I was like, 'What game am I even playing?' It was like a reeducation."

After Berhalter ascended to the job of national team head coach, the reality of his job conflicted with the way he likes to work. The national team manager is at once regarded as the country's highest-ranking coach, although there is no formal hierarchy, and yet also not given the time to do much substantive coaching.

Forced to prioritize, Berhalter decided to devote most of his time with the team to cultivating a familial culture. He worked to introduce and cement ideas, to restore rigor to the work, and, before all of that, he wanted to make national team camps fun again. On one national team trip, they hiked up a mountain in the Swiss Alps. They trained like Navy SEALs for a day at a naval base. They spoke to a NASA astronaut in Houston. They went to see *Free Solo,* a movie about free climbing. One night during the 2021 Gold Cup, the federation rented out a comedy club where the players, coaches, and staffers took turns roasting one another, Berhalter included, to the delight of everyone in the room. The head coach did the same kind of work with his own staff, taking his fellow coaches on a retreat to Montana to hike, bike, bond, and plan.

The new generation of players, led by Christian Pulisic, Tyler Adams, and Weston McKennie, came to refer to it as The Brotherhood, but this new camaraderie was no natural thing. Rather, the tightness of the new national team was managed in minute detail. At early team meals, for instance, players were assigned tables, often with a coach placed in their midst to guide the discussion as everyone got to know one another. Staff consulted with the players on what games or activities they would like during their downtime in camps and then participated, to narrow the gap between the two groups. It all contributed to an unusual closeness on the national team, the benefit of starting over with young, malleable players.

Berhalter was approachable, once counseling a crying Weston McKennie through his girlfriend problems. And Berhalter was sunny, just like his staff. This, too, was by design. "It's a learned habit," Berhalter said. "I believe people tend to skew negatively. How do I bring positivity? When we lose a game, I'm not happy but I have to show I'm happy. Because—guess what?—the sun rises the next day, the world is not ending. And players need to feel that. Because people take losses really hard. People are down. And when the leader is down, it brings people further down. In those moments, it's about being really intentional lifting people up."

In this environment, a new generation coalesced into the kind of unit that had helped the U.S. team thrive in the past while harnessing an unprecedented wealth of talent. Berhalter did this by being flexible rather than dogmatic. He loosened up tactically when his favored system proved unsuitable to the talent at hand. When the players told him that afternoon practices didn't actually accommodate their jet lag because it disrupted their routine, he changed the schedule. When the players wanted to make social justice statements through their "Be the Change" campaign, Berhalter helped them strategize. Players expected a kind of strictness with their clubs but wanted more leeway with the national team. Berhalter complied, abandoning food restrictions and loosening up camps.

When Weston McKennie violated the team's COVID-19 rules by spending a night outside the team's bubble and then bringing an unauthorized person into it, Berhalter suspended him for a pair of crucial World Cup qualifiers but didn't cast him out. He signaled that McKennie would be held accountable, no matter his importance to the team, which missed him badly in his absence, but after the midfielder apologized to the team, Berhalter offered him a path back.

In the same vein, Berhalter didn't bring down the hammer during the 2019 Gold Cup when four players returned to the team hotel at 4 a.m., several hours after curfew. Instead, he started a dialogue over what might be a more realistic curfew.

Taken together, Berhalter's responses to these episodes reflected an acknowledgment that he commanded a young team of sociable men who would sometimes make mistakes. By empowering his players, he transformed discipline into something organic. "It became like this culture that sort of policed itself in a lot of ways," said goalkeeper Matt Turner.

Power, likewise, was shared among the players. For years, the captain's armband rotated while a leadership council of seven players spoke on behalf of the team. "Our team is a democracy," said Tyler

Adams, who was eventually elected as the sole captain. "Everyone has a vote in everything. I think that's super-important when you can have a team that's player-led. But never with too much power, where the players can feel that they run the team. There's a very fine line between us having that power and Gregg making big decisions still."

It was hardly coincidental that curating a culture was a subject that interested Gregg Berhalter deeply before he took the national team job. He spent years reading about management techniques and unconventional approaches to team building, pondering how they might be applied to soccer. He went to see retired general Stanley McChrystal, who commanded U.S. forces in the wars in Iraq and Afghanistan. Berhalter read books on open-mindedness, risk, decision-making, leadership, community, and habit formation, and he sought out their authors to help him shape his own thinking, even going on some author-led retreats. He joined exclusive communities of executives and decision-makers from across industries. The coach even spoke in a kind of corporatese.

Berhalter's quest for self-improvement was perpetual. And if unusual new roles—a substitutes coach!—might broaden the coaching staff's skill set, Berhalter would consider creating them.

20 | Born in the USA

The U.S. men's national team program may have been quick to capitalize on the opportunity in the softening notion of nationality, but it also benefited substantially from plain good fortune.

Like the time when Dave van den Bergh, then the head coach of the under-15 U.S. boys' national team, called his old club Ajax to inquire about a fullback playing there named John Hilton, who transplanted himself from Los Angeles to join the famed Dutch academy. A coach there told Van den Bergh that, by the by, Ajax had another player in its youth ranks with an American passport, a fellow fullback named Sergiño Dest. His Surinamese American father had served in the U.S. Army during the Vietnam War. While stationed in Germany, Kenneth Dest met a Surinamese woman on one of his trips to Amsterdam. Sergiño was born in Almere, just east of Amsterdam, in November 2000. Ajax wasn't terribly high on Dest, on account of his oddness and indiscipline. The free-spirited Dest worked hard on the field but could be flaky and stubborn off it. Crucially, he was also not on the radar of the Dutch youth national team program.

Nine months older than Dest, Timothy Weah was the first of three future men's national teamers born in New York City in a further series of lucky strokes for the U.S. men's soccer team—a list that does not include Johnny Cardoso, also destined for the USMNT, who was born over in New Jersey before his parents moved back to their native Brazil three months later. Clar Duncan, a Jamaican émigré to New York, worked as a customer service representative for a Chase bank branch in Manhattan when, in the early 1990s, George Weah walked in. The Liberian striker was in the prime of a glittering soccer career that would make him the first, and still the only, African to win the Ballon d'Or award for the world's best player of the year.

The next year, Folarin Balogun was born in Brooklyn when his family visited from Nigeria. When the Baloguns moved to London, Folarin wound up in the Arsenal academy. The year after Folarin was born, Amina Musah, a Ghanaian immigrant living in Italy, went to visit her uncle in the Bronx, safe in the knowledge that she had ten weeks or so left in her pregnancy and therefore plenty of time to return home before having the baby. But a complication in her pregnancy prevented her from flying back home. And so Yunus Musah, like Balogun and Tim Weah, was born on American soil. Musah, too, eventually wound up in London and in the Arsenal academy, becoming Balogun's teammate.

In his youth career, Dest managed to evade the elaborate mechanisms the sport has implemented to weed out oddballs like him. In the Ajax academy, he forever questioned his exasperated coaches on drills and workouts and anything else he could possibly second-guess. He was something of a loner on the days when he remembered to go to school. Dest didn't so much march to the beat of his own drummer as sway to the free jazz playing in his head. He never heeded those who doubted his talent, even though he didn't establish himself as a starter on Ajax's youth teams until he reached some of the older age groups. He just pressed on, imperturbable. He surprised Ajax when he not only made the first team but also wrested a starting job and thrived.

Dest didn't speak much English when the U.S. first called him up to its under-17 team in 2016, but he felt a kinship to the country that his father had fought for. Besides, the Netherlands still showed no interest. It wasn't until late 2019, once Dest had become an Ajax regular and rumors swirled of a move to FC Barcelona or Bayern Munich, that the Dutch came calling. U.S. head coach Gregg Berhalter and technical director Earnie Stewart—whose own background was almost identical to Dest's—flew to Amsterdam and made their case. Dest felt a sense of loyalty to the American program, which called him up consistently before he was a household name, and stuck with it.

Less than a year later, Dest was off to Barcelona. He spent a season playing alongside Lionel Messi. When the latter left for Paris Saint-Germain, Messi's Barca teammates dressed in suits and ties for the somber occasion of his globally watched farewell press conference—all except for Dest, who was clad in a basketball jersey and shorts. Dest reportedly forgot about the event and had to be tracked down on the beach by club officials. With the U.S., he proved every bit as nonconformist as advertised. When Weston McKennie ran a pool tournament during a national team camp, Dest decided he would play by different rules than everybody else. He liked to eat an entire baguette before games. When he scored a stunning, game-tying goal for the U.S. against Costa Rica in October 2021, he did so both with his weaker left foot and with a shoelace that was untied.

"When Sergiño first came into the team, no one talked to him too much because he was just a quiet guy," recalled Tyler Adams. But Dest grew on them. "He's quite the character when he's comfortable. He's so relaxed and calm in every situation. Even before a game you make jokes with him."

If he didn't always fit in with his other teams, Dest eventually wove neatly into the tightly knit fabric of a young and ambitious U.S. national team. So, too, did Tim Weah, who never wavered from the U.S. program even though he was also eligible for Liberia, Jamaica, and

France. Weah shouldered the weight of his father's fame but didn't always benefit from it. He spent his childhood hearing from others what a great man his father was. Yet he didn't see the great man much—George was still playing for the first few years of Tim's life and then launched a political career. Tim's first coach was his mother, aided by his sister, rather than his father. He learned about his dad's career largely from the internet.

Around his fourteenth birthday, in 2014, Tim moved to Paris to join the academy at Paris Saint-Germain, one of the clubs where his father had starred. Four years later, and six weeks after George Weah was sworn in as Liberia's president, Tim Weah made his professional debut for PSG. Twenty-four days after that, Tim made his first U.S. senior national team appearance. In less than two months, he had become a member of a nation's first family, the first team of a juggernaut soccer club, and a national team that would soon take him to the World Cup.

Yunus Musah committed to the U.S. program in early 2021 after representing four different England youth national teams and captaining England's under-15 team, which featured future superstars Jude Bellingham, Cole Palmer, and Jamal Musiala. Musah, a midfielder, was also eligible for Ghana, from which his parents hailed, and Italy, where he had spent most of his childhood. It was conceivable that even Spain should become an option at some point—Musah left the Arsenal academy for Spanish powerhouse Valencia CF when he was sixteen. The idea of a home country is a nebulous thing in the Musah family. His father, Ibrahim, left Ghana for Nigeria when he was sixteen himself, pressed on to Libya, and then got a visa to live in Italy—the alternative was Japan. Ibrahim struggled in Italy, often sleeping on the street or in a car as he settled in with little help from local government, riding a bike two hours each way to his job. Once he finally established himself, he married Amina, a fellow Ghanaian. They still found it hard to make ends meet in Italy and moved with their five children to London.

A devout Muslim who eats halal, prays five times a day, and fasts during Ramadan whether he has games to play or not, Yunus inherited his father's hazy sense of citizenship. His tether to the United States was thin when the U.S. came calling. This choice was a matter of some introspection to him, forcing him to consider deeply what he thought of as home. "It's a tough decision to make, to commit forever," he said—once a player appears in a competitive, senior-level game for one country or files for a one-time switch, he is committed forever. Musah loved each of his countries in its own way. His identity was a mosaic. Musah decided to go with his birth country. The U.S. offered a clear path, a wide-open competition for places in the midfield—much more so than with Ghana, England, or Italy. It was the same kind of leapfrogging move he had made as a sixteen-year-old by turning his back on Arsenal in favor of Valencia: He'd get to the next level quicker. Although he could have signed with just about any English club, he moved to a new country in pursuit of opportunity with an abiding faith that things will work out—this was the Musah way, after all. Now that it was time for Musah to pick a national team, the English angled for the loyalty of the do-everything central midfielder as well, but, as Mexico had done with Ricardo Pepi, they proposed that he begin with the under-21 national team.

The promise of an immediate place on the senior national team, as opposed to a detour through the youth pipeline, proved persuasive for the U.S. on several occasions—a benefit to having a rebuilding program light on established players. Musah appreciated the USA's faith in his readiness to play for the senior team right away. Besides, he enjoyed the company of his new teammates, quickly feeling entrenched in the group. The next summer, Weah traveled to New York City with Musah and showed him around. Then, Musah visited Weston McKennie in South Florida, where Jedi Robinson passed through as well. "For a young player coming into this team, it's quite straightforward because there's a lot of young players," Musah said. "A similar generation, a similar vibe. A young player feels comfortable."

The USMNT never gave the hard sell to its recruits, believing the team's tight-knit locker room would sell itself. Sure enough, once committed, Musah turned around to help in the successful recruitment of yet another dual national, the German-born Malik Tillman. During one national team camp, the players borrowed a van so that they could take Tillman to Chick-fil-A for the first time, forging an unbreakable covenant in fried chicken.

Musah then aided in the campaign to land Folarin Balogun, who also had his pick of national teams—the U.S., England, and Nigeria. Like Musah, Balogun had zoomed through England's youth national team system—with a brief sojourn to a tournament in the Czech Republic with the U.S. under-18s. The U.S. coveted Balogun and pursued him for two years, but during a breakout campaign with twenty-one league goals for Stade de Reims in France, the fourth most in Ligue 1 in the 2022–23 season, other suitors emerged. Balogun considered himself a kind of international free agent. The U.S. had no clear first choice at its striker position. If Balogun joined up, he would instantly become the single-season record holder for goals scored in a major European league by a U.S. men's national teamer.

As he sorted through his feelings on the matter, Balogun took a trip to New York to explore the city and country where he had been born. Then he visited Orlando during a break from his club season, turning down an invitation to England's under-21 national team, where the English hoped to warehouse Balogun until the senior team needed him—the same plan rejected by Musah. "We cannot go and give first-team call-ups to someone just because we don't want them to go somewhere else," England senior national team manager Gareth Southgate declared.

Balogun's trip was supposedly a vacation, but the USMNT not-so-coincidentally happened to be in town as well. Balogun discreetly met interim head coach Anthony Hudson for a meal and had dinner with several leading national team players, including Musah and Arsenal teammate Matt Turner. Internet sleuths worked out that a mural in a photo Balogun posted on Instagram, which he thought was nondescript, placed him in Orlando. "I showed the picture to my agent to see if it was OK before I posted it," Balogun recalled. "To be fair, I couldn't make out that I was in America from the picture." Once the word was out, the New York Yankees and the Orlando Magic both welcomed Flo, as he is nicknamed, to games and offered him personalized jerseys, assisting in what had become a cross-sport recruitment effort. National team fans flooded Balogun's social media accounts with pleas to pick the United States, a campaign so overwhelming that he said it helped make up his mind—abetted by his parents, who also pushed Balogun toward the United States. Two months later, he committed to the USA.

Balogun was swayed by the American promise to slot right into the first team. Once FIFA paperwork came through formalizing the switch, Balogun posted a hype video to his social media accounts, announcing that he was "coming home" and sending the fan base into rapture. The Americans now had a handful of highly coveted players with multiple passports.

A promising national team career can aid a player's rise at the club level. An appearance at a World Cup, or even in a youth national team game of any sort, immediately raises a player's stock in the global market. Which is to say that the choice of a national team is more than just a triangulation of identity. Balogun, ultimately, made a practical decision that aligned with his emotions—or perhaps one guided the other. England's striker position was nailed down by at least two veterans who were unlikely to relinquish their grip on it anytime soon. And there were plenty of other prospects competing with Balogun to be next in line. Nigeria, meanwhile, featured Victor Osimhen up front, one of the world's most prized strikers—who was, at twenty-four, only three years older than Balogun. By the spring of 2023, the U.S. still had vacant jobs, starting positions that could be won in short order, even though the team had already been through a World Cup.

Daryl Dike, a striker who has made occasional appearances for the U.S., was also eligible for Nigeria, whose national soccer teams his sister and male cousin represented. "At the end of the day, you want to go where you can develop, where you can compete, where you can help the squad," he said. "Because once you make that decision, you're not able to switch. It becomes part of your footballing identity, what country you represent."

Open admissions of this mercenary thinking, however, have drawn criticism. "It's always weird to me when countries are fighting over a player and the player hasn't decided where he wants to play," said Landon Donovan, a dual national himself. His father is Canadian, and Landon retains an intense pride in that part of his identity, rooting for Canada in every sport unless it faces the United States. "But I felt American through and through and I was only ever going to play for America, if America allowed me to," he said. "So the idea that national teams are fighting over a player who may or may not pan out just seems so backwards to me. If you want to play for the greatest country in the world, say you want to play for the USA. If you don't, no problem. There's no animosity, play for whoever you're passionate about. What I've also experienced, unfortunately, is players who have played for our national team who are not proud of the U.S., who in many cases have barely stepped foot in the U.S. If you have to be convinced to play for the country, you probably shouldn't play for the country."

Donovan's views, which others share, may feel a little old-fashioned.

As nationalities get ever more mixed up in a world where migration patterns only seem to accelerate, this tussle for talent will persist. It isn't just a matter of whether the United States should pursue talent that is only partially American. Because an inverse battle has also begun. Soon enough, the USMNT will be fighting to hang on to its own homegrown prospects. In the spring of 2023, the Argentinian federation, having just won the 2022 World Cup in Qatar, announced that it would open a national training center and several youth academies in Florida. The objective? To pursue American talent with Argentine roots.

The Making of a National Team: Weston McKennie

For most of a night and much of a day in 2016, Weston McKennie paced up and down the same hotel hallway. He called friends, rambling through his anxiety for hours. Slowly, painfully slowly, the hour neared when he would hear whether Schalke 04, storied German club, incubator of elite talent, would be taking him on for its development team. A first-class ticket to the top. At eighteen years old, he'd be on his way. Even those who failed to break into the first team at Schalke tended to have solid professional careers.

It was between him and one other player for a single spot. If Schalke turned him down, he'd be off to the University of Virginia. He did not want to go to the University of Virginia. No matter how much his father and older brother insisted that he take the full scholarship, spend four years playing college soccer, and become the family's first college graduate. Weston didn't care about any of that. It was professional soccer for him. Only ever soccer. He'd looked through the course catalogue at UVA. Nothing in it excited him. Going to college was a plan B type of thing. But he had no plan B, just as they had taught him in Bradenton, before he was no longer welcome in Bradenton.

Here, now, in this hallway had arrived another inflection point, keeping him dangling yet again between the only life he had ever imagined for himself and the abyss. Like all the times he was cut from the youth national teams. Like when the overzealous coach nearly pushed him out of a game. Like the years when his body refused to grow as quickly as all the other boys' did, leaving him as the undersize kid with all the technical talent who hoped to God that his body would finally catch up.

Then came the call. In spite of everything, Weston McKennie was a professional soccer player.

John McKennie wanted to pick Alaska for his next posting in the United States Army. His then-wife, Tina, lobbied for Germany. The McKennies went to Germany. The military family had never lived anywhere for longer than four years since Weston, the youngest of their three children, was born at Fort Lewis in Washington in 1998. So a six-year-old Weston and the rest of the McKennies left Fort Lee in Virginia for the Rhine Ordnance Barracks in Kaiserslautern.

Weston was an energetic child and determined to join in whatever his older brother John Jr. was doing. To beat him at it, if he could, no matter the eight-year age difference. Wes was athletic. His father had been a football player in high school, his mother a hurdler. Most of all, he was outgoing. "He could make friends with a turtle," Tina recalled. They opted to live off base in a little town called Otterbach. Call it providence if you believe in that kind of thing, but the elementary school across the street from the house had a gymnasium where kids played pickup soccer. It took just a few weeks for Weston to get sucked into a game with teenagers, where he hollered for the ball even though he had never played and the others towered over him. A family friend began teaching Weston the sport, making him dribble around apples and kick the ball at a brick wall. Weston McKennie scored eight goals in his first organized soccer game. The next year, he moved up two age groups. All this in a country that has won four men's and two women's World Cups.

In March 2006, the U.S. men's national team came to Kaiserslautern for a friendly against Poland. Tina surprised Weston by keeping him out of school and taking him to a meet and greet with Landon Donovan and Carlos Bocanegra at Ramstein Air Base. They stood in line for several hours and got their picture with the two stars. Donovan signed Weston's cleats, but only after noting how smelly they were. They watched the snowy game, too. That summer, the World Cup came to Germany and Weston went to a fan festival for the U.S.–Italy game, a 1–1 tie, in downtown Kaiserslautern. The experiences were life-changing. Weston made up his mind about what he was going to be.

When Weston was ten, Tina and the children moved to Little Elm, Texas, a suburb on the north side of Dallas, while John went to Fort Bragg in North Carolina for his final posting. In Texas, Weston hopped to better and better teams until an overzealous coach on a travel team crushed him with pressure. Things came to a head in the final of a tournament in California. "Weston looked at me—and I'll never forget the look, it still makes me emotional—like, 'Mom, help,'" Tina recalled. Weston helped his team win the tournament, and then he quit. "If he'd stayed, he would have lost the passion for the game."

As it happened, FC Dallas had tryouts for its youth academy

around that same time. The club already knew who Weston McKennie was when he showed up and invited the eleven-year-old to try out for its under-13 team. Weston arrived with a friend. But when it came time to partner up for warmups, Weston went right up to the team's captain, its biggest and obviously best player, and announced to him that they would be doing the passing drill together. "It's really interesting that an eleven-year-old that doesn't know anybody would not get a ball with his buddy and pass back and forth," recalled Chris Hayden, who ran the academy. "It was a really curious moment for me in an early interaction with this really talented kid to just see his personality." Weston made the team. Of course he did. He was just that kind of athlete. He was a running back and a kicker on his middle school's football team as well. When the scheduling of the two sports began to conflict, Weston told his mom that he liked gridiron football 99.8 percent, but soccer 99.9 percent—his decision was made.

Tina challenged Weston, predicting before games that the star player on the other team would get the best of him. That fired him up. More often than not, Weston proved his mom wrong. "I've always wondered about how I brought him up," she said years later. "His friends would go to midnight movies and he couldn't. I always made him eat pasta four hours before a game. When his friends went for sleepovers, he couldn't go because he had a game the next day. I've said to him, 'I often wonder if you resent me for taking some of your childhood.' He said, 'No, Mom.' And I said, 'Good, because I wouldn't change a thing.'"

The day a group of youth national team scouts came to watch the FC Dallas academy scrimmage, Weston was sick. He didn't know the scouts were coming; Tina did. She coaxed him into playing the game anyway, without telling him why. He scored four goals.

He had always played up by a year or two. This was becoming a problem. As a teenager, Wes was small for his age. While his peers gained height and muscle, he did neither. "He wasn't pudgy, but he wasn't chiseled, I'll put it that way," Hayden said. "He was not very tall and going through puberty a little bit late." Weston's technical ability wasn't in question. It's just that when the other kids hit their growth spurts and you don't, the game becomes a lot more difficult.

He made the under-15 national team, but he wasn't a starter. As his peers drew the notice of Europe's big clubs, Weston stood on the sidelines. "He had a very different trajectory," said under-15 national team coach Dave van den Bergh. "Whereas Christian Pulisic was sought after at an early age, I don't know how many European teams were even aware of Weston McKennie."

He was good enough to make it to Bradenton for the under-17 residency, but, again, not so good, or big, that he got to play much. A younger player in the same position kept making the team's traveling roster instead of him: Tyler Adams. McKennie stayed behind in Florida as the team went on yet another trip without him. He started to fall behind his age group. He was cut from the residency midway through the 2014–15 school year and sent back to Dallas, a stinging humiliation and a rare decision at the academy, which was designed for players to stay for the whole year. "Weston, at that age, hadn't physically matured and he hadn't matured as a person yet," said under-17 head coach Richie Williams. "He wasn't physically strong enough."

There's a certain kind of logic that explains the historical difficulty in identifying soccer talent in the United States. By outward appearances, soccer looks something like a track meet. To an untrained eye, a high-level match unfolds as an unrelenting jumble of sprints and jumps and slide tackles, interspersed with long stretches of jogging. The further you look back into soccer's archives of game footage, in fact, the more physical the sport appears. The original English style of play was appropriately dubbed "kick and rush." Belt the ball forward and tear after it. Muscle the other team off the ball and smash it at the goal. That was, for many decades and by broad consensus, the way the game ought to be played.

The sport has become faster to the point of being unrecognizable from the brand of soccer played as recently as the 1990s. Elite players typically cover somewhere between six and eight miles over the course of a ninety-minute game, doing so on squishy grass and in a syncopated cadence of stops and starts. At the highest level, they do this two or three times a week, not counting the miles covered in practice.

It is tempting, then, to think of soccer as an innately physical sport, for which the best specimens ought to be selected. For generations, American coaches picked out the biggest, fastest players they could find, overlooking scores of clever and gifted players who didn't fit the mold.

The trouble is that, up close, soccer is less like an NFL scouting combine than a chess match for the available space on the field. Players move in highly orchestrated patterns, attempting to keep the field large when in possession of the ball and small when without it, opening up corridors of space or sealing off vacant pockets. As soccer evolves, the tactics grow more complex with it. Enmesh yourself deeply in the game and you will pick up on the sport's strange patois, talking of "half-spaces" and "rest defense" and "inverted wingers." In this environment, skillful and cerebral players thrive no matter their size. Eventually, the spoils accrue to the ones who can connect the dots in this blur of movement, like an astrophysicist peering at a whiteboard of equations and spotting the patterns in them. Some of the best playmakers of their generation, such as Xavi Hernández and Andrea Pirlo, could barely beat their coaches in a footrace. The pantheon of greatest-ever soccer players must include Pelé, Diego Maradona, Johan Cruyff, Lionel Messi, and Cristiano Ronaldo, give or take. But out of those, only Ronaldo stands taller than 5 foot 10.

And yet, American coaches at every level sought out brawn.

The manicured soccer fields of the academy and practice facility sprawled behind the FC Dallas stadium in Frisco. The wind whipped down Tornado Alley, offering some respite from the baking heat of a late-May afternoon. On one of the fields, the under-13 FC Dallas team played a travel team from Louisiana called Elite something-or-other—a name chosen to evoke excellence and exclusivity in exchange for a lot of money from eager parents. FC Dallas's team consisted mostly of non-white players. The other team was all white but for one player.

This is where Weston McKennie returned after being sent away from Bradenton. The rejection had devastated him. His mom believed he might stop playing soccer altogether, because Weston didn't do things he didn't enjoy and he had always promised that his soccer career would be over the minute he stopped having fun. Still, he persisted. And his patience would finally be rewarded. A few years earlier, when Weston fretted that he might never grow, Tina had taken him to get his growth plates tested. The test predicted a 6-foot-1 frame. "Yes!" Weston shouted. "That's a great midfielder size!" When he came home from Bradenton, it finally happened for him. He grew taller, thinner, and stronger. He may have missed out on the under-17 World Cup with the national team, but he led his FC Dallas youth academy team to a national championship, restoring his confidence.

The next year, in 2016, the under-19 national team called him—a team that existed to create a kind of backdoor path for late bloomers—and he became perhaps its best player. Out of somewhere in the proximity of nowhere, Weston became a major prospect. "He was always undersized and then all of a sudden he started to grow and became a physical force," Van den Bergh said. "His attributes are ridiculous. That, paired with the soccer he had in him, made him into the player he is now. We always knew that he was a good player. I never thought he was going to be this influential."

A generation earlier, perhaps even a few years earlier, getting sent home from Bradenton ended a career. Now, however, Weston could fall back on a strong academy program. He was fortunate that he spent the last years of his youth in the vicinity of FC Dallas academy. The dearth of high-level youth academies—especially those under the umbrella of Major League Soccer teams, which don't charge exorbitant fees—remains a slow-moving crisis. "The challenge we have is there's not enough of these environments compared to other countries," Chris Hayden said. "There's four hundred professional clubs in Spain, and that's in a country the size of Texas. And we have three MLS teams in Texas and a handful of other upper-level environments."

The Dallas–Fort Worth area, in a market of about 7.6 million people, has just one professional club and one professional academy. The wider Madrid region has a million fewer residents, yet, at any given time, counts about a dozen clubs that are either fully professional or semiprofessional. They all have youth systems. Madrid has twelve times as many spots for elite youth players as Dallas does, for a smaller population. This sobering arithmetic helps explain why the Spanish have churned out world-class national teams for many decades and the U.S. hasn't. A Spanish boy with any talent and passion for soccer at all will almost certainly be found and nurtured. An American boy with the exact same gifts and proclivities faces far longer odds of being discovered.

"We could develop, in my mind, a world-class team just from the population center in Dallas," said Hayden. "If we find the right players at the right age, any of those players could become the next Messi or the next Ronaldo. What you need is high-level programs for *all* of those kids, regardless of financial background or ethnicity."

Globally, lots of players who turn out to be the biggest stars of their generation weren't the transcendent talent of their age group at the youth levels. So perhaps they didn't make the team at the biggest clubs' academies. Instead, they came up with some smaller club, and then moved up to a bigger one. The pool was big enough for all that talent to stay in the water. But when those smaller clubs don't exist, the paths to the pros are fewer, and those would-be world-beaters wash out.

Weston McKennie got lucky. If his family had settled in one of the many places in the country without an MLS academy, chances are you'd never have learned his name.

McKennie had already committed to playing college soccer at the University of Virginia when he called his mother from an under-19 youth national team camp in Los Angeles. "Mom," he announced. "We're going to Germany."

When?

Tomorrow.

Schalke 04 offered McKennie, who was about to turn eighteen, a trial, an opportunity to practice with its development team for a few days and, if he made enough of an impression, sign a contract. "I always wanted to return to Germany because it was like a second home to me," McKennie said. He flew home to Dallas and, as quickly as they could, Tina and Wes scurried back to the airport to fly to Europe. On the way, he called UVA to let the school know that he was decommitting, so sure was McKennie of his future. The coach told him that he would hold his scholarship for five days, because, as he put it, it would take several players to replace one Weston McKennie.

When he got to Gelsenkirchen, the club's academy director was stunned that McKennie spoke German, which he never lost after they returned stateside from Otterbach. The director offered a piece of advice in case McKennie made the team: Don't get caught in public with "your little friend down the road." That would be Christian Pulisic, already playing for the first team of Borussia Dortmund, Schalke 04's archrivals.

The family members pushing for McKennie to go to UVA had made no substantial progress in convincing him that he ought to be a college man. He understood that spending time in the college ranks, where teams are hamstrung by strict limitations on the amount of time they can be on the field, would slow the momentum his career had finally gathered.

Schalke offered McKennie a spot and he signed his first professional contract when he turned eighteen. The club put him up in a building with a dozen other Schalke prospects where a house mom kept them all in line. By May 2017, at the tail end of his first season in Germany, he rose out of the academy team and made his debut with Schalke's first team. By November, he scored on his senior U.S. national team debut, just after turning nineteen.

After three full seasons with Schalke, McKennie moved to Italy's serial champions Juventus when several Premier League clubs were reportedly also interested. In Turin, he shared a locker room with Cristiano Ronaldo, one of the greatest players ever. McKennie was starstruck, sure, but he remained himself. A camera caught him quipping to Ronaldo and his famously fat-free physique, "Bro, you wish you had this body." A bemused Ronaldo peered back at McKennie, who never lost his jowly baby face and retains an unusually bulky build for a soccer player.

He got regular games in Turin, just as he always had even when he seemed out of his depth. But he faded from the lineup and was farmed out, spending a disappointing half season with Leeds United in the Premier League, where fans scapegoated him—and his, well, unorthodox physique—for the team's relegation. McKennie returned to Juventus by default, absent serious offers for his services. The club messaged his outcast status without ambiguity: It assigned no locker or parking space to Weston McKennie—soccer clubs can be pointlessly petty like that. Yet under a coach who made no secret of his indifference to him, Weston went right on back to overperforming, becoming a key player for that same skeptical manager, Max Allegri. *Tuttosport*, one of several Italian daily sports newspapers, named Weston as Juventus's best player of the first half of the season. McKennie would, in fact, lead his team in assists over the course of the 2023–24 campaign with ten—four more than anyone else. When Allegri was inevitably given credit for discovering a player who had been under his nose the entire time, he conceded that he had not, in fact, "transformed" Weston. "I just told him during the summer that he had a great chance of staying at Juventus as long as he started running on July 15 and stopped on May 26," Allegri joked. Weston, evidently, had complied. By the time the season ended, Allegri was gone and McKennie was regarded as a key player.

When a new manager arrived, he announced that Weston was among the eight players he expected the club to unload. Yet two weeks later, McKennie was on the nineteen-man game-day roster for Juve's season opener. Five days after that, the club signed him to a contract extension. McKennie was in the starting lineup for Juve's first Champions League game of the season and scored a goal. "Weston can do everything," his new coach, Thiago Motta, eventually conceded. "It's a fortune to have players of this quality." By the middle of the season, Motta had named McKennie team captain for a Champions League game. Before long, Thiago Motta was fired, too, but Weston McKennie remained an occasional team captain.

There is a star-like quality to McKennie that makes his rise seem preordained. Whenever a camera points at him, he makes a face, strikes a pose, or begins to dance. If a microphone happens to be around, he will grasp it given the chance and begin to entertain whoever might be able to hear him. During a press conference, he is liable to suck air through the straw of his empty drink, rattling the leftover ice cubes in the cup just as a teammate is talking. And then he'll break into a grin so disarming that all is instantly forgiven. "Weston is a big, exploding ball of fun and character," Antonee Robinson said. "He loves attention. But he's not a big ego. He's a lovely guy."

McKennie never switches off. If there is a dial that controls him, he has either never found it or chosen to leave it turned to ten at all times. "He's a guy who has a lot of energy, man," Ricardo Pepi said. "Me, I'm not a morning person. I wake up and I'm still groggy, still kind of grumpy. But then Wes walks into the room, this guy is screaming."

The national team locker room appreciates him for what he brings. "He's really important to the group," said Tim Weah, McKennie's teammate on both the national team and at Juventus for several years. "He's someone who brings the team together. Wes is always excited. It's a good thing. If everyone was just quiet, it doesn't make it a team. You need personality, and Weston has that personality."

McKennie is an unusual character, brash yet charming, and an unconventional midfielder. He isn't shaped like your typical waifish soccer player. He's stocky, yet a physical marvel, possessed of the prized endurance to run hard for all ninety minutes and athletic enough to both win headers in the air and get the ball back for his team on the ground. He has a precise pass that can unlock a defense when paired with his keen reading of the game. "Every attribute you could want for a soccer player, he has," Gregg Berhalter said. This is all the more remarkable for the fact that Weston didn't watch sports very often growing up—he still doesn't watch soccer today. As an adult, he devoured the Harry Potter books and movies, inspiring his signature magic wand goal celebration, and would rather spend time in this fantasy world than engage with his very real profession. He rarely saw the U.S. men's national team play until he was *on* the U.S. men's national team. His ignorance of the team's fraught history may be an asset—baggage you don't know your team has cannot burden you.

For many of the crucial teenage years, when the ceiling of soccer players is typically ascertained, McKennie was an afterthought. Too small. Christian Pulisic and Tyler Adams, among the standout talents of their generation, were practically guaranteed a future on the senior national team from the time they put on a junior national team jersey. McKennie, meanwhile, clung on for dear life to the only plan he had. His dreams were always teetering at the edge of what was truly possible.

You wouldn't know it now. McKennie makes a point of signing autographs for fans—but first he pretends to walk past them, then turns around with a wide smile. He celebrates trophies with childlike abandon. He gets whimsical streaks of bright colors dyed into his hair.

McKennie travels extensively during the off-season, in Portugal one day and Monaco the next, clearing his head, seeing new places, getting his mind off soccer, visiting friends, going to music festivals. He hired a piano teacher in Italy, where he also had a live-in photographer for a spell, to document the high life. He mused about opening a Chick-fil-A, a Wingstop, and a Chili's in Italy, evidently dissatisfied with the local food offerings. He made his agent bring ranch dressing when he came to visit in Turin. McKennie lightly insulted his Juve teammates by showing up to practice in some old shorts and sandals—not done in Italy, where soccer players are expected to dress in the finest fashion anytime they report for team duty. He visibly upset those same teammates in a viral clip from an Amazon docuseries by recommending they put ranch on their pizza. Then he proclaimed that he didn't drink Italian coffee, deepening their distress. "If I drink espresso," McKennie explained, fully aware that a camera was rolling, "I shit myself."

Sometimes, his commitment to doing and saying whatever pops into his head lands him on the wrong side of the rules. During the height of the COVID-19 pandemic, McKennie was twice suspended from his teams, once by Juventus and once by the national team, for egregiously violating isolation rules. Just as soon as he returned to the national team following a two-game suspension—a self-inflicted wound for a side that badly missed him in his absence—he set up a pool tournament for his teammates in the hotel, taking a good amount of their per diem money. Somehow, he stayed popular in the locker room.

Nobody seems to stay mad at McKennie for very long. He's too lovable. Besides, he delivers when it counts. "He's one of the best competitors you'll find," Adams said. "He won't let you down. There's never a bad performance."

In that combination of attributes—the joy and the play—even McKennie himself might lose sight of what he offers the team. "Wes believes that the energy he brings is most valuable to the team—this approachable, easygoing, fun-loving guy that binds people together," Gregg Berhalter said. "And there's definitely that side of it. But, in my opinion, the most valuable attribute he brings to the team is intensity and focus. When he turns that on, we're *really* difficult to beat. When he's going all the way to the edge but never going over it. He's right there and guys are behind him and you can feel it."

McKennie's peripatetic childhood made him adaptable in his soccer career, settling in quickly whenever he moved clubs, adjusting to tricky situations. "My background, coming from a military family, plays a lot in my personality," he explained. "Everywhere we moved, I had to make new friends, adapt to new cultures, new situations, and new environments. So moving around to different countries starting at a young age definitely benefits my situation now."

Before every game, Tina and Weston text. She gives him pointers on his game, even after he played splendidly at the 2022 World Cup in Qatar. Challenges him. Cajoles him. And then she'll watch him play on a monitor while she's at work at the Veterans Administration in Florida. From afar, she watches Weston live his plan A.

PART VII

A Golden Generation, Maybe

2022–2024

21 | Rehearsal

In Doha, the capital of Qatar, a dog park isn't merely a square of battered grass surrounded by a fence, but an elaborate dog obstacle course, like the kind you see on TV competitions. As if every pooch in Doha, of which there seem to be virtually none in late 2022, is some kind of world-class canine athlete. A narrow park between major thoroughfares contains not just a pond but also a sort of oasis with water features and swan boats and a pedestrian bridge but no pedestrians. A public pool is framed by tall towers of spiraling waterslides but contains no swimmers. On a playground, all the play structures are also miniature versions of the city's landmarks. The many stretches of grass are impossibly green, in spite of the prohibitive climate. And then you look up, where all manner of tall and jagged buildings poke into the cloudless sky from various angles. The architecture of the place is stunning yet also entirely incoherent, as if someone leafed through a catalog of Western skyscrapers and ordered one of everything.

Until the 1960s, Doha was a middling harbor town that subsisted on pearl diving. The oil and gas sucked from beneath the Persian Gulf transformed it into a dreamscape, rapidly grafted onto the arid sand. A strange place to stage the 2022 World Cup and for the United States men's national team to conduct a kind of general rehearsal for its home tournament in 2026. Qatar, which had very little soccer culture, was so unlikely a host that even FIFA, an organization that sequesters itself in a magical reality of imperviousness, had its doubts. Its own inspection report pointed out that the Qatari summer was too hot for high-level soccer and the nation too little to host the planet's biggest mega-event.

Still, FIFA swooned in the face of Qatar's dazzling bid book, the master plan for which had been drawn up in part by Albert Speer Jr.—the son of Adolf Hitler's favorite Third Reich architect, trading on the same name. FIFA's executive committee handed the tournament to Qatar over the USA in a 14–8 final round vote in 2010, a process shot through with corruption. Within five years, eleven of the twenty-two voters were suspended, banned, fined, under investigation, or indicted over their role in the decision, while another five had retired, died, or lost their seat in the face of allegations. That's not counting the two executive committee members who had already been suspended ahead of the vote when they were caught seeking bribes. Disgraced former FIFA president Sepp Blatter, who oversaw the vote, conceded that Qatar had been "a mistake," as if that might redeem him somehow.

Still, FIFA never seriously entertained the possibility of moving the World Cup to another host country. Never mind Qatar's appalling record on human rights, LGBTQ+ rights, and women's rights, and its woeful treatment of more than two million migrant laborers who served the country's three hundred thousand citizens. By *The Guardian*'s estimate, some 6,500 migrant workers from India, Pakistan, Nepal, Bangladesh, and Sri Lanka died while working to remake Doha for a four-week event—a sparkling city that doubled as a massive tomb.

Despite twelve years of preparation and the $220 billion price tag—more than three decades' worth of World Cups and Olympic Games put together—an inexplicable number of logistical issues hadn't been figured out when the tournament started, like concessions at the opening game. Doha was a city remade but also one still very much under construction. Just off main thoroughfares, sidewalks and pavement were missing. Migrant workers had been moved out of view, sent home or awaiting work in miserable, faraway camps. But they were also everywhere, building things and serving people, cleaning places that needed no cleaning. Three men to a job, all of them eager to do something useful, to be retained, but mostly just standing around. At a concession stand in the stadiums, half a dozen cashiers might implore you to entrust your order with them, all waving frantically to beckon you to their empty lanes. The police were bored, too, many thousands of them, far outnumbering their usefulness. So they peered into the middle distance or approached their tedious work with too much gusto, checking for the banned rainbow motifs on fans or telling reporters that they had to unwrap their energy bars because of branding conflicts.

It was a dry World Cup, save for FIFA's stadium luxury boxes and a few licensed hotel bars where imported beer and wine sold for eye-watering prices. A Potemkin World Cup: one that looked and sounded like a World Cup but somehow didn't feel like one. Too much artifice. Free face-painting stations. A booth offering "complimentary team flags" and a "banner evaluation area"—checking for rogue rainbows, lest anyone be reminded of the natural fact of homosexuality—just beyond the marble VVIP entrance with an actual red carpet. Not enough fans, who could only be found in large numbers around the tourist traps—the Corniche and the Souq Waqif—even though the tournament was compressed into a single city. An empty Fan Fest, surrounded by forlorn food trucks. Fan villages built out of shipping containers or desert tents that had intermittent running water. Folklore that came not from fans singing and dancing and drumming, but from hired performers in colorful, neutral outfits, put there by the organizers. An Elvis impersonator, among other musical non sequiturs mixed in with the Arab and Asian music troupes and dancers to bring a local flavor to the first Arab World Cup. And an app that you could not refuse, doubling as your Qatari entrance visa and tracking your every movement. An oppressively monitored and clumsily staged World Cup.

An antiseptic World Cup, maintained by an army of street sweepers—enough of them to lay siege to a major metropolis. One of them worked on the median of a nondescript road at 1 a.m., pushing the bristles of his broom against nothing at all. At 2 a.m., a lawn crew cut the grass outside the colossal Qatar National Convention Centre, toiling in the dark.

The U.S. team had lived up to expectations. Christian Pulisic and Weston McKennie and Tyler Adams and all the rest performed. The Americans had beaten Iran and made it out of the group stage of the 2022 World Cup, doing about as well as they could have reasonably been expected to. What else could they achieve? How high could this team climb?

In seven elimination games at the World Cup going back almost a century, the U.S. prevailed in only one knockout-stage game, against Mexico in 2002. Winning another one: That would be the barrier to break through in 2022. The brutal arithmetic of the World Cup commands that once the tournament moves beyond the group stage, every match is winner takes all. Lose and your tournament is over just as soon as the final whistle chirps through the stadium. Now the U.S. had to play the Netherlands, a three-time World Cup finalist. Such were the breaks of the World Cup: If the Americans had hung on for the win against Wales, or found a breakthrough goal against England, they would have played a much weaker Senegal rather than the Netherlands. Instead, they faced about as tall a task as the Americans might have imagined. Yet they were determined not to be daunted by the Barcelona and Liverpool and Inter Milan stars on the Dutch team. Or by Louis van Gaal, the manager who had been reshaping the sport since the 1990s and hadn't lost in sixteen months since taking over the Dutch national team.

Van Gaal was effusive about Gregg Berhalter and the United States. "The USA has demonstrated that it has an excellent team," he said before the game. "I would even say one of the best teams. I think that they are an example of what a good team is supposed to be."

Each night before the Americans played a game in Qatar, Gregg Berhalter conducted the same exercise. He asked a single question, and the players would take turns answering it. Before facing Wales, Berhalter wanted to know what playing at the World Cup meant to them. On the night of Thanksgiving, the eve of the England game, they all shared what they were thankful for. The night before the Holland game, goalkeeper Matt Turner took his turn to explain why he wanted to beat the Netherlands. But he didn't speak about himself. He spoke about Sergiño Dest, who had broken into the national team around the same time as Turner. Dest, who was born and raised in the Netherlands, had a hard time picking between the Dutch and the American national teams. "It would mean more than anything to me if we could win this game for Serg," Turner spoke that night. "Because I know how much he struggled with that decision and I'm so happy he's here and I want to win it for him."

Berhalter took it as confirmation that the team's cohesion, the brotherhood it liked to speak of, was also its biggest strength. "We had moments like that, where you're so thankful for these guys that they're sharing," he said, marveling at the emotional vulnerability of the generation in his charge. "The beauty of working with twenty-something-year-olds is they'll say shit like that. My generation, we wouldn't answer a question like that."

Just two minutes after kickoff, Tyler Adams won the ball high up the field and dinked it over the Dutch defense. It fell right before the feet of Christian Pulisic, who connected with the ball squarely but didn't give it enough direction. Dutch goalkeeper Andries Noppert made a routine kick save. It would turn out to be the game's if-only moment.

The Dutch sat back. Oranje defended comfortably, letting the Americans tire themselves out with largely pointless possession. The Yanks weren't precise enough to find a path through the forest of orange jerseys, and whenever they lost the ball, the Dutch scampered away with it. The Netherlands scored twice before halftime by capitalizing on mistakes. At last, in the seventy-sixth minute, U.S. striker Haji Wright shanked a low ball from Pulisic only for it to arc strangely into the Dutch net. The Americans were back in it. Then, the U.S. left yet another opponent alone. Another Dutch goal. 3–1. Game over. World Cup over.

The U.S. was not obviously outplayed, outclassed, or outpunched; it was punished for its errors. Two of the major expected-goals models, which quantify the quality of scoring chances but differ somewhat, gave the Dutch a mere 0.2 advantage, which suggested that the game's chances had been virtually even. Another actually awarded the U.S. a tiny 0.04 lead in expected goals. What's more, the Americans had almost 60 percent ball possession and outshot the Dutch 17–11, forcing twice as many fouls. "They go like crazy, like hell," Noppert said of the Americans after the game. "They're working together. They don't give up."

In Qatar, U.S. Soccer president Cindy Parlow Cone, who won a Women's World Cup and two Olympic gold medals as a longtime member of the U.S. women's national team, noticed a shift in the men's team. "Going into any match now, our men's national team believes that they can win," she said. "It was kind of the first major tournament that I saw our men's national team have this true belief."

But none of that was any consolation now. The Americans showed themselves to be both worthy and naïve, promising and unpolished. They crumpled onto the turf of the Khalifa International Stadium. Tyler Adams covered his face in his jersey. "When you look at that game, I'm not going to sit here and say Holland was better than us," he later said. "We dominated for a majority of the game; we made them uncomfortable. It's probably the first time in a long time where people will say, 'Wow, this U.S. team has something special.' There were so many ups and downs in the past three years and then when you put four performances like that out on the field, it really gives people something to be excited about."

Berhalter exchanged hugs with his players. He consoled a tearful Tim Weah. Pulisic stared blankly as his teammates came and went, trying to commiserate with him. They were slow to leave the field. Because once they stepped off, it really was over. A few players sat on the bench, their heads buried in their hands.

Long after the game, DeAndre Yedlin, a Buddhist, stood in the field's center circle barefoot with three teammates. Their hands were folded in prayer, their eyes closed, chins lowered, silently meditating. A while later, Yedlin wheeled his massive, suitcase-size speaker—through which he and Weah had carried out their work as team DJs—out of the stadium for the last time, pushing it past Weston McKennie.

"We have four years now to focus—I can't wait," McKennie said on his way to the team bus. "This tournament has really restored a lot of belief and respect to U.S. soccer. We've shown that we can beat giants eventually. We may not be there yet, but we're definitely on our way."

In soccer, four years is an awfully long time. A lot can happen, as the U.S. would find out soon enough.

22 | The Reyna Brouhaha

Gregg Berhalter was twelve years old when he first started playing soccer with Claudio Reyna. They became best friends. When Claudio's father, a former professional in Argentina and their club team coach, steered Claudio to the more competitive high school soccer team at Saint Benedict's Prep in Newark, Gregg enrolled as well. The Catholic school was big on leadership and community-building through weeklong hikes and the like.

Bruce Arena recruited Claudio to the University of Virginia and pursued Gregg, too, although only as a walk-on without a scholarship. Berhalter was a good player but a physical late bloomer who didn't grow his first chest hair until he was twenty-two. The University of North Carolina didn't offer him a scholarship, either—although it would after his freshman year—but Gregg decided to commit there anyway. "I needed to go somewhere else," Berhalter said. "Three years with Claudio in high school was great, but I felt like the sidekick."

Gregg and Claudio stayed close and reunited in national team camps, both breaking into the senior team in 1994 and growing into mainstays. On his first day at UNC, Gregg met Rosalind Santana, a soccer player herself. They soon started dating. Rosalind's roommate and teammate, Danielle Egan, became her best friend. Danielle met

Claudio when she reached the women's national team—locked out of her room in the hotel the two national teams shared, she wandered into the men's dining room and Claudio offered her a slice of his pizza. They started a relationship as well. They were now a pair of couples made up of best friends, which only drew them closer. Claudio and Gregg were in each other's weddings. The women spoke daily for three decades. Before long, they simply became the Reynas and the Berhalters. Each couple had four children. A new generation grew up together.

The second of the Reyna children, Giovanni, was precocious and possessed the same talent that made his father one of the best American midfielders ever.

The Reynas' firstborn child, Jack, who was three years older than Gio, died of cancer at thirteen, devastating the family and making it more protective of Gio. Claudio, the former captain of the national team and a technical director for U.S. Soccer and two MLS teams, wielded his clout with emails and calls, advocating for favorable treatment for his son. As Gio rose through the youth game, flashing his ample gifts, Claudio frequently complained to U.S. Soccer about Gio's youth national team coaches or the referees assigned to his games. In one 2018 email to a federation official, Claudio lamented that one of Gio's games was refereed by a woman. "Can we get real and have male refs for a game like this," he wrote in a typo-strewn missive. "Its [sic] embarrassing guys. What are we trying to prove? A game like this deserves bettr [sic] attention."

Gio followed in Christian Pulisic's footsteps and left the United States for the Borussia Dortmund academy at sixteen. He made his senior U.S. national team debut in November 2020, the day before he turned eighteen. Berhalter, by then the national team head coach, likened it to "putting a family member in the game." (Berhalter's son Sebastian, meanwhile, played for Austin FC, where Claudio Reyna was the technical director.) Although Gio was injured a lot, it didn't take long for him to establish himself as perhaps the most technically gifted player on the new national team—which, by extension, probably made him the most promising American soccer player ever. He once dribbled through seven Mexican opponents on a single play, the sort of thing he did almost as a matter of routine but that nobody else had ever managed in an American jersey before.

A week before the U.S. kicked off the 2022 World Cup, Gio Reyna turned twenty. He was not 100 percent fit, owing to yet another injury, but he expected to play a lot regardless, even though Berhalter had settled on a starting eleven that left Reyna on the bench. Before the opening match against Wales, the head coach told Reyna that he would play a limited role that day—albeit not for the entire tournament, as Reyna would later claim. During a scrimmage against a Qatari club team before the World Cup, Gio grew petulant and demonstratively ambled about. Berhalter talked to Reyna about his unprofessional performance, but Gio's lack of effort continued in practice. Berhalter didn't play Reyna at all against Wales. After the game, Claudio texted U.S. Soccer sporting director Earnie Stewart, his old teammate. "What a complete and utter fucking joke," Claudio wrote. "Our family is disgusted in case you are wondering. Disgusted at how a coach is allowed to never be challenged and do whatever he wants." He sent a similar text to men's national team general manager Brian McBride, who had also been a longtime teammate, calling the federation a "political clown show." When the Reynas and Berhalters, traveling with the team as part of the federation's arrangements for families and friends, were assigned to the same bus, Danielle refused to board it. At a luncheon the following day, she uttered a vague threat to a federation staffer with no involvement on the soccer side, referring to Gregg Berhalter's habit of sporting Air Jordans along the sideline and feeding his players balls with behind-the-back basketball passes. "Once this tournament is over, I can make one phone call and give one interview, and his cool sneakers and bounce passes will be gone," Danielle Reyna reportedly said.

Things came to a head on Thanksgiving 2022, the day before the U.S. would play England. Gio Reyna's behavior had not improved. Fearing that he might poison team chemistry, the coaching staff and federation officials discussed whether to send Reyna home, understanding that such a move would become the dominant narrative of their World Cup campaign—not even in 1998 had a player been sent home. Still, they were prepared to do it. With Reyna's World Cup hanging by a thread, the national team brain trust decided to give Gio one last chance to apologize to the team and correct his lack of effort. Reyna did both and got to stay.

Around the same time, McBride and Stewart met with Claudio and Danielle Reyna. "You guys don't even know what we know about Gregg," Claudio said.

In the midst of the Reyna family drama, Berhalter had to guide a young team through the mayhem of a World Cup, forcing him to observe one of his own edicts on the importance of responding to adversity. "When this stuff happened, I was thinking to myself, 'I talk to my players all the time about this. Now it's time for me to live this,'" Berhalter later said.

Gio played eight minutes against England, getting all of four touches on the ball. He didn't appear at all in the third group-stage game against Iran and played a forgettable second half of the round of 16 elimination at the hands of the Dutch.

On his return from the World Cup, Gregg Berhalter stopped over in New York City on December 6 to attend the HOW Institute for Society's Summit on Moral Leadership—where "diverse leaders from varied fields" would gather "to stimulate and inspire fresh thinking and concerted actions to help answer the most vital questions we face as a society." Berhalter spent the day listening to talks by the likes of the Walmart CEO, the vice president of the Philippines, and administrators from several prominent universities. He was onstage himself for a Q&A late in the day. At the end of a twenty-two-minute session, Berhalter answered a single question from the audience of a hundred-odd people, on challenges to his moral leadership. "In this last World Cup, we had a player that was clearly not meeting expectations on and off the field," said Berhalter. "One of twenty-six players, so it stood out. As a staff, we sat together for hours deliberating what we were going to do with this player. We were ready to book a plane ticket home, that's how extreme it was." Berhalter spoke of how the unnamed player made amends with his teammates and how the entire thing was a shining example of the team living its values.

The rules of the conference were clear. Anything said in the room could only be shared publicly if the speaker's identity was anonymized. A miscommunication with a publicist, however, somehow landed a transcript of the Berhalter conversation in a newsletter five days later, with his name on it. *The Athletic*, which had been piecing together the story on its own, reported just hours after the quotes leaked accidentally that the player in question was Gio Reyna. That same night, an irate Claudio and Danielle Reyna called Earnie Stewart to complain about Berhalter's indiscretion. At the end of an hour-long call, Danielle told Stewart that Berhalter had assaulted Rosalind in 1992, when they were freshmen in college. "'Gregg beat the living shit out of her in a back alleyway,'" Stewart recalled Danielle telling him. Then she said that the Reynas didn't plan to make this public, but that they were considering telling other people about it. Stewart came away with the distinct impression that they were setting in motion a plan to ensure that Berhalter's contract as national team head coach would not be renewed. Still, Stewart felt compelled to report the allegation to the federation's legal counsel. After all, the federation had just been leveled by an avalanche of bad PR over an equal pay fight with its women's national team—a fight that forced President Carlos Cordeiro to resign—and accusations that it hadn't done enough to stop abusive coaches in the National Women's Soccer League it bankrolled.

U.S. Soccer commissioned an investigation from a law firm. Until it concluded, the federation would delay talks about renewing Berhalter's contract, which expired on December 31, 2022, just twenty-eight days after the Americans' World Cup run ended. To that point, Berhalter had been favored to keep his job with the federation, having impressed Stewart and McBride.

The day after the investigation was triggered, Gio chimed in himself, posting a message on Instagram that acknowledged his lack of effort while calling out Berhalter for speaking out of turn. On January 3, 2023, the newly unemployed Berhalter put out a public statement as well. "In the fall of 1991, I met my soulmate," wrote Berhalter, before confessing in detail that he had kicked Rosalind when he was eighteen. "There are zero excuses for my actions that night; it was a shameful moment and one that I regret to this day. . . . The lessons learned from that night over three decades ago became the foundation for a loving, devoted, and supportive relationship, which we honored and celebrated with our twenty-fifth wedding anniversary this past weekend."

The next day, it was Danielle Reyna's turn to publish a statement, explaining why she had made the allegation to Stewart. "I was absolutely outraged and devastated that Gio had been put in such a terrible position, and that I felt very personally betrayed by the actions of someone my family had considered a friend for decades," she wrote. "I told Earnie that I thought it was especially unfair that Gio, who had apologized for acting immaturely about his playing time, was still being dragged through the mud when Gregg had asked for and received forgiveness for doing something so much worse at the same age."

The law firm's report filled in the details. In January 1992, Gregg and Rosalind got into an argument in a nightclub in Chapel Hill, North Carolina, apparently sparked by Berhalter's jealousy. They were both drunk and yelled at one another as they left the club. Outside, Rosalind pushed Berhalter and scratched his face. Berhalter pushed her to the ground and kicked her twice in her upper leg before a passerby tackled him to the ground and ended the altercation. Rosalind required no medical attention and pressed no charges. They both reported the incident to their respective soccer coaches, who took no further action. The next day, Berhalter sent Rosalind a note of apology and a mixtape, but she wouldn't talk to him. So he steered clear of her for the rest of the school year. He sought counseling and even assigned himself community service at an adolescent female correctional facility, according to the report. Rosalind called Berhalter in the fall of 1992, and they reconciled. They have been together since.

The investigation turned up "no information to suggest that Mr. Berhalter engaged in another physical assault against Mrs. Berhalter, or anyone else, in the last 31 years" or violated any disclosure rules when he was hired by U.S. Soccer. Investigators, in fact, commended him for being forthcoming and accountable. "We were less impressed with the Reynas' cooperation during the investigation," read the report.

The report concluded that Danielle Reyna's accusation was timed to get Berhalter fired. "We know of nothing that would have prevented Mrs. Reyna from making her report to U.S. Soccer at any time prior to December 11, 2022," the report noted. "When she made this report, she had known about the 1992 Incident for more than thirty years, and Mr. Berhalter had been Head Coach for four years." Indeed, the couples had remained close until the 2022 World Cup.

In the end, the whole episode, which made global headlines and tempted even the usually demure BBC into devoting a four-minute segment to it, was tawdry, embarrassing, and mutually destructive. "Really, the biggest pain for me was for my family," Berhalter said.

"That's where it really hurt." Upon the report's release, Claudio Reyna resigned from his position as sporting director of Austin FC.

"There's always going to be situations where parents or club head coaches are upset with the national team head coach," USMNT general manager Brian McBride said. "Those things happen all the time. It normally never comes out. I think Gregg got a little comfortable when he was told that everything was going to be off the record. When it all got out in the press, that's when it started getting ugly."

By the time the investigation concluded in mid-March, clearing the way for Berhalter to return, Earnie Stewart had taken a job with PSV Eindhoven in the Netherlands to be closer to his family and Brian McBride had left the federation as well. Much like in 2018, a new technical director would have to be hired before appointing the next head coach.

Matt Crocker joined the federation from Southampton of the Premier League in mid-April. Crocker rehired Berhalter, with whom he had no prior relationship, in mid-June 2023, after an exhaustive, analytics-driven interview process in which the returning head coach outperformed the other finalists. The rehiring didn't sit well with everyone. Was there really not another person suited to the job, perhaps one with less baggage?

23 | The Reset

Eleven fit and well-groomed men sat around a long table in the meeting room of a swanky hotel. They each wore the same bright-red polo shirt under a gray zip-up hoodie, both emblazoned with the U.S. Soccer crest. The table was littered with laptops, water bottles, and espresso cups, and all around them stood whiteboards scribbled with schedules, tactical formations, meeting agendas, principles, objectives. Gregg Berhalter and his staff of nine coaches and data analysts had assembled to analyze the video footage from the morning's practice session. The eleventh man was Jason Lee, the team's leadership coach, a middle-aged Englishman whose job was effectively to coach the other coaches on coaching. This was the second of the three meetings the coaches would hold on a Friday in the middle of the men's national team's annual January camp in 2024.

It was 4 p.m. when the meeting started, the shadows growing longer in the afternoon sun while the wind whipped up the palm trees outside the second-floor windows, the outer bands of a storm approaching Orlando. To this point in the day, the players, coaches, and staffers had adhered closely to a detailed schedule. But there was no clock on this meeting. They had all night if they needed it.

Twenty-five players started this two-week camp and essentially constituted a national B team. With only a few exceptions, they sat somewhere toward the bottom of the depth chart in their positions. These were marginal national team prospects. Historically, the point of the January camp was to give the domestically based national team players some extra practice during the long Major League Soccer off-season, while their colleagues playing overseas slogged through the middle months of their club campaigns. It was a casual affair back then, dubbed "Camp Cupcake" by the players. Every now and again, a player will use the January camp to vault into the A team, but that's rare. Just one player in camp had been on the twenty-six-man roster at the 2022 World Cup fourteen months earlier. If even two or three here in Orlando made it onto the 2026 World Cup team, this endeavor would be a great success. A series of glorified off-season workouts for long-shot talent is what this really was. In the context of the national team, the stakes couldn't have been lower.

But Berhalter wanted every camp to be run at the same speed: all out. No matter who the opponent was, or which players were available, every squad would be treated like the A team. The men's national team would travel with all thirty-two full-time staffers, toting around all 250 trunks of gear and setting up their recovery lab, equipment room, coaches' room, and communications room, taking over much of the hotel at which it stayed.

So here they were, the coaches and the analysts, poring over every little detail, frame by frame, from a practice session they had just run. To an outsider—even one with a lifelong love for soccer—the repetitiveness of the video analysis over a few hours was crushingly boring. But Berhalter had a terrific time. He loved this stuff.

That morning, the coaches assembled in a small theater at Orlando City Soccer Club's practice facility to go over the video they had picked out to show the players. When the team, mostly players in their early twenties, walked in, the coaches snapped to attention. The players filed by the coaches and gave them each a fist bump or a hand clasp, even though the entire group had had breakfast together not that long ago. The greetings were mandatory, after all.

The subject of the day's video session was the team's pressing scheme. Berhalter and his staff wanted the players to charge at their opponents as a unit in an effort to win the ball or, at a minimum, disrupt the other team's buildup play. Berhalter paced the front of the room in shorts and a tight, red quarter-zip, same as all the other staffers, pointing out mistakes documented in three quick video sequences but cloaking them in a series of compliments on all the things the players had done well. He called on most of them to analyze the footage, smiling as he asked questions. They answered like young men everywhere when called on by a teacher: apprehensively, lacking authority, with answers that sounded like questions. Berhalter gave encouraging responses, even when the answers were very wrong. Then assistant B. J. Callaghan took over and broke the team into small groups, where they discussed defensive principles before reporting back. The energy and dynamic felt a lot like that of a college class. Which passes from the opponent trigger the USA's press? Who springs the trap? To which opponent does every player move? Who rotates where on the second pass? How do they shift when the opponent manages to move the ball through their press? In slow-motion replay, it all looks a bit like a high society dance in eighteenth-century England, with partners shuffling through an intricate pattern, joining and twirling and separating again.

Next, the team practiced in what used to be the Houston Astros' spring training facility, now converted into a soccer field—a metaphor for the trajectory of the two sports, maybe. High overhead, a giant eagle's nest sat perched on a light stanchion. A bald eagle atop another stanchion presided over practice, sometimes peering over, unimpressed, at the drone a coach had sent up to record the action.

On the field, every line and cone and dummy and ball had been placed in exact accordance with a document sent around that morning that contained a detailed rundown of practice: staff assignments, drills, objectives, tactical shapes, player groupings, and so on. The coaches warmed up separately with a game of pig in the middle. Berhalter showed off, doing tricks. As the players laced up, the head coach hyped everyone up. But they all knew what he expected from them: total intensity from the players for the length of a short, well-orchestrated session. Attention from the staffers, too—no phones, face the field. No sunglasses. No ankle socks. Anybody whose feet touched the grass had to be in soccer cleats, even the videographers. It rained in swirls of warm droplets, but nobody broke stride as the silent, stone-faced players moved through the drills, running like hell for a few minutes until a shrill whistle released them for some rest.

Now, around the long table, there was no escaping it: Berhalter and his staff were having a meeting about a meeting, discussing how the morning's video session with the players had gone. Berhalter fretted that, at half an hour, the session ran too long, stretching the attention spans of the young men.

The coaches then analyzed the practice session drill by drill, with each coach assessing the exercise he had been responsible for. Berhalter challenged them constantly. Were the turnaround points for a running drill in their optimal position? Did the coaches demand too much deceleration of the players, increasing the risk of injury? Was the spacing of the playing area ideal, creating enough congestion while still leaving open passing lanes? Of a ball exercise in which players quickly clipped the ball around in a complicated pattern and then moved on to the next station, Berhalter wanted to know whether the passing asked of them was "psychologically safe." Was the drill too hard, in other words, and did it present a danger of demoralizing the players? His staff had to show Berhalter their work, to explain their thinking—because it all must reflect deep thought. Did they think they stopped practice too often to instruct and correct? Or not enough? Should they acquire a pricey portable big screen that could be wheeled out onto the field to give the players feedback in real time? They decided against it—too disruptive. A debate broke out on the ideal dimensions for the pressing drill, the main event of practice

Satisfied that the format of practice had been well covered, they moved on to watching the actual practice footage. On a big screen at the end of the room, the coaches played, paused, discussed, rewound, replayed, discussed, rewound again, discussed some more, and on and on, for each sequence. Each touch and every step were noted and considered. "That's interesting," Berhalter said every now and again. Sometimes, the coaches disagreed and debated, bringing in a whiteboard with the outline of a soccer field and magnets representing players, just to make their points.

They looked for patterns and behaviors. On the screen, Duncan McGuire, a young striker for Orlando's MLS team, struggled to execute the press, amusing the coaches at first. He looked lost, drifting far from his tight banks of teammates—a tendency made all the more obvious by the drone's bird's-eye angle. There was no hiding in the film session. The coaches grew exasperated by him. The lab rat was not moving through the maze as he was supposed to.

"I have a crazy idea," Berhalter announced at one point, his signature Air Jordans resting on the meeting table. "Anybody see AZ as a fullback?" AZ was Aziel Jackson, a twenty-two-year-old midfielder for St. Louis City, who had impressed the room with his ball recoveries.

They wouldn't need all night after all. Picking through every last frame of the hour-ish practice session would take them three hours, although they planned to show footage to the players after dinner. But there was always the next day, when they would scrimmage Argentinian powerhouse River Plate, producing more footage to pick through. And every day of camp after that, each presenting more chances to talk for hours and hours about tactics and process and performance.

Less than six months later, Berhalter and his staff would be gone.

When Gregg Berhalter was invited to interview for his old job, he was on the brink of accepting a job as manager of Club América, the juggernauts of the Mexican league. But he craved closure on his time managing the U.S., and he saw more untapped potential. In the middle of his six-month absence from the team, he traveled to England to study the work of some other coaches and catch up with the seven national team regulars then active in the Premier League. The bond with his players had survived the scandal. So had the culture he built. While Berhalter was gone, two of his assistants ran the team—Anthony Hudson and then, when the Englishman departed for a job in Qatar, B. J. Callaghan. Virtually nothing changed and the team continued to win. The A team thumped Mexico 3–0 and then claimed its second straight CONCACAF Nations League title. The U.S. 2023 CONCACAF Gold Cup, however, yielded a disappointing semifinal exit to Panama on penalty kicks, albeit with the B team.

When the Reyna incident first surfaced, Berhalter sent a note to each player on his World Cup roster to express his regret. Once reinstalled, the coach, in typical Berhalter fashion, consulted an expert in mediation before mending his relationship with Gio, and the affair was put to bed in Reyna's first camp back under Berhalter.

At last, they could turn their attention to 2026. Berhalter was acutely aware of the fact that all three of his predecessors on the national team had markedly worse second World Cup cycles than their first go-rounds. Only Arena even made it to his second World Cup, where his team went winless. Bob Bradley lasted only a year into his second cycle, and Jürgen Klinsmann barely made it halfway.

Playing on home soil at the 2024 Copa América, the Americans were supposed to build on their 2022 World Cup run. Take another step. Build momentum. Win a knockout-stage game if at all possible, and break through that vexing barrier. But there were issues from the outset. A host of USMNT regulars had fallen out of favor with their club teams and had barely played in the last months of the season. Berhalter would later volunteer that he had become too reliant on a regular starting lineup and therefore couldn't turn to alternatives with more minutes in their legs. Meanwhile, the staggered arrival of the American players to their training camp meant that the full team had just two days in June to practice as a group before their first warm-up game against Colombia—an ominous 5–1 loss. A 1–1 tie with Brazil four days later soothed only some of the concerns.

The Americans dispatched a tame Bolivia 2–0 in their tournament opener, although not convincingly. The campaign fell apart in the second game against Panama. The otherwise even-keeled Tim Weah lashed out at an opponent with a punch in the eighteenth minute and was sent off. His now-outnumbered teammates took the lead but couldn't hold it in a 2–1 loss. A 1–0 stumble to Uruguay in a game remembered most for some comically bad refereeing sealed the Americans' group-stage elimination-cum-humiliation.

"This Copa América I just got completely wrong," Berhalter later said. "From the preparation period to the execution in tournament.

We had higher aspirations, and we didn't reach our goals in that tournament and that's disappointing. This is a group that always reached our checkpoints; we never really fell short of what we had to do. A number of different factors were the reason why, but in the end we didn't play well enough. And we paid the price."

In breaking down his own failures, Berhalter diagnosed his fixation on the collective. "I was so focused on the team that I forgot to keep challenging the individuals," he said. "There was a lot of focus on what we could do together, but there were certain guys that needed some jarring and some pushing. And I don't think I did that well enough in Copa América."

In the middle of the tournament, Berhalter's six-player leadership council approached him with a concern. They wanted him to demand more of them, to be more critical, to yell at them more. "Guys, there's six of you right here and you're telling me you're not happy with the standards," Berhalter responded. "I believe you can do something about it."

For half a decade, the head coach had nurtured a young team with a loose hand in hopes that it would eventually come to run itself, that its closeness and culture would generate its own momentum. "There really was this player-ownership model that I wanted to implement, where the players are the coaches and coaching each other and very critical of each other," Berhalter said. "That was the final step that they just weren't ready for. That was an issue. They just wanted more direction."

In the wake of Copa América, the mood shifted. Suddenly, the prevailing question was whether the team had stagnated or, worse, was simply overrated. Had a golden generation been willed into existence, gussied up with a coat of high-gloss paint masking a very ordinary batch of soccer players? Had they only made it to Europe at such early ages because the bias against Americans was slowly eroding? And did all those opportunities leave them coddled, shorn of the hunger that had powered their predecessors?

All the old existential questions were posed again. That pesky inferiority complex rushed back from whatever nook it had been stashed for the last few years. Now the team's brotherly culture was blamed for a perceived indiscipline.

When coaches are under fire, you tend to see the same thing play out: The methods once credited for success are recast as liabilities. The USMNT was supposedly thriving exactly because of its closeness and doggedness just months earlier. Now it stood accused of being sloppy and indifferent. Berhalter was unpopular with a subset of the fans from the moment of his appointment. He tried to do too much, or not enough. He tinkered too much, or not enough. He was too rigid. Or he gave his players too much freedom. While he retained broad support within the federation, the clamor grew too loud to ignore after the calamity at Copa América. All the metrics that had made him the strongest candidate to coach the team when he was rehired didn't count anymore.

"When we rehired Gregg, we were really clear that there were some milestones along the way and some key tournaments that we needed to see some progress in," said Matt Crocker. "We had to acknowledge that the Copa América results weren't as we anticipated and had all hoped for. We're judged on results. The wins are really important. And we didn't get enough wins."

After Copa América, Berhalter and his family went to his parents' house on Long Island, where the entire extended family gathered. Nine days after the loss to Uruguay, Berhalter went to a private room to take a phone call from Crocker, who fired him. The conversation only took a minute or so. "I came out and said, 'Hey, I just got fired. On to the next chapter,'" Berhalter recalled. It was around 10 a.m., too early for a drink.

"At the end of the day, as a coach at the international level, you've got to win," U.S. Soccer president Cindy Parlow Cone said later. "As harsh as that sounds, it's the way it is. And while I think we owe a lot to Gregg and all that he has done for our men's national team throughout the years, both as a player and as a coach, we felt as a federation that it was time to go in another direction."

If the point of the United States cohosting the 2026 World Cup with Mexico and Canada is to move the sport forward by generating that hard-won, needle-moving excitement, you can't contest it with a team enveloped in negativity, whether or not that negativity is justified. Berhalter expected to be given a chance to make amends for a failed summer. He still retained the highest winning percentage of any head coach in USMNT history. The long-term strategy was geared toward 2026, not 2024. But he understood that the backlash over the bad results made him vulnerable. "I think there was outside momentum that made it very difficult for U.S. Soccer," he said. "I'm not questioning U.S. Soccer's decision at all. They had to do what they had to do, and I blame myself for not performing in the Copa América. Sometimes when there is this negativity, you want something new, something fresh."

Berhalter retained his faith that his now-former players were special. That it was no coincidence that they started for Milan and Juventus, in the Premier League and in the Bundesliga. That they were Champions League regulars. And all the other accomplishments their national team predecessors merely aspired to. "It's a generation like we've never seen before," he said. "I still believe that. I really do. You have setbacks as a program. It's really about how you respond to those setbacks."

The program was moving on without him, rebooting in the middle of the most consequential World Cup cycle in its history.

Epilogue

The origins of Mauricio Pochettino's soccer career sound fantastical, but they are confirmed facts.

He was born in a speck of a town called Murphy in a rural part of Argentina. His father, Hector, was a farmer who worked his 250-odd acres of land by himself, yielding enough to feed the Pochettinos and a tad more to sell. Their farmhouse had no indoor plumbing, and no heating. If Mauricio wanted to watch something, he had to wait for his father to get off his tractor so that its battery could be wired to the TV.

He did judo and played volleyball—since the latter was what the girls all played—but soccer had an unbreakable hold on him. When he was little, Mauricio hoped for rain, because when his father couldn't work the land, he was free to kick the soccer ball around with his three sons. Pochettino became a take-no-prisoners hardman on the soccer field when he was ten or so, after an opposing goalkeeper pulled his shorts down during a game. "It pissed me off so much," Pochettino later said. "I cried and cried because I felt so powerless on the pitch." It remains the great humiliation of his life. "The most insufferable part was the fact that I didn't have the balls to react." The next time an opponent provoked him, some years later, Pochettino punched him.

As a teenager, Mauricio rose at 6 a.m. to go to an agricultural school. At 5 p.m., he boarded a bus and rode it for three hours to Rosario, the nearest major city, to practice with Rosario Central, a top-tier club. Around the same time, another future household name climbed the ranks. Marcelo Bielsa, a young coach in charge of the reserve team at Rosario's other big club, Newell's Old Boys—whose academy Lionel Messi would pass through several decades later—went out into the countryside looking for talent. Pochettino was tired and decided not to go to the tryout—he already had a team, after all. Bielsa heard about him anyway and set off to find Pochettino's house. He and a fellow coach arrived at 1 a.m. and talked their way inside. Mauricio was asleep, but the coaches asked to see his legs. The Pochettinos obliged and lifted the duvet for the coaches to take a peek. Duly convinced by the boy's size, they petitioned Hector Pochettino to let his son practice with Newell's, Central's archrivals.

The boy woke up heedless of what had happened. He had no interest in defecting to the enemy but was convinced by his grandfather and set off on the three-hour journey to Rosario once again. Bielsa put Pochettino in a scrimmage, and after just five minutes and a few touches of the ball, took him out of the game. Bielsa had seen enough. From then on, Pochettino was a Newell's player. He turned professional at sixteen and made his debut in the frightfully violent Argentinian First Division the next year—as a central defender no less, a particularly physical position. Bielsa, for his part, became the most influential coach of his generation, spawning an army of *bielsistas*.

Pochettino, the pubescent professional, lived in a tiny apartment in Rosario with practically nothing in it but a gas heater that almost asphyxiated him one night and a picture, by his bed, of Diego Maradona lifting the 1986 World Cup: "I always went to sleep with Maradona looking down on me." Then, Maradona signed with Newell's late in his career and roomed with Pochettino the night before games. "I didn't sleep for the first few nights, I just looked at him," Pochettino recalled. He fulfilled his military service in one of the last years it was compulsory in Argentina, going around in uniform when he wasn't playing. The only part of it that bothered him was the youthful trauma of losing his long, jet-black hair to a pair of Argentine army clippers.

When at twenty-two it came time for Pochettino to leave Newell's, he passed over more lucrative offers to sign with Espanyol, Barcelona's second club, because he liked the city. He made the Argentina national team—coached by Bielsa—and played twenty games for his country, including three at the 2002 World Cup, where he surrendered a controversial, game-losing penalty to England. He spent a few years with Paris Saint-Germain and Girondins de Bordeaux—picking them in no small part for their abundant wine-tasting opportunities—before finishing up his playing career back at Espanyol.

Fearing the black hole that swallows up newly retired athletes who go from a highly orchestrated life to a void of free time, Pochettino immediately set to work on a degree in sports management. Meanwhile, he earned his coaching certification as an intern with Espanyol's women's team. Before long, he became the Espanyol men's team's third coach of the 2008–09 season, a campaign that saw Espanyol the team teeter on the brink of relegation to Spain's second tier. In need of a miracle, Pochettino hiked 7.5 miles up the Montserrat mountain to ask for the intervention of La Morenata—the Virgin of Montserrat—at the abbey dedicated to her. In Pochettino's first few games, Espanyol not only tied Messi's mighty FC Barcelona, but beat the cross-town rivals at their own stadium for the first time in twenty-seven years. Espanyol also steered well clear of relegation.

Pochettino managed Southampton next, despite not speaking a word of English and working through a translator. He guided the club to eighth place in the Premier League, equaling its best-ever season. By 2014, he managed perennially underachieving mega-club Tottenham Hotspur. When he was finished with Spurs five and a half years later, he had posted the club's highest-ever points tally in the Premier League, its highest league ranking since 1963, and its first season without losing a game at home in fifty-two years. Also, he had brought Tottenham to the first Champions League final in its history—which didn't protect him from being fired just five months later. Then followed eighteen fraught months at Paris Saint-Germain and a lone, unhappy season with Chelsea.

Like many before him, Pochettino's second career as a coach turned him into a workaholic. He plans practices and games in almost maniacal detail. He demands a lot from his players, too. Like Bielsa's, his practice sessions are famously grueling. His teams tend to skew young and play an exhausting high-pressing system. Yet for all his sophistication as a coach, Pochettino, who consults video breakdowns and analytics and the many specialists working under him, ultimately relies on his gut. He once benched a player for picking lasagna from the clubhouse menu before practice—even though the club had made it available, this was an abhorrent choice to the coach.

Save for the outsize importance he attaches to lunch choices, most of Pochettino's methods—emphasizing fitness, intensity, and positional discipline—are more or less indistinguishable from those of his modern managerial peers, although he is more successful than most of them. Where he stands apart is in his reliance on the occult, leaning on his own spiritual cocktail, which he mixed up along his journey through soccer. Much of what we know of the private Pochettino comes from the 2017 book *Brave New World: Inside Pochettino's Spurs*. The first inkling that this will be a strange tome stems from the foreword, penned by Pochettino's wife, Karina. "He's like the ocean in that he's plentiful and strong," she writes of her husband, "he flattens all that lies before him and he is relentless."

Brave New World is a quasi-autobiography and a sort of diary of Pochettino's 2016–17 season, his most successful year at Tottenham. It is part memoir and part management manual. But it also contains passages of uncommon candor, about Pochettino's pain over drifting apart from his parents and brothers, who cannot fathom his life and can't quite separate their boy from the celebrity; fretting over his ongoing battle with his own waistline; a meditation on ego ("The idea of drifting over to the dark side worries me"); and several love letters to wine. "Whenever I am slightly down, I like to smell Argentinian wine," Pochettino writes. "It makes me happy and takes me back to my country, to recognisable places, to when I was a boy, the redolence of the countryside. . . . If I am challenged to some blind wine tasting, I quickly suss out which one is Argentinian."

The real insight, however, lay in his worldview, in his belief that "lemons absorb negative energy and cleanse the air, which is why I have a tray of them in my office." Mauricio and Karina believe in something they call universal energy, a sort of life force that operates in parallel to their Catholicism.

"We all have the potential to see the energy that surrounds objects and people, although not everyone has honed that sense," Pochettino writes. "For whatever reason, I've been able to develop an ability which allows me to see others' auras. . . . I gradually learnt how to develop that sixth sense.

"I need data and tests, but what most influences my decisions is my ability to see if the right energy is flowing. I can foresee things that are going to happen and the associated consequences, or which path each player is going to take. I can see it in their auras.

"I also believe nothing happens by chance, that there is a reason for everything," Pochettino writes. "Since those early days I've had the ability to notice something powerful that you can't see, but does exist. A vital force, an energy field that makes the world go round, an aura that accompanies people, which gives lots of information about them. . . . It helps me break down day-to-day life, comprehend things, even possibly my own past."

If he manipulates the energy correctly, Pochettino believes, he has the power to chart his own destiny. Nevertheless, he has tried other experimental methods to improve his teams as well. Walking on hot coals. Leaning into an arrow pressed against the throat until it snaps, rather than pierces the skin. Hypnosis. That kind of thing.

Whether correlation or causation, the results of Pochettino's work are inarguable. Even in the jobs that haven't gone well, he knew success. Paris Saint-Germain won the French league in his only full season as its manager. He won his final five games in charge of Chelsea, finally mustering some cohesion out of its haphazardly assembled squad. He left Chelsea anyway, free to take on a new challenge.

Mauricio Pochettino trotted down the aisle steps of the auditorium, the first glimpse of the long-awaited man in the flesh. "Morning, morning, morning," he chirped, without making eye contact with an audience that had grown to a hundred people, before disappearing through a side door.

Here he was at last—right? That had really been him?—however briefly, almost two interminable months after the first reports that the Argentine was the favorite to become the new United States men's national team head coach. Physical evidence that this was really happening, the manifestation of U.S. Soccer's breathtaking coup, of its "super stretch" candidate.

Pochettino reemerged some minutes later, no longer clad in a hoodie and leisurewear but sporting a white dress shirt, a tightly fitting navy blue suit, black dress shoes with big buckles, and a U.S. Soccer pin on his jacket lapel. He took a seat in the front row of a theater on the twenty-fourth floor of a glass Manhattan skyscraper. We were here, Andrés Cantor, a famous Hispanic soccer announcer, announced to the room of reporters, officials, and federation guests, to welcome "one of the most sought-after managers in the world."

A hype video of men's national team footage played to deafening music. And then Pochettino and three beaming U.S. Soccer officials—federation president Cindy Parlow Cone, CEO JT Batson, and technical director Matt Crocker—took their seats behind a desk on the stage. This was, Parlow Cone declared, a "monumental day for U.S. Soccer."

For the next forty-five minutes, Pochettino answered questions from the media, speaking languidly to the wall of cameras in his halting English—still heavily accented even after working in England for eight years. Pochettino laughed easily, cracked jokes whenever he thought of one. He frequently referred to the new bosses flanking him, who were seldom addressed by the reporters in the room.

Pochettino—keenly aware that he was now working in the only country in the world where the women's national soccer team is a bigger deal than the men's—said a few media-savvy things about wanting to learn from the U.S. women's coach, Emma Hayes, whose path he crossed at Chelsea. "The women's team is going to be our inspiration," he said. "Our objective is to match their results and their philosophy."

"We need to really believe in big things," Pochettino proclaimed. "We need to believe that we can not only win a game, we can win the World Cup. Because if not, the journey is going to be so difficult."

Some of his answers delivered in Spanish revealed more of Pochettino's personality. Asked if being an Argentine, which is to say a countryman of the reigning men's world champions, meant that he held some sort of special ingredient, Pochettino pounced on the opportunity to further his own mystique. "The Argentinian coach, like the Argentinian player, has value because of how we feel, how we are, because of our character, for our passion," Pochettino said in Spanish. "Soccer is passion and emotion. And who better than an Argentine to translate this emotion that is soccer?"

The questions asked that morning all circled the same query: *What are you doing here?*

Mauricio Pochettino could have had just about any coaching job in soccer. The English national team needed a new manager to take over a world-class squad primed to compete for World Cup and European Championship trophies for several more years. It was surely only a matter of months before one of the juggernauts of European club soccer, Manchester United or Bayern Munich or Real Madrid or AC Milan or all of them, decided to dump their head coach. United had considered Pochettino just months earlier before sticking with their embattled incumbent—for the time being. Pochettino had been linked to the Real Madrid job in the past; FC Barcelona, too. As one of the game's preeminent managerial names, it was a given that he should be on the shortlist for any high-profile position that opened up. All he had to do was wait around and let the offers come to him. There would probably be another eight-figure salary in it.

After all, the affable Argentine had already managed three of the sport's biggest clubs. Chelsea was still paying him $13 million to sit at home and *not* coach their team. Certainly his last two jobs had been brief. But that had more to do with the reigning chaos at those clubs than Pochettino's body of work. And he could still count on a great deal of credit for turning Tottenham from a dysfunctional laughingstock into a Premier League contender.

Whichever way you looked at it, bagging Pochettino to coach its men's national team into the 2026 World Cup was a triumph for U.S. Soccer. But there were two distinct perspectives to take. The first cast his signing as a kind of culmination in a decades-long pursuit. Securing the commitment of one of the world's most famous and accomplished coaches conferred upon the men's program a prestige it had never known before. It validated all those years of yearning and striving, the toil of hundreds of people who had made it their life's work to bring the team into the upper echelon of the global game. Pochettino was the final piece in a puzzle painstakingly laid and ready to be fully revealed and marveled at by the 2026 World Cup.

Looked at another way, signing Pochettino to a salary more than double what Berhalter had made was an act of desperation. Two years on from a tantalizing performance at the 2022 World Cup by a very young American team, the march of what was labeled a golden generation had stalled. Copa América was seen as a kind of dress rehearsal for the 2026 World Cup. Rather than proving that it was ready to go toe to toe with some of South America's powerhouses, the U.S. team had faceplanted on the big stage. Two months later, and two days before Pochettino signed his name on U.S. Soccer stationery, the USMNT lost meekly to Canada, the first time their northern neighbors had defeated the Yanks on the road since 1957. Rather than energetic and hungry and overflowing with talent, the Americans looked lethargic and uninterested and overrated.

If the United States Soccer Federation headquarters were equipped with alarm bells, they would have been blaring.

Something about the backlash to Berhalter felt hysterical and oddly disproportionate to his performance. All the same, U.S. Soccer responded as it had when it moved on from Bob Gansler in 1991 and Bob Bradley in 2011: replacing a homegrown coach with the most famous foreigner it could find.

Technical director Matt Crocker was the point man on coaching hires. He wanted a manager with a track record of developing young players, winning, and playing attractive soccer—all, if possible, with enough panache to charm the American public. He divvied his list of a hundred potential coaches into three buckets: pie-in-the-sky "super-stretch" candidates, reach candidates, and previous candidates. "I very clearly stated that I only wanted coaches from the A bucket," recalled federation president Cindy Parlow Cone. "I was like, 'Let's find out what it's going to take, and we'll figure out a way to pay for it.' Because this was just too big a moment for our team and our country to not at least see if it was feasible to get one of the best coaches in the world."

The A bucket consisted of the sport's biggest one-man brands, men known just by their last names: Klopp, Zidane, Tuchel, Vieira, Benitez . . . Pochettino. If the pool of candidates had been a tad thin when Berhalter was rehired—a long time out from the World Cup and in the wake of public embarrassment—the federation was pleasantly surprised by how much interest there was in the job this time around. "As soon as we'd made the decision to part ways with Gregg, your phone starts ringing pretty quickly," said Crocker. "And the types of people that were reaching out to show an interest, and the amount of people that we spoke to in the initial stage, was significant. I felt like it was quality and quantity."

Even the super-stretch names were keen on a conversation.

Other than the timing and the appeal of leading a team with a lot of upside and relatively low expectations through a World Cup on home soil, something else was working in U.S. Soccer's favor: money. If the sport of soccer had matured, so had the nation's attitude toward it. It had hosted a World Cup in 1994, after all, making a deep impression on children who had since grown up and risen to positions of influence. "There's a generational change in American business and government leadership, where lots of the people in power are now soccer people," said JT Batson, the federation's millennial CEO and secretary general. "That's not how it was. Now, our generation grew up playing and loving the game and are now running some of the biggest corporations in the world, or with very important roles in finance, government, and philanthropy."

"The federation is just in a different place than it was even two years ago," explained Parlow Cone. Sponsorship earnings had skyrocketed. So had the number of billionaire backers willing to chip in for special projects, like hiring a world-famous coach. "I'm in a different financial situation than any of my predecessors were. U.S. Soccer is now in a position to be able to bring in and retain the best people, across the federation."

A federation delegation made almost a dozen trips to Europe to speak to six candidates in person. Jürgen Klopp, the charming German who had just left Liverpool and sat atop U.S. Soccer's wish list, ultimately demurred. Crocker had worked with Pochettino at Southampton when the former was the club's youth academy director. U.S. Soccer's representatives met Pochettino and his coaching staff in Barcelona, where he lived whenever he wasn't in London. They brought the Argentine oenophile a bottle of California cabernet. A ninety-minute meeting turned into a four-hour one. And then another one two days later. There were presentations and counter-presentations. Crocker and his colleagues were honest about the team's flaws; a well-prepared Pochettino already had a good sense of the USMNT and the job. "I was very impressed that they had done their research," Batson said. "They knew our player profiles, they knew our pool, they had analyzed our games. They called a ton of people."

That Pochettino intended to take the job was established quickly, but unwinding his ongoing Chelsea contract and working out a buyout for him and his staff took time as word of negotiations leaked, filling USMNT fans with a blend of glee and anxiety as the matter dragged on. To afford making Pochettino one of the highest-paid international coaches in the world, the federation needed help from several sponsors and donors who had committed their financial support at the outset of the coaching search.

But they got their savior in the end.

In soccer manager-speak, Pochettino had been tempted by the project. Top coaches love a project, a job that doesn't just demand wins and trophies but also presents some distinct challenge, an opportunity to leave a legacy. The home team of the biggest World Cup ever, now there was a project. A team with ample talent, apparently, but a potential not nearly tapped.

Pochettino explained that he was attracted to America for its can-do attitude, for its open-mindedness on new ideas and approaches, for its elite sporting culture, and for the relative absence of politics from the national team program compared with Europe's biggest clubs. "My family sees the fire in my eyes," he said.

There were questions about whether the time constraints of the international game would allow Pochettino to implement his finely orchestrated tactical systems. And whether they would work at all when he couldn't simply buy the players he needed, limiting him instead to whoever happened to hold an American passport. He promised to be pragmatic. "We are going to try to respect our philosophy, but the priority in soccer is to win," he explained. "People sometimes say, 'That's my philosophy, and I'm going to die with my idea.' No, I want to live. Because life is amazing. I want to be clever, and I want to win. I don't want to die."

If he had once been labeled a *bielsista* ideologue, this fifty-two-year-old version of Pochettino seemed less concerned with convincing the game's purists than with persuading a new nation. "We are in the USA," he said. "To convince our fans to join us, the aesthetic is important. We want to play nice, exciting, attacking football. We need to educate our fans. Because together we need to build that confidence and trust, so that we can arrive in two years really competitive in a sport that maybe wasn't born here but that is starting to belong here."

There is something deeply physical about Pochettino. He's a large man, for starters. He stands six feet tall and walks upright, a frame elongated by a double helping of brown hair that no longer falls onto his shoulders the way it did when he was a rugged defender. When you meet him, his hand doesn't merely shake yours but coils around it. He'll clasp it with his other hand, touch you on the shoulder. He's a fanatical hugger. "I remember every day him coming through everybody's office and he would pretty much hug everybody in the club," Crocker said of their time together at Southampton.

As a defender, Pochettino used his body to bully attackers—"I'd say to the striker, 'If you're going to get past me, think twice about it, because I'll kill you.' Of course I didn't, but at least he thought that I might." Casual pictures away from the field showed him draped over his teammates. Now, as a coach, he demands that the players use up every drop of their endurance, even in practice. Tim Ream, whose USMNT career had already spanned fourteen years and nine permanent and interim head coaches, labeled Pochettino's first full practice session as the hardest he'd experienced with the national team. The coaches wanted players to sprint at full capacity in every drill, and even instructed them on running form. Between drills, Pochettino had a habit of dispensing such forceful backslaps that Ream grew mildly concerned that some of his smaller teammates might get knocked down.

Mauricio Pochettino loves to talk, even in a language he still doesn't entirely command. Speaking to a few reporters next to the Austin FC practice field on a hot Texan fall afternoon before his debut as U.S. men's national team head coach the following night, he talked and talked. He joked and cajoled and alternately spoke seriously and lightly. As he spoke, he shifted endlessly in his seat, slouching and then leaning forward, his arms in constant motion. A pair of glasses dangled from the collar of his maroon U.S. Soccer warmup jersey. Every now and again, the religious icon hanging from a bracelet—Jordi, the patron saint of Catalonia, a present from Pochettino's son that he rarely takes off—clanked onto the plastic picnic table.

He apologized whenever he accidentally said "football" instead of "soccer." The subject he kept returning to was enjoyment. He'd been enjoying the job a lot so far—or "enshoying" it, as it came out in his accent. But the USMNT's players needed to "enshoy," too. The camps and practice and the games. An unrepentant players' coach, Pochettino believes that people function at their best when they are at ease and in a familiar environment—a view diametrically opposed to Jürgen Klinsmann's a decade earlier. For all the intensity on the field, Pochettino's first camp had been laid-back away from it, with far less programming than Berhalter tended to squeeze into the day. There was more freedom for everyone, players and staffers alike. "They need to be happy," Pochettino explained. "They need to enshoy the way they will be in the camp. It's our responsibility to create a very nice environment."

Besides, where the U.S. needed the most work, Pochettino felt, was in its mental strength. "We need to evolve as a team in our mentality, in our attitude, in our arrogance, in the way we need to compete," he said. What counted was performance on the field.

At Q2 Stadium in Austin on October 12, 2024, loud cheers greeted Pochettino the moment he walked onto the grass for a pregame interview. The American Outlaws hung a banner behind one of the goals depicting the new manager as Ted Lasso, the über-positive gridiron football-turned-soccer coach in the eponymous hit comedy series, above the word BELIEVE—a "shock" to the coach, he would later say with a laugh. Pochettino had been talking about belief a lot, just like the fictional Lasso. "Belief is a word that is powerful," he had said in one such instance. "You can have an enormous talent, you can be clever, but in football you need to believe, believe that all is possible." U.S. Soccer handed out posters at the game with Pochettino on them, and the words BELIEVE and CREER.

Everywhere he went that day, Pochettino was stopped for pictures, for autographs. In the tunnel on the way to the field, coming onto the field, leaving the field, in the hallways to the locker room. It didn't end. The burden of the celebrity coach. Come game time, the stadium announcer called out the American lineup—Matt Turner! Antonee Robinson! Yunus Musah! Christiaaan Puliiisiiic!—and then offered an unusual addendum. "And for the first time . . . your head coach, Mauriciooo Pochettinooo!" A roar rose from the stands, perhaps louder even than the one Pulisic had gotten.

The U.S. played a friendly against Panama, the very team that had triggered the Americans' undoing at Copa América. Pochettino mostly stood along the sideline with his arms crossed. He wore a black suit jacket over a black T-shirt and a black pair of sneakers. And his bracelet, of course. He paced, waved his arms to give instructions, clapped his hands over his head whenever the U.S. won the ball back quickly and high up the field. The Americans scored early and late in the second half. Each time, Pochettino pumped his fists. A convincing 2–0 victory. A page turned, vengeance for a Copa loss he wasn't around for. After the final whistle, Pochettino hugged every player and every staffer. Not quick, good-job hugs. Long ones. Full chest-to-chest contact. Two arms wrapped around the recipient for several seconds.

The players walked over to the supporters' section of the stands. Cheers. Pochettino, the wily veteran of crowd manipulation, waited for the players to saunter off and headed over to the fans last, like the headline musical act, holding off until the audience reached fever pitch. Louder cheers. They chanted his name.

"Po-che-tti-no!"

"Po-che-tti-no!"

"Po-che-tti-no!"

The subject of their adoration stood before them and took it in, smiling. When the chanting flagged, he whipped his hands up to keep the fans going. They obliged. Whatever you say, boss. Things were looking up again. Was this the future? Maybe. It could also be the past again. In the thrum and euphoria, nobody could say. Least of all Pochettino.

There would be more challenges over the following year, a period marred by mercurial performances and results as Pochettino tried out new players and tactics and struggled to reignite a complacent team. There was encouragement, too, from hard-fought friendly wins over Australia and Paraguay in the fall of 2025, just before they were both revealed as 2026 World Cup group stage opponents. A 5–1 thumping of Bielsa's Uruguay put an exclamation point behind this five-game undefeated run.

But however this experiment turned out, the USMNT would arrive at a second World Cup on U.S. soil as a team remade. The Americans would no longer be seen as tourists, like in 1990, or as unworthy hosts, as in 1994. Their decades of effort had elevated them to a new status: that of an ascendant program, hoping to summit sometime soon. If a few things broke right, they could make their mark on the world's game. The United States men's national team knew well that World Cups are fickle.

Some Inadequate Thank-Yous

After we agreed a deal for me to write this book, my first editor, Rick Kot, asked me a question that stumped me: "Why does the U.S. feel like it needs to win the World Cup?" As I stumbled through an explanation, Rick's parrot, Lou, who had gone by Louise for the first few decades of his life until a newly invented test revealed his actual sex, stared at me over Rick's shoulder, unblinking, skeptical. I said something about how it had to do with a kind of American sporting exceptionalism. And with the assumption that the United States ought to be good at any sport it takes seriously.

But it was a valid question. Why had the United States men's national team set out on this tortured, often painful journey? What compelled it to begin the steep trek from complete international irrelevance to a place where, if things went very well, they would not embarrass themselves on the global stage? Surely the U.S. couldn't hope to ever win the World Cup, right? Out of the two-hundred-odd countries that play soccer, only eight countries ever have. Some of the world's leading soccer nations have yet to win the thing. Even England, the self-styled home of the game, finds itself on the wrong side of a sixty-year drought.

Why did a nation that already dominated the world in so many other sports feel the need to also conquer the one that at least half the world was better at: men's soccer? Why bother when those countries had every cultural and sporting advantage? The misery would far outweigh the catharsis, surely.

I spent the next three years seeking to answer that question by retracing that road from the dark ages of American men's soccer to a present that is hardly without issues but is, by comparison, positively luminous. The men's national team is not there yet, but when you step back and take the macro view, the amount of progress made in a few generations is fairly miraculous.

In the end, the simple retort to Rick's question is, I think, that the personalities and ambitions of most everyone involved in the senior men's national team were such that it hadn't occurred to them not to strive for a spot among the sport's elite. Not everyone got it right, but they all pushed to improve the program.

I had a lot of help in answering this question.

David Patterson reached out with the idea for this book and became my agent, my sage counselor, and my friend, ably assisted by Chandler Wickers. Rick Kot acquired the book at Viking and then passed it off to Allison Lorentzen, helped by Camille LeBlanc and Sonia Gadre, who artfully whittled all my words down to the good stuff. The rest of the team at Viking that worked on this book gave me as pleasant an experience as I think a first-time author could have. They were Anna Brill, Emily Fishman, Bridget Gilleran, Andrea Schulz, and Kate Stark.

I am grateful to all of the players, coaches, U.S. Soccer officials, and others quoted throughout this book for speaking to me, whether briefly or at length. I'm also grateful to those who told me things and whose names aren't in the book. They know who they are.

The Pepi family was particularly hospitable in having me in their home. The Sullivans are wonderful people and I enjoyed getting to know them—thanks again to Evan Whitson for the introduction.

There are hundreds of U.S. Soccer employees, past and present, whose names most soccer fans will never know, but whose monumental efforts brought the sport to where it is in this country. I particularly want to thank Neil Buethe and Michael Kammarman for their help. They vouched for me again and again, which went a long way with the people I needed to speak to me.

Also of great help were Adam Klionsky, Gina Miller, and Chris Winkler, who deftly run PR for their respective MLS teams and went out of their way for me. Agents Rich Motzkin and Ron Waxman convinced some of their clients that speaking to me was worth their time.

At *The Ringer*, Conor Nevins commissioned the profile on Gregg Berhalter that got the ball rolling on this book and then, as usual, made it much better. Aric Jenkins has done the same for me there ever since. Alex Abnos and Tom Lutz are my editors at my other writing home, *The Guardian*, where they save me from my half-cooked ideas and sharpen the good ones. At earlier stops in my career at ESPN and Yahoo! Sports, James Martin, Joe Lago, and Joey Gulino made me better.

Dan Leydon made the delightful illustrations throughout this book and was a delight to work with.

My oldest friend, Frank Grinaert, was a creative sounding board for all the artsy bits. So was Asha Fuller, who also managed to make my face look respectable on the book's jacket. Asha and the rest of the Wolfcocks (reader, don't ask . . .) offered brotherhood, merriment, and a bottomless tolerance for my errant long balls.

Pablo Maurer, Henry Bushnell, and Brian Straus generously shared quotes and other material from their own reporting. Paul Carr gave me access to his archive of U.S. games at World Cups. Andy Clayton, Luke Cyphers, Matt Doyle, Simon Kuper, Jeff MacGregor, John Miller, Cas Mudde, Brian Phillips, and Brian Straus read parts or all of the manuscript and offered helpful notes.

Andy Das and James Tyler are my fellow travelers in soccer media and a constant source of support and humor.

At Marist University, Drs. Kevin Lerner, Jackie Reich, and Thom Wermuth were enthusiastic supporters of this book from the very start and arranged for a leave so I could write it. The university also supported my reporting travel. And the Marist library and its digital archives were essential. Monica Schott did her usual heroic work wrestling my receipts into submission.

Ricardo Martinez-Paz, my student at Marist, and now my friend, was a first-rate researcher and brought a degree of organization to the project that I could only aspire to. I can't wait to see all the things he will accomplish in sports media.

My in-laws, Mark and Mary Elin, were ever supportive and ready with a meal or an incisive edit.

My mother, Ingrid, successfully imbued me with her love of books. On the other side of the ledger, she failed spectacularly in passing on her hatred of soccer. But she never once wavered in her support of my teenage dream of becoming a sportswriter, no matter how far-fetched it must have seemed.

You would not be holding this book if it were not for my wife, Steph Carnes. It is little coincidence that my sudden onset of ambition coincided with our meeting when we were twenty-one. She has made me want to improve a little bit on every one of the thousands of happy days we have shared. She is my first reader and my last, just as she is the first and the last person I think about every day. I adore her.

Last but never least, our son, Lukie, is a guiding light with his energy and his humor and curiosity and his joy. He's not that keen on soccer either.

On Sources and Such

I figure I conducted some 150 interviews for this book. Quotes without attribution to a specific outlet came from one of my own interviews. When they didn't, I tried to give judicious credit. If I missed any, I enclose my humble apologies for the oversight.

This book focuses on four decades of national team history. Listing the hundreds—maybe thousands?—of articles from which I mined little nuggets or big storylines would add untold pages to this book. Instead, I will list the outlets that I leaned on, as anyone compiling the history of a single institution must: AmericanSoccerNow.com; *The Athletic*; *Bleacher Report*; ESPN.com; *Esquire*; FBRef.com; FiveThirtyEight.com; GrantWahl.com; *The Guardian*; *Hard Gras*; *London Review of Books*; *Los Angeles Times*; MLSSoccer.com; *The New Yorker*; PhillySoccerPage.net; *The Players' Tribune*; *Pro Soccer Wire*; *The Ringer*; *SB Nation*; *Soccer America*; *Sports Illustrated*; USSoccer.com; *Vice*; *The Washington Post*; Yahoo! Sports.

I would be remiss, however, if I didn't single out a few reporters whose work was especially useful. Steven Goff; Brian Straus; Henry

Bushnell; the late, great, and much-missed Grant Wahl; Doug McIntyre; Jeré Longman; Jeff Carlisle; and Pablo Maurer, Sam Stejskal, and Paul Tenorio.

The passage on the origins of the soccer/football divide stands on the shoulders of an exhaustive paper written by the venerable soccer economist Stefan Szymanski, at the University of Michigan.

Roger Bennett's narrative podcast *American Fiasco* for NPR on the 1998 World Cup campaign was instructive.

Books are made out of books, as Cormac McCarthy put it. Mine was made, in ways small or big, out of the below:

Allaway, R., & Jose, C. (2011). *The United States Tackles the World Cup.* St. Johann Press.

Arena, B., & Kettmann, S. (2018). *What's Wrong with Us? A Coach's Blunt Take on the State of American Soccer After a Lifetime on the Touchline.* Harper Collins.

Balague, G. (2017). *Brave New World: Inside Pochettino's Spurs.* Weidenfeld & Nicolson.

Bolsmann, C., & Kioussis, G. (2021). *Soccer Frontiers: The Global Game in the United States, 1863–1913.* University of Tennessee Press.

Bunk, B. (2021). *From Football to Soccer: The Early History of the Beautiful Game in the United States.* University of Illinois Press.

Dohrmann, G. (2022). *Switching Fields: Inside the Fight to Remake Men's Soccer in the United States.* Ballantine Books.

Dure, B. (2019). *Why the U.S. Men Will Never Win the World Cup: A Historical and Cultural Reality Check.* Rowman & Littlefield.

Elder, A. (2022). *New Kids in the World Cup: The Totally Late '80s and Early '90s Tale of the Team That Changed American Soccer Forever.* University of Nebraska Press.

Foer, F. (2005). *How Soccer Explains the World.* Harper Perennial.

Glanville, B. (1973). *The Story of the World Cup: The Essential Companion to Germany 2006.* Faber and Faber.

Hopkins, G. (2010). *Star-Spangled Soccer: The Selling, Marketing and Management of Soccer in the USA.* Palgrave Macmillan.

Howard, T. (2014). *The Keeper: A Life of Saving Goals and Achieving Them.* Harper.

Kirschbaum, E. (2016). *Soccer Without Borders: Jürgen Klinsmann, Coaching the U.S. Men's National Soccer Team and the Quest for the World Cup.* Picador.

Kuper, S. (2003). *Football Against the Enemy.* Orion Paperbacks.

Mandis, S., & Wolter, S. (2021). *What Happened to the USMNT: The Ugly Truth About the Beautiful Game.* Triumph Books.

Markovits, A. (2001). *Football to Soccer: The Early History of the Beautiful Game in the United States*. Princeton University Press.

Phillips, H. (2022). *Generation Zero: Founding Fathers, Hidden Histories and the Making of Soccer in America*. Dickinson-Moses Press.

Pulisic, C. (2022). *Pulisic: My Journey So Far.* Rizzoli.

Sugden, J., & Tomlinson, A. (1994). *Hosts and Champions: Soccer Cultures, National Identities and the USA World Cup*. Ashgate Publishing Limited.

Vecsey, G. (2015). *Eight World Cups: My Journey Through the Beauty and Dark Side of Soccer.* St. Martin's Griffin.

Wahl, G. (2018). *Masters of Modern Soccer: How the World's Best Play the Twenty-First-Century Game*. Crown Archetype.

Wangerin, D. (2008). *Soccer in a Football World: The Story of America's Forgotten Game.* Temple University Press.

Wangerin, D. (2014). *Distant Corners: American Soccer's History of Missed Opportunities and Lost Causes*. Temple University Press.

White, G. (2022). *Soccer in American Culture: The Beautiful Game's Struggle for Status.* Temple University Press.